T0328448

VOLUME 613

SEPTEMBER 2007

THE ANNALS

of The American Academy of Political
and Social Science

PHYLLIS KANISS, *Executive Editor*

Advancing Research on Minority Entrepreneurship

Special Editors of this Volume

TIMOTHY BATES
Wayne State University

WILLIAM E. JACKSON III
University of Alabama

JAMES H. JOHNSON JR.
University of North Carolina at Chapel Hill

SAGE Publications
Los Angeles • London • New Delhi • Singapore

Origin and Purpose. The Academy was organized December 14, 1889, to promote the progress of political and social science, especially through publications and meetings. The Academy does not take sides in controverted questions, but seeks to gather and present reliable information to assist the public in forming an intelligent and accurate judgment.

Meetings. The Academy occasionally holds a meeting in the spring extending over two days.

Publications. THE ANNALS of The American Academy of Political and Social Science is the bimonthly publication of the Academy. Each issue contains articles on some prominent social or political problem, written at the invitation of the editors. Also, monographs are published from time to time, numbers of which are distributed to pertinent professional organizations. These volumes constitute important reference works on the topics with which they deal, and they are extensively cited by authorities throughout the United States and abroad. The papers presented at the meetings of the Academy are included in THE ANNALS.

Membership. Each member of the Academy receives THE ANNALS and may attend the meetings of the Academy. Membership is open only to individuals. Annual dues: $84.00 for the regular paperbound edition (clothbound, $121.00). Members may also purchase single issues of THE ANNALS for $17.00 each (clothbound, $26.00). Student memberships are available for $53.00.

Subscriptions. THE ANNALS of The American Academy of Political and Social Science (ISSN 0002-7162) (J295) is published six times annually—in January, March, May, July, September, and November—by Sage Publications, 2455 Teller Road, Thousand Oaks, CA 91320. Telephone: (800) 818-SAGE (7243) and (805) 499-9774; Fax/Order line: (805) 499-0871; e-mail: journals@sagepub.com. Copyright © 2007 by The American Academy of Political and Social Science. Institutions may subscribe to THE ANNALS at the annual rate: $612.00 (clothbound, $692.00). Single issues of THE ANNALS may be obtained by individuals who are not members of the Academy for $34.00 each (clothbound, $47.00). Single issues of THE ANNALS have proven to be excellent supplementary texts for classroom use. Direct inquiries regarding adoptions to THE ANNALS c/o Sage Publications (address below). Periodicals postage paid at Thousand Oaks, California, and at additional mailing offices.

All correspondence concerning membership in the Academy, dues renewals, inquiries about membership status, and/or purchase of single issues of THE ANNALS should be sent to THE ANNALS c/o Sage Publications, 2455 Teller Road, Thousand Oaks, CA 91320.Telephone: (800) 818-SAGE (7243) and (805) 499-9774; Fax/Order line: (805) 499-0871; e-mail: journals@sagepub.com. *Please note that orders under $30 must be prepaid.* Sage affiliates in London and India will assist institutional subscribers abroad with regard to orders, claims, and inquiries for both subscriptions and single issues.

THE ANNALS

© 2007 by The American Academy of Political and Social Science

Editorial Office: 3814 Walnut Street, Fels Institute for Government, University of Pennsylvania, Philadelphia, PA 19104-6197.
For information about membership* (individuals only) and subscriptions (institutions), address:
Sage Publications
2455 Teller Road
Thousand Oaks, CA 91320

For Sage Publications: Rachel Mayer (Production) and Sandra Hopps (Marketing)

From India and South Asia, write to:
SAGE PUBLICATIONS INDIA Pvt Ltd
B-42 Panchsheel Enclave, P.O. Box 4109
New Delhi 110 017
INDIA

From Europe, the Middle East, and Africa, write to:
SAGE PUBLICATIONS LTD
1 Oliver's Yard, 55 City Road
London EC1Y 1SP
UNITED KINGDOM

*Please note that members of the Academy receive THE ANNALS with their membership.
International Standard Serial Number ISSN 0002-7162
International Standard Book Number ISBN 978-1-4129-6026-7 (Vol. 613, 2007) paper
International Standard Book Number ISBN 978-1-4129-6025-0 (Vol. 613, 2007) cloth
First printing, September 2007.

The articles appearing in *The Annals* are abstracted or indexed in Academic Abstracts, Academic Search, America: History and Life, Asia Pacific Database, Book Review Index,CABAbstracts Database, Central Asia: Abstracts &Index, Communication Abstracts, Corporate ResourceNET, Criminal Justice Abstracts, Current Citations Express, Current Contents: Social & Behavioral Sciences, Documentation in Public Administration, e-JEL, EconLit, Expanded Academic Index, Guide to Social Science & Religion in Periodical Literature, Health Business FullTEXT, HealthSTAR FullTEXT, Historical Abstracts, International Bibliography of the Social Sciences, International Political Science Abstracts, ISI Basic Social Sciences Index, Journal of Economic Literature on CD, LEXIS-NEXIS, MasterFILE FullTEXT, Middle East: Abstracts&Index, North Africa: Abstracts&Index, PAIS International, Periodical Abstracts, Political Science Abstracts, Psychological Abstracts, PsycINFO, Sage Public Administration Abstracts, Scopus, Social Science Source, Social Sciences Citation Index, Social Sciences Index Full Text, Social Services Abstracts, SocialWork Abstracts, Sociological Abstracts, Southeast Asia: Abstracts& Index, Standard Periodical Directory (SPD), TOPICsearch, Wilson OmniFileV, and Wilson Social Sciences Index/Abstracts, and are available on microfilm from ProQuest, Ann Arbor, Michigan.

Information about membership rates, institutional subscriptions, and back issue prices may be found on the facing page.

Advertising. Current rates and specifications may be obtained by writing to The Annals Advertising and Promotion Manager at the Thousand Oaks office (address above).

Claims. Claims for undelivered copies must be made no later than six months following month of publication. The publisher will supply missing copies when losses have been sustained in transit and when the reserve stock will permit.

Change of Address. Six weeks' advance notice must be given when notifying of change of address to ensure proper identification. Please specify name of journal. POSTMASTER: Send address changes to The Annals of The American Academy of Political and Social Science, c/o Sage Publications, 2455 Teller Road, Thousand Oaks, CA 91320.

ANNALS

OF THE AMERICAN ACADEMY OF
POLITICAL AND SOCIAL SCIENCE

Volume 613   September 2007

IN THIS ISSUE:

Advancing Research on Minority Entrepreneurship

Special Editors: TIMOTHY BATES
WILLIAM E. JACKSON III
JAMES H. JOHNSON Jr.

FORTHCOMING

The Biology of Political Behavior
Special Editors: JOHN R. HIBBING and KEVIN B. SMITH
Volume 614, November 2007

The Epidemic of Childhood Overweight
Special Editor: AMY JORDAN
Volume 615, January 2008

The Politics of History in Comparative Perspective
Special Editor: MARTIN O. HEISLER
Volume 616, March 2008

Fostering Research on Minority Entrepreneurship

By
ROBERT D. STROM

This special issue of *The Annals of the American Academy of Political and Social Science* presents work that is vitally important to our nation's future. At the Ewing Marion Kauffman Foundation, we see entrepreneurship and educational achievement as the levers that will create a society of self-sufficient individuals and a growing economy. Entrepreneurship is a means for individuals of all backgrounds to lift themselves out of poverty, to create jobs for other citizens, and to ensure that innovation and creativity continue to revitalize the country. Entrepreneurship, in fact, has been the engine behind the United States' unprecedented economic growth over the past decade and has offered opportunities for immigrants, minorities, and women to climb the ladder of economic success throughout our nation's history.

However, there continues to be a need to increase the number of successful entrepreneurs in the United States. Ensuring that all Americans—and new immigrants—have access to entrepreneurship and to the tools they need to be successful entrepreneurs will result in higher employment, less poverty, more innovation, and higher living standards for everyone. To that end, we see a need to bolster the institutions that support entrepreneurial

Robert D. Strom directs the Ewing Marion Kauffman Foundation's commissioned research, working with the nation's top scholars to advance knowledge in entrepreneurship. He has also served on the collegiate and youth entrepreneurship teams during his tenure at the foundation. Previously, he was a visiting professor at the Bloch School of Business at the University of Missouri at Kansas City and vice president of the National Council on Economic Education. He has also been assistant vice president for public affairs at the Federal Reserve Bank of Kansas City, president of the Missouri Council on Economic Education, a professor of economics at the University of Missouri at Columbia, and a member of the economics department at Miami University in Oxford, Ohio.

DOI: 10.1177/0002716207303403

development and the training of entrepreneurial leaders for America's global knowledge economy. It is also important that we engage in a vigorous debate regarding policies that will foster a more entrepreneurial environment for all Americans and that we bring people together as a networking hub to stimulate the flow of ideas and action. We must work to break down barriers to entrepreneurship for all individuals and for minorities and women, in particular.

While self-employment has historically been a means for minorities and women to enter the mainstream of the economy, barriers to entrepreneurship for these groups remain. Census data indicate that the rates of entrepreneurial activity for blacks lag significantly behind those for whites, and the rate for women is much lower than the rate for men.[1] Furthermore, data suggest that meaningful and sustained gaps exist in the growth of new businesses for minorities and women.[2]

The first step toward closing these gaps is to understand them. Recognizing that too few scholars pursue research on minority and women's business development, the Kauffman Foundation supports work on the changing demographics of entrepreneurship and the barriers to business ownership faced by these groups. But addressing these barriers—and meeting our other goals—also requires a deeper understanding of entrepreneurship more generally. As such, we also encourage research on a wide range of other topics, from firm productivity and entrepreneurial finance to entrepreneurship's contribution to the economy and the formation, growth, and death of firms and industries.

It is also important that we engage in a vigorous debate regarding policies that will foster a more entrepreneurial environment for all Americans and that we bring people together as a networking hub to stimulate the flow of ideas and action.

High-quality scholarship allows us to learn more about this important economic phenomenon, inspires a national conversation about policies that foster entrepreneurship, and informs our programmatic efforts to educate tomorrow's entrepreneurs. Furthermore, the research findings that result from these efforts, published in journals such as *The Annals*, lead to scholarly dialogue that inspires yet more research in the field. In fact, building this field—making a place for entrepreneurship in the academic community—is essential.

Entrepreneurship is relatively new to the academic community. While the subject has been included in business school course catalogs for years, very little scholarly investigation examines the workings of entrepreneurship or the policies that are most conducive to the formation and growth of new businesses. In the past decade, however, the number of schools teaching entrepreneurship has swelled and a wide variety of peer-reviewed journals have begun publishing research on the topic.

Over the past decade, the Kauffman Foundation has worked to foster this trend by supporting defined research projects (both small and large) conducted at universities and public policy think tanks and by creating entrepreneurship research centers at seven leading universities. These schools have created interdisciplinary communities of researchers studying entrepreneurship and have used their funding to award competitive grants for small research projects on their campuses. Senior scholars interact with more junior faculty and give students an opportunity to study the topic, as well.

It is also important to train the next generation of scholars conducting cutting-edge research on entrepreneurship through doctoral consortia and junior faculty programs at various professional associations and other venues that bring young scholars together and allow them to interact with senior faculty who share their interest in entrepreneurship. The Kauffman Dissertation Fellowship Program encourages the study of entrepreneurship at the early stages of academics' careers and generates high-quality research in the broad field of entrepreneurship and is intended to launch a cohort of world-class entrepreneurship scholars. Fellows are encouraged to approach the topic from a wide range of disciplinary perspectives, from strategy, management, and organizational behavior, to public policy, finance, sociology, and economics. As the earlier recipients of these fellowships are now teaching at preeminent universities, they share their interest and expertise in entrepreneurship with today's young scholars.

The Biannual Kauffman Prize Medal for Research in Entrepreneurship also recognizes the work of young scholars in the field. Initiated in 2004, this award recognizes an individual scholar under the age of forty who has made the most significant contributions to research in the field of entrepreneurship. Recipients are selected by a small committee of senior scholars. These awards draw attention to innovative scholarly work, encourage promising young scholars with great potential to advance the field, and further build interest in entrepreneurship across disciplines.

Finally, the conferences that led to the series of papers contained in this volume are a key piece of the effort to encourage young scholars. The Research Conference on Entrepreneurship among Minorities and Women, held in 2004 and 2005 at the University of North Carolina at Chapel Hill's Kenan-Flagler Business School, brought together junior and senior faculty members from universities throughout the country to discuss research on minority and women's entrepreneurship. Large sessions as well as smaller breakout groups and one-on-one meetings allowed for vigorous discussion and learning throughout the conferences. The wide range of social science disciplines represented at the conference offered varied perspectives on both content and methodology. Topics discussed range from access to capital and barriers to business development, to entrepreneurial behavior models, microenterprise, and data for the study of entrepreneurship. A research grant competition for additional work in the field of minority and women's entrepreneurship followed each conference. In 2006, the scholars convened once again to discuss research by both senior faculty and the grant recipients from the previous two years. This volume publishes these papers, sharing the knowledge that came out of these conferences and hopefully inspiring further work in this important domain.

Bringing together multidisciplinary approaches to entrepreneurship, a focus on training the next generation of scholars, the pursuit of research on entrepreneurship among minorities and women, and the effort to inspire dialogue about entrepreneurship between academics throughout the country, the Research Conference contributed to our understanding of this important topic. Not only will these articles inform the development of programs to encourage high-growth minority and women-owned businesses, but also they advance policy conversations regarding barriers to business development and contribute significantly to efforts to build the field of entrepreneurship.

Notes

1. Robert W. Fairlie, *Kauffman Index of Entrepreneurial Activity National Report, 1996-2005* (Kansas City, MO: Ewing Marion Kauffman Foundation, 2006).

2. U.S. Census Bureau, *Characteristics of Business Owners: 2002* (2006), http://www.census.gov/prod/ec02/sb0200cscb.pdf.

Advancing Research on Minority Entrepreneurship

By
TIMOTHY BATES,
WILLIAM E. JACKSON III,
and
JAMES H. JOHNSON Jr.

Background and Context

Creation of viable small businesses entails (1) involvement of skilled and capable entrepreneurs who have (2) access to financial capital to invest in their business ventures and (3) access to markets for the products of their enterprises. It is often suggested by those who regularly invest in small businesses that the first of these three building blocks—skilled and capable entrepreneurs, or the management team—is the most important. However, gaining management skills and capabilities require opportunities to acquire certain educational and business-related experiences.

Among minority business enterprises (MBEs), discriminatory barriers have often interfered with efforts to obtain access to these educational and business-related experiences as well as the other two building blocks of business viability. Specifically, these barriers often result in overly small, less profitable, and generally less viable firms (Bates 1997). The uniqueness of minority-owned businesses is rooted in the higher barriers that they encounter when attempting to access these fundamental building blocks. The whole process is more difficult for minorities than it is for whites.

Applicable barriers limit access to financial capital and product markets; access to skills and work experience that facilitate firm formation are sometimes limited. These barriers handicap minority self-employed and small-business owners in multiple ways. Barriers often result in overly small and less viable firms, relative to those owned by nonminorities. The greater incidence of marginal firms, in turn, causes heightened failure rates among minority-owned businesses. Barriers, finally, discourage some potential minority entrepreneurs from ever taking the plunge into self-employment.

DOI: 10.1177/0002716207303405

When scholars first began to collect and analyze data describing MBE performance, many argued that minority businesses—being few in number and small in size and scope—were collectively insignificant (Brimmer and Terrell 1971; Osborne 1976; Tabb 1979). Cross-sectional data indicated that minority businesses were heavily concentrated in several lines of personal services and retailing that held minimal potential for growth. Andrew Brimmer—the nation's first African American to serve on the Board of Governors of the Federal Reserve System—predicted a bleak future for MBEs, concluding that minority-owned firms typically lacked the managerial and technical competence needed to compete successfully in the business world (Brimmer 1966).

In fact, MBEs have grown rapidly in recent decades, albeit from a small base. Larger-scale MBEs—those generating gross revenues exceeding $1 million annually—have grown at a rate three times faster than the overall minority business community (Bates 2006). Employer firms have surpassed the growth rate of MBEs lacking paid employees. Among black-owned enterprises nationwide operating in the business-services niche, for example, total employment has grown explosively, from 12,432 employees in 1982 to 156,974 employees in 1997 (U.S. Census Bureau 2001; Bates 1998). In other industry niches, such as food stores, firm numbers and paid employment showed no growth during this period.

There is a pronounced dichotomy in the twenty-first-century minority business community. Numerous traditional lines of business—personal services and small-scale retailing—reflect the continuing relevance of traditional barriers. Rapid growth in larger-scale ventures reflects declining barriers, widening opportunities for those with the education, expertise, and experience to move into more remunerative lines of business.

Distinct traces of a racial-caste system shaped the minority-business community throughout most of the twentieth century; college-educated minorities were particularly trapped. Minorities who attended college were hemmed in by social attitudes about which occupations were appropriate. Between 1912 and 1938, for example, 73 percent of black college graduates nationwide became either teachers or preachers (Holsey 1938). The few entering professions—law, medicine, dentistry—served an all-black clientele. Caterers, shoe shiners—even barbers— might serve white clients, but black college graduates rarely did. This sort of

Timothy Bates is a distinguished professor of economics at Wayne State University. His current research focuses upon the minority-oriented venture capital industry and the roles that small businesses might play in revitalizing low-income urban areas.

William E. Jackson III is a professor of finance, professor of management, and the Smith Foundation Endowed Chair of Business Ethics and Integrity in the Culverhouse College of Commerce at the University of Alabama. His research interests focus on financial markets and institutions, corporate governance, small-firm finance, and political economy. He received his PhD in economics from the University of Chicago.

James H. Johnson Jr. is the William Rand Kenan Jr. Distinguished Professor of Entrepreneurship at the University of North Carolina at Chapel Hill. His research focuses on how demographic and global economic forces affect minority- and women-owned business growth and development.

hemming in is what shaped and narrowed minority-owned small businesses: a few doors were held open, but many were closed. Merit still mattered in this caste system, but the range of alternatives people entering careers faced was narrowed. Thus, the size of the middle class was artificially restricted, and the nature of the resultant small-business community was circumscribed (Myrdal 1944).

Distinct traces of a racial-caste system shaped the minority-business community throughout most of the twentieth century; college-educated minorities were particularly trapped.

Minority entrepreneurs have thus catered largely to a clientele of fellow ethnic-group members. When they ventured into the broader marketplace, opportunities were limited to those that white society felt were appropriate to their inferior status. Traditional service occupations—ironing shirts, shining shoes, preparing and serving meals—were commonly found suitable by the dominant society (Light 1972).

Andrew Brimmer (1966) developed an opposing interpretation of minority business patterns, based on the assumption that owner preferences shaped industry composition. Because the pattern of tiny minority firms heavily concentrated in traditional fields was merely a reflection of owner preferences, growth, if generated by supportive public policies, would simply translate into creation of more beauty parlors and barbershops. Declining segregation and discrimination, he concluded, would not promote development of the black business community. Brimmer and Terrell (1971) made job creation extrapolations based upon the assumption that further minority business creation would be in those industries "where they are already concentrating." Brimmer and Terrell omitted "firms in transportation, manufacturing, and construction. This omission was not accidental; rather, it resulted from the basic fact that there are few Negro-owned firms competing in these types of business" (304-6).

The disproportionate concentration of MBEs in the personal services field particularly strained the Brimmer position that owner preferences guided industry choice. Personal services, the area of greatest MBE concentration and overrepresentation, was also the least profitable line of small business, on average, and the field in which financial capital requirements for business startup were lowest (Pierce 1947; Bates 1973, 1997). In a world of reduced constraints and expanded opportunities, would MBEs continue to concentrate so heavily in this niche? In fact, they would not.

The nature of the minority business community is much different today than it was throughout the twentieth century. As size and scope have expanded, business diversity has flourished. The growing lines of minority enterprise today are dominated by large-scale firms that often serve a racially diverse clientele. Increasingly, these enterprises sell to other businesses, including large corporations. MBEs operating in the broad marketplace are commonly run by college-educated owners. Areas of particularly rapid growth include the skill-intensive services: finance, business services, and various professional services. These areas are called emerging lines of minority enterprise because the presence of minority owners has been minimal, historically.

The nature of the minority business community is much different today than it was throughout the twentieth century. As size and scope have expanded, business diversity has flourished.

To comprehend the growth dynamic in the diverse and rapidly evolving minority business community, it is useful to track changing conditions through time. The essential point to understand is that the nature of the minority business community is derivative of broad social, economic, and political forces. A lessening of discrimination has generated a powerful growth dynamic that is gradually transforming the minority business community. Its future composition may derive from expanded opportunities offered by a less discriminatory society, or it may reflect growing constraints imposed by evolving discriminatory barriers.

Overview of This Issue

The entrepreneurship literature appearing to date in social science and business journals has comprehensively described self-employment and small business ownership among both African Americans and Asian immigrants. Surprisingly absent is a similarly comprehensive literature analyzing entrepreneurship among Hispanic Americans. Beyond sociological studies of Cubans self-employed in Miami, scholars have rarely explored this topic.

This special issue on minority entrepreneurship offers two articles that together mark the most extensive discussion and analysis of Hispanic entrepreneurship to be found in scholarly journals to date. Bárbara Robles and Héctor Cordero-Guzmán (this volume) review the existing fragmentary literature and then present up-to-date statistics describing Hispanic-owned firms operating in the United States. One issue facing researchers is the fact that the aggregate grouping of "Hispanic" appears to be inappropriately "masking the intra-group differences in human and financial capital resources of Latino/Hispanic small business startups."

Mexican Americans are by far the largest subset of self-employed Latinos in the United States. They account for roughly 45 percent of all Latino self-employment and small-business ownership. Magnus Lofstrom and Chunbei Wang explore rates at which male Mexican Americans entered into self-employment nationwide in the 1990s. Nonminority white males were about twice as likely as Mexican-Hispanic males to be self employed, and reasons for this differential were investigated using the 1996 panel of the Survey of Income and Program Participation (SIPP). Their analysis demonstrates that the lower rates typifying Mexican Hispanics are due to lower entry into higher barrier industries; "barriers" in this instance refer to the classification of firm types by human- and financial-capital intensiveness. Absent high barriers, Mexican males are actually more likely than nonminority whites to enter into self-employment.

This special issue features three articles examining the financial-capital barriers that powerfully shape the nature of the minority business community. Alicia Robb and Robert Fairlie (this volume) review both household net worth and borrowing constraints that limit black-owned businesses' access to capital and credit. Black households nationwide possess, on average, one-eleventh as much personal wealth as whites. Robb and Fairlie note that

> Starting with this disparity, blacks are much less likely to start businesses than are whites, which results in a substantially lower rate of business ownership. Even . . . black entrepreneurs who are successful in starting businesses . . . invest much less capital at start-up on average than white entrepreneurs. Lower levels of start-up capital among black businesses appear to also limit their ability to grow and succeed. (47)

They conclude that "racial disparities in start-up capital contribute to higher failure rates, lower sales and profits, and less employment among black-owned businesses" (47).

Numerous studies in the scholarly literature reinforce Robb and Fairlie's conclusions. Even the mainstream business press has picked up this theme. Back in 1992, the Roper Organization polled 472 black-business owners nationwide for the *Wall Street Journal* to gauge how they viewed their own firms, as well as black businesses generally. Asked why there were so few black-owned firms in the nation, 84 percent responded that "black-owned businesses are impeded by a lack of access to financing" (Carlson 1992, R 16). Asked to cite specific problems impeding operations in their own firms, 61 percent indicated that "obtaining sources of capital" was a major problem; 54 percent listed "access to credit" as a major problem. These were the two most common major problems identified by the surveyed black-business owners.

Even when controlling statistically for small business traits (size, age, firm industry of operation, and the like) and owner traits (age, education, experience, etc.), banking and venture-capital investors provide less funding to MBEs than to white-owned firms (see Cavalluzzo and Cavalluzzo 1998; Bates and Bradford 1992; Blanchflower, Levine, and Zimmerman 2003; Cavalluzzo and Wolken 2005). Summing up and evaluating a wide range of studies on discrimination, Holzer and Neumark (2000) observed, "We think it fair to say . . . that the evidence is most consistent with continuing discrimination against blacks in business lending" (503).

A highly innovative analysis by Ben Craig, William Jackson III, and James Thomson (this volume) pursues a logical implication of the reality of constrained financing available to MBEs. They empirically test the hypothesis that greater availability of small-business loans has a positive impact "on economic performance in markets with a high percentage of potential minority small businesses." Greater small-business loan availability in high-minority markets, they demonstrate, translates into higher average levels of employment in those same markets. This result is important because it provides objective evidence that financial constraints on MBEs may be binding. That is, MBEs may have positive net present value projects that go unfunded because of credit market failures.

According to Timothy Bates and William Bradford (this volume), the very existence of discriminatory barriers limiting capital access to minority ventures creates an underserved market, and hence, attractive opportunities are available to firms capable of identifying and serving MBE financial-capital needs. Their analysis of venture-capital-fund investing demonstrates that the returns to the minority-focused funds are certainly no lower—indeed, slightly higher—than those of mainstream funds. Furthermore, the market risk of investments in MBEs made by minority-oriented venture-capital (VC) funds is not higher than the risk of the mainstream funds. Bates and Bradford conclude that minority-focused VC funds are investing in an underserved market niche that offers attractive returns.

Turning to large and successful African American–owned businesses, Thomas Boston and Linje Boston (this volume) explore why some firms achieve higher growth rates than their peers. Defining a firm as a "gazelle" if it was achieving annual employment growth of 20 percent or more annually, Boston and Boston identified 208 gazelles that were black-owned; their traits and strategies were compared, in turn, to 927 other ventures growing at lower (or negative) rates. The authors conclude that "the real explanation of high growth remains a 'black box' " (129).

The next article, by Jeffrey Robinson, Laquita Blockson, and Sammie Robinson, differs from the articles discussed thus far in that it delves into more subjective determinants of business behavior that are not easily subjected to statistical analysis. Based on qualitative, in-depth interviews of sixty-two African American women-business owners, they seek to explore the experiences of these entrepreneurs in their own words. This analytical technique has certain advantages over the common alternative of econometric analyses of databases. The richer detail achievable in a qualitative interview is useful for capturing nuances of issues that may be overlooked by statistical analysis.

Candida Brush, Daniel Monti, Adrea Ryan, and Amy Gannon, in their article, pursue a detailed analysis of a sample of twenty-nine entrepreneurs who participated in a Boston-based technical assistance program. In the process, the authors illuminate the concept of "civic enterprise." Most of the subjects are characterized as blending personal business and community improvement goals in the operation of their urban enterprises. Rather than falling into a strict social motivation versus profit motivation dichotomy, most of the ventures are found to combine both objectives.

Finally, Bárbara Robles, in her second contribution to this volume exploring minority entrepreneurship, examines individuals living in areas of the United States bordering Mexico who have received earned income tax credits (EITCs). She specifically targets EITC recipients who either use their EITCs to fund self-employment activities, or who are interested in knowing more about self-employment and microbusiness ownership. Self-employment is an increasing activity among low-income Hispanic families residing in border regions that are often economically depressed. Can micro enterprise, patched with other income sources, raise family incomes? Can EITC funds help to finance these activities? The longer-term research agenda being pursued by Professor Robles is addressing those issues.

Concluding Remarks

On balance, the articles constituting this special issue reveal a vibrant field of research that seeks to enhance our understanding of the nature and prospects for self-employment and small business ownership among African Americans and Latinos. Much of this research is pioneering in nature. Many of these articles push forward the boundaries of scholarly knowledge in the entrepreneurship field. Now, as a consequence, we know a great deal more about the development trajectory of minority entrepreneurship in the United States.

References

Bates, Timothy. 1973. *Black capitalism: A quantitative analysis.* New York: Praeger.
———. 1997. *Race, self-employment, and upward mobility.* Baltimore: Johns Hopkins University Press.
———. 1998. Job creation through improved access to markets for minority-owned businesses. In *The black worker in the 21st century: Job creation prospects and strategies,* ed. Wilhelmina Leigh and Margaret Simms. Washington, DC: Joint Center for Political and Economic Studies.
———. 2006. The urban development potential of black-owned businesses. *Journal of the American Planning Association* 72 (2): 272-91.
Bates, Timothy, and William Bradford. 1992. Factors affecting new firm success and their use of venture capital financing. *Journal of Small Business Finance* 2 (1): 23-38.
Blanchflower, D. G., P. B. Levine, and D. J. Zimmerman. 2003. Discrimination in the small business credit market. *Review of Economics and Statistics* 85 (4): 930-43.

Brimmer, Andrew. 1966. The Negro in the national economy. In *American Negro reference book*, ed. John David. Englewood Cliffs, NJ: Prentice Hall.

Brimmer, Andrew, and Henry Terrell. 1971. The economic potential of black capitalism. *Public Policy* 14 (2): 289-308.

Carlson, Eugene. 1992. Battling bias. *Wall Street Journal*, April 3.

Cavalluzzo, Ken, and Linda Cavalluzzo. 1998. Market structure and discrimination: The case of small businesses. *Journal of Money, Credit, and Banking* 30 (4): 771-92.

Cavalluzzo, Ken, and John Wolken. 2005. Small business loan turndowns, personal wealth and discrimination. *Journal of Business* 78 (5): 2153-78.

Holsey, Albon. 1938. Seventy-five years of Negro business. *The Crisis* 45 (7): 241-42.

Holzer, Harry, and David Neumark. 2000. Assessing affirmative action. *Journal of Economic Literature* 38 (3): 483-568.

Light, Ivan. 1972. *Ethnic enterprise in America*. Berkeley: University of California Press.

Myrdal, Gunner. 1944. *An American dilemma*. New York: Harper & Brothers.

Osborne, Alfred. 1976. The welfare effect of black capitalists on the black community. *Review of Black Political Economy* 6 (4): 477-84.

Pierce, Joseph. 1947. *Negro business and business education*. New York: Harper & Brothers.

Tabb, William. 1979. What happened to black economic development? *Review of Black Political Economy* 9 (4): 392-415.

U.S. Census Bureau. 2001. *1997 economic census: Minority- and women-owned businesses*. www.census.gov/epcd/mwb97/metro (accessed December 20, 2001).

Latino Self-Employment and Entrepreneurship in the United States: An Overview of the Literature and Data Sources

By
BÁRBARA J. ROBLES
and
HÉCTOR CORDERO-GUZMÁN

While significant attention has been paid to the growth of the Latino population and its contribution to the U.S. labor market, less scholarly and popular media attention has focused on Latino self-employment, entrepreneurship, and business growth. A review of interdisciplinary research literature on Latino entrepreneurship over the past twenty-five years indicates a gap in our knowledge about the accelerated growth in Latino small business ownership across the United States. The authors provide an overview of the current state of research on Latino entrepreneurial activities and recommend a broader research agenda that includes community-based organizations as part of the entrepreneurship landscape in urban and rural high-density Latino communities.

Keywords: Latino entrepreneurs; small business owners; self-employment; community-based organizations; country of origin; transnationalism; biculturalism

Bárbara J. Robles joined the College of Public Programs at Arizona State University as an associate professor in August 2005. She currently sits on the Board of Economic Advisors for the U.S. Hispanic Chamber of Commerce. She is a coauthor of The Color of Wealth: The Story behind the U.S. Racial Wealth Divide *(New Press, 2006) and author of* Asset Accumulation and Economic Development in Latino Communities: A National and Border Economy Profile of Latino Families *(Filene Research Institute, 2006). She is a research fellow at the Filene Research Institute.*

Héctor Cordero-Guzmán is a professor and chair of the Black and Hispanic Studies Department at Baruch College of the City University of New York and a member of the faculty in the PhD programs in sociology and urban education at the CUNY Graduate Center. He is working on a book titled Organizing Migration *on the role of community-based groups, organizations, and service providers in the migration process; the adaptation of immigrants; their political representation and incorporation; and the maintenance of ties to communities of origin.*

NOTE: This research was supported by a grant from the Kauffman Foundation. We benefited from presentations and discussions surrounding minority business and entrepreneurship research at summer conferences hosted by the University of North Carolina at Chapel Hill.

DOI: 10.1177/0002716207303541

Introduction: Latinos and Entrepreneurship

The Latino population in the United States displays considerable diversity by national origin[1] and dynamic generational status from recent arrivals to families that have lived in the United States for generations. In 2005, the U.S. Census reported more than 42.7 million Latinos residing in the United States (14 percent of the total U.S. population) and projects a Latino population of 102.6 million by 2050 (24 percent of the total U.S. population).[2] Traditional Latino communities in the United States (Phoenix, New York, Los Angeles, Miami, San Antonio, and Chicago) continue to report in-migration, while new urban and rural areas have begun to attract Latino families. These new Latino gateway areas have experienced high growth rates (Raleigh-Durham, Las Vegas, Atlanta, and Des Moines) with a corresponding increase in Latino self-employment and small business formation.

The most recent results from the *Hispanic-Owned Firms: 2002* (U.S. Department of Commerce 2006a) indicate that 1.57 million Hispanic-owned businesses operate in the United States (see tables 1 and 2). The significant growth rate of 31 percent (three times the rate of the national average, 10 percent) between 1997 and 2002 among Latino establishments has outpaced all other U.S. populations. Hispanic-owned firms generate more than $222 billion dollars in receipts and sales. Despite this growth, only 29,184 (1.8 percent) Hispanic-owned firms report receipts of $1 million or more. Hispanic-owned firms encompass country of origin diversity where 44 percent are Mexican, 10 percent Cuban, 7 percent Puerto Rican, 38 percent "Other Hispanic/Latino/Spaniard" (U.S. Department of Commerce 2006b). Additionally, of the 1.57 million Hispanic-owned businesses, 13 percent (199,601) have paid employees and employ approximately 1.5 million workers. The data indicate that the bulk of Latino-owned firms and small businesses are heavily represented in the nonemployer segment of the Latino entrepreneurship universe. Clearly, very different policy prescriptions are required for such diverse segments of the Latino entrepreneurial community.[3]

Our article sets out to provide a brief overview of the interdisciplinary research examining Latino entrepreneurial activity spanning the past twenty-five years. Since the topic is not limited to one discipline, we profile the various data sources most commonly employed in conducting research on Latino business and self-employment measures. Although we conclude our review by indicating the substantive limitations in both current data availability and previous policy initiatives, we are encouraged by the debate among Latino small business scholars who have pioneered investigating Latino entrepreneurial activity in the United States. We end our article with recommendations that include a broader scope of research and policy designed to (1) acknowledge the financial capital start-up and expansion needs of experienced corporate and business-trained Latino entrepreneurs; and (2) connect the less educated, nonemployer Latino micro-entrepreneur with community-based organizations offering basic financial resource and entrepreneurial support services.

TABLE 1
U.S. HISPANIC FIRMS BY PAID EMPLOYEE, 2002

	Hispanic Firms	Percentage of Hispanic Firms	Total Sales ($1,000s)	Percentage of Total Sales
Total firms	1,573,600	100.00	221,976,823	100.00
No paid employees	1,373,999	87.32	42,420,721	19.11
With paid employees	199,601	12.68	179,556,102	80.89

SOURCE: U.S. Department of Commerce (2006a).

TABLE 2
U.S. HISPANIC FIRMS BY PAID EMPLOYEE SIZE, 2002

	Total Hispanic Firms	Percentage of Hispanic Firms with Paid Employees	Total Sales ($1,000s)	Percentage of Total Sales
With paid employees	199,601	100.00	179,556,102	100.00
Firms with no employees	36,765	18.42	6,692,253	3.73
1-4 employees	99,611	49.91	28,300,879	15.76
5-9 employees	31,498	15.78	26,619,230	14.83
10-19 employees	18,406	9.22	26,973,834	15.02
20-49 employees	9,021	4.52	29,474,968	16.42
50-99 employees	2,790	1.40	19,461,192	10.84
100-499 employees	1,327	0.66	27,218,362	15.16
500 or more employees	183	0.09	14,815,385	8.25

SOURCE: U.S. Department of Commerce (2006a).

Research Literature Overview

We believe an important contribution to understanding the accelerating growth in Latino entrepreneurial activity is to catalog the strands of research that capture Latino entrepreneurship in its various formulations. This entails assessing scholarly work in the areas of economic and business development, migration, small business, firm behavior/organizational studies, sociology, economic anthropology, cultural geography, community studies, the informal economy, and studies of micro-enterprise lending. To date, the scant research within economics, business, and sociology tends to focus on Latino entrepreneurship with attention to immigrant versus native-born ethnic self-employment rates and small business formation. Recent research on micro-enterprises and the informal economy has begun to emerge that focuses less on the immigrant and native-born divide and more on the contribution of micro-businesses in the formal and informal economies of Latino neighborhoods and ethnic enclaves.

Self-employment studies

The literature appearing in economic and business journals (Bates 1987, 1990, 1997; Olson, Zuiker, and Montalto 2000; Fairlie and Meyer 2003; Fairlie 2004; Lofstrom 2002; Flota and Mora 2001; Mora and Davila 2006) assess the labor market barriers to Hispanic populations and focus on self-employment rates of the native-born and foreign-born as well as describing business owner characteristics. Educational attainment rates, individual or family personal wealth, customer demographics, age of enterprise, age of owner, and particularly access to financial capital have been identified as significant variables in explaining Latino[4] self-employment rates and business ownership success and failure. Many of the studies report that barriers in traditional labor markets and low human capital acquisition tend to be the driving forces behind the growth of self-employment activity among Latinos, especially the foreign-born. These studies trace out the connections between mainstream labor market opportunities and challenges and provide empirical evidence comparing Latino self-employed earnings to Latino worker earnings. The results have been mixed: for particular socioeconomic groups (disadvantaged male youth), self-employment produces higher earnings than wage-work; however, these results do not hold for female disadvantaged youth. Further research may provide more information about intergenerational links to self-employment income as well as spatial (community) characteristics linking self-employment outcomes directly to place-based factors.

Many of the studies report that barriers in traditional labor markets and low human capital acquisition tend to be the driving forces behind the growth of self-employment activity among Latinos, especially the foreign-born.

Bates (1990) described Mexican American self-employment and argued that the aggregate grouping of "Hispanic" may inappropriately mask the intragroup differences in human and financial capital resources of Latino/Hispanic small business start-ups. The diversity among the various countries of origin communities combined with their unique immigrant experiences are important features driving the Latino entrepreneurial landscape (Delgado 1998; Ruiz-Vargas 2000; Carvajal 2004; Mora and Davila 2006). From the Mexican-origin studies, findings and recommendations require a degree of consideration for culturally based entrepreneurial behaviors. One cannot simply extrapolate and predict similar entrepreneurial patterns without taking into account the country of origin, transnational ties to the home country, location of business (ethnic enclaves versus mainstream markets), and parallel sociodemographic profiles of the group in question. There is a significant difference between exporting patterns of Latino firms when assessing intragroup comparisons. Latino self-employment and small business studies have consistently focused on the native-born and immigrant differences among the Latino populations in the United States (Fairlie 2004, 2005; Lofstrom 2002; Toussaint-Comeau 2005). From these studies emerge recommendations that include thoughtful policy actions focused on human capital remediation or acquisition, access to financial resource information and planning, mentoring programs to expand business ownership in areas other than the service sector, and a greater cultivation of a diverse customer base and increased entrepreneurship programs at universities and community colleges.

Small business credit market studies

An equally important research literature on the small firm market (minority and nonminority), business credit and channels of financial capital access, provides evidence of low rates of capitalization for small businesses with particular characteristics and located in certain industry sectors. Small business lending decisions by suppliers of credit, information technology embedded in automated credit scoring, and market forces that have changed the nature of location-based banking relationships between banker and business owner appear as important areas of study in this literature. These market studies provide information on the variables that hinder access to formal commercial credit by minority-owned firms and small businesses. Not surprisingly, many of the same variables that appear in self-employment studies also appear as explanatory variables in models of commercial credit accessibility studies. Although these studies do not focus exclusively on Latino-owned firms and small businesses, they do include information about aggregate Hispanic access to commercial credit markets and government guaranteed small business loan programs (Cavalluzzo and Wolken 2005; Cavalluzzo, Cavalluzzo, and Wolken 2002; Blanchflower, Levine, and Zimmerman 2003; Bitler, Robb, and Wolken 2001; Craig, Jackson, and Thomson 2006).

Firm organizational studies

A growing literature has arisen on the characteristics and behaviors of entrepreneurs, their decision making within firms and small businesses, and particularly nascent entrepreneurial and firm expansion decision making. This area of research has relied on a combination of small area surveys, gender-based surveys (Latina entrepreneurship), and industry sector data. What most of these studies have in common is a descriptive assessment of Latino entrepreneurs; they seek to answer the question, Who are Latino business owners? From small survey (generally mail-in or telephone-respondent-based) data, they profile the "typical" Hispanic entrepreneur. What emerges from these studies are acculturation and degree of ethnic identification metrics, business problem-solving and performance measures, identifying life-cycle growth and/or structural stages of the business, and working capital and financing decisions (Vincent 1996; Shim, Eastlick, and Lotz 2000; Raijman and Tienda 2000; Ruiz-Vargas 2000). These studies also tend to characterize entrepreneurial performance and characteristics along gender lines (Sarason and Koberg 1994; Shim and Eastlick 1998; Zuiker et al. 2003; Pearce 2005).

Entrepreneurship, ethnic enclaves, and economic/community development studies

A complementary strand of literature that parallels the self-employment and small business studies appears in the sociological, informal economy, and community studies literature. These studies describe characteristics of Latino ethnic enclave business owners and ethnic niche markets while focusing on similar measures examined in the self-employment literature. Additionally, variables that incorporate intergenerational dimensions of entrepreneurial skills, family and community social networks, neighborhood resources, and nonprofit organizations that support ethnic and immigrant economic adaptation and civic engagement appear with varying degrees as important resources for initiating entrepreneurial activities (Aldrich and Waldinger 1990; Logan, Alba, and McNulty 1994; Sanders and Nee 1996; Raijman 2001; Portes, Haller, and Guarnizo 2002; Edgcomb and Armington 2003; Cordero-Guzmán 2005; Pearce 2005; Robles 2002, 2004). Although most of the studies focus on the linkages between Latino or ethnic community resources and entrepreneurship, economic development and community studies of distressed local economies also recognize the importance of minority small business viability for local economy and community development (Rondinelli, Johnson, and Kasarda 1998; Light and Gold 2000; Valenzuela 2001; Johnson 2002; Robles 2006; Cordero-Guzmán and Auspos 2006; Cordero-Guzmán and Becerra 2007) (see Table 3).

Latino Data Sources: Aggregate and Country of Origin Identifiers

Scholars conducting research on Latino self-employment and entrepreneurship have employed a wide variety of governmental data sources that include but

TABLE 3
LITERATURE SURVEY FOR LATINO ENTREPRENEURIAL ACTIVITY BY AUTHOR AND YEAR

	Latino Immigrant	Latino Native-Born	Latino Ethnic Enclave	Latino Subgroup	Latina
Self-employment	Sanders and Nee (1996); Fairlie and Meyer (1996, 2003); Fairlie (2004, 2005); Lofstrom (2002); Pearce (2005); Touissant-Comeau (2005); Mora and Davila (2006)	Bates (1987, 1990, 1997); Olson, Zuiker, and Montalto (2000); Flota and Mora (2001); Fairlie and Meyer (1996, 2003); Zuiker et al. (2003); Fairlie (2005); Mora and Davila (2006)	Sanders and Nee (1996); Delgado (1997, 1998); Raijman and Tienda (2000); Raijman (2001)	Bates (1990); Fairlie and Meyer (2000); Fairlie (2004); Lofstrom (2002); Flota and Mora (2001); Pearce (2005); Mora and Davila (2005, 2006)	Zuiker et al. (2003); Pearce (2005)
Small business and credit markets	Kasarda and Johnson (2006)	Vincent (1996); Shim, Eastlick, and Lotz (2000); Bitler, Robb, and Wolken (2001); Cavalluzzo, Cavalluzzo, and Wolken (2002); Blanchflower, Levine, and Zimmerman (2003); Cavalluzzo and Wolken (2005)	Logan, Alba, and McNulty (1994); Delgado (1997, 1998); Carvajal (2004)	Logan et al. (1994); Delgado (1997, 1998); Carvajal (2004)	Sarason and Koberg (1994); Shim and Eastlick (1998)
Micro-business	Edgcomb and Armington (2003)	Edgcomb and Armington (2003)	Rochin (1998); Edgcomb and Armington (2003); Robles (2006)	Rochin (1998); Edgcomb and Armington (2003)	Robles (2002, 2004)

Entrepreneurship	Sanders and Nee (1996); Raijman and Tienda; (2000); Raijman (2001); Valenzuela (2001); Portes, Haller, and Guarnizo (2002); Cordero-Guzmán (2005); Kasarda and Johnson (2006); Mora and Davila (2006); Cordero-Guzmán and Becerra (2007)	Valenzuela (2001); Mora and Davila (2006)	Aldrich and Waldinger (1990); Rochin et al. (1998); Raijman and Tienda (2000); Raijman (2001); Gold and Light (2001); Mora and Davila (2005); Cordero-Guzmán (2005); Robles (2006); Cordero-Guzmán and Auspos (2006)	Rochin et al. (1998); Raijman and Tienda (2000); Raijman (2001); Gold and Light (2001); Ruiz-Vargas (2001); Morawska (2004); Lippard (2005); Mora and Davila (2006)	Shim and Eastlick (1998)

are not limited to the Survey of Small Business Finances (SBF; Federal Reserve Board of Governors), Panel Study of Income Dynamics (PSID; University of Michigan, Ann Arbor), Public Use Microdata Dicennial Surveys at the 1 and 5 percent levels (PUMS; U.S. Census Bureau), Current Population Survey (CPS; U.S. Census Bureau), Characteristics of Business Owners (CBO; U.S. Census Bureau and IRS-proprietary), Survey of Income and Program Participation (SIPP; U.S. Census Bureau), Non-Employer Statistics (NES; U.S. Census Bureau), and National Youth Longitudinal Survey (NYLS; U.S. Bureau of Labor Statistics). Other researchers have turned to private data sources such as Dun and Bradstreet, the National Federation of Independent Businesses, as well as small sample surveys based on national and local Hispanic Chamber of Commerce member lists.

The data collected on Latino business owners and the self-employed have improved over time. Continuing analyses of the available data, however, creates further questions arising from scholarly findings for this particular community.

The data collected on Latino business owners and the self-employed have improved over time. Continuing analyses of the available data, however, create further questions arising from scholarly findings for this particular community. For example, does successful management of small or micro-businesses despite low levels of education and low family wealth relate to a family member (especially an extended family member) having owned a business? We know business training has an important impact on probable business success, but for particular communities, Puerto Rican and Dominican, family business operations may serve the role of corporate or university education. Since Hispanic sample sizes within these business owner data sets are limited to begin with, it is very difficult to assess the country of origin business characteristics of El Salvadorans, Dominicans, and other Latino groups. For researchers seeking to understand the entrepreneurial activities of particular Latino groups, the PUMS and CPS are the only large data sources that specifically capture Latino country of origin data. Table 4 outlines some of the characteristics and limitations of the available databases that include a Latino sample.

TABLE 4
SURVEY OF LATINO ENTREPRENEURSHIP DATA SOURCES

			Available Data Sets					
	PUMS[a]	CPS[a]	Survey of Business Owners	Characteristics of Business Owners[b,c]	NLSY[b,a]	SBF/Federal Reserve[b,c]	Survey of Consumer Finances[b]	Small Surveys[b,c]
Frequency of data collection	Every 10 years	Annual	Every 5 years	Discontinued (?)		~Every 5 years	Every 3 years	Proprietary
Selected variables								
Hispanic	X	X	X	X	X	X	X	X
Native	X	X			X			X
Foreign-born	X	X			X			X
Year of entry	X	X			X			X
Country of origin	X	X	X[d]	X[d]	X[d]			X
Gender	X	X	X	X	X	X	X	X

NOTE: PUMS = Public Use Micro Sample 1 and 5 percent of decennial census; CPS = Current Population Survey, annual; NLSY = National Longitudinal Survey of Youth—NLSY79 has years 1979-2004 (rounds 1-21) and NLSY97 has years 1997-2005 (rounds 1-8); SBF = Survey of Small Business Finances.

a. Surveys designed for socioeconomic and demographic responses.
b. Small or limited sample size of Hispanic respondents.
c. Surveys specifically designed for small business responses.
d. Hispanic country of origin breakdown is limited to Mexican, Puerto Rican, Cuban, and Other.

Assessing Latino Country of Origin Self-Employment:
A PUMS Data Example

One of the continuing issues among Latino entrepreneurship researchers is the lack of sufficiently large data samples for specific country of origin analysis. The PUMS at the 1 and 5 percent levels from the decennial census provides sufficient observations to increase our understanding of the self-employment experiences of individual Hispanic groups. The most compelling reason for employing this data source is the degree of detail provided on a state-by-state, county-by-county, and urban/rural geographical level of the various Latino subpopulations engaged in self-employment, either full-time or part-time. Moreover, it provides information on educational attainment levels as well as immigrant versus native-born characteristics.

Using the 1 percent database for New York City, we find that South Americans, specifically Peruvians (11 percent) and Colombians (12 percent), have the highest rates of self-employment, with Cubans (10 percent) and Dominicans (8 percent) displaying the next highest rates, and Mexican (7 percent) and Puerto Rican (6 percent) rates trailing. However, when parsing the data by educational attainment, it turns out that Mexican college graduates (11 percent) have one of the highest self-employment rates, with Domincans just under 10 percent and Puerto Rican college graduates at 6 percent. We find, as have other researchers, the Latino self-employed are more likely to be foreign-born and in New York, Latino self-employment increases with educational attainment. Finally, we find that in New York, the average Latino self-employed have higher annual earnings ($25,658) than do the average Latino workers ($19,357). This higher average earnings outcome has a downside: in New York, the average self-employed Latino works more hours per week and more weeks per year than the average Latino worker.

Clearly, the self-employed as described in the PUMS database are only one segment of a very diverse Latino entrepreneurial landscape. However, we note that the largest segment of the Latino business community is the nonemployer segment (87 percent); thus, the more we know about this sector by country of origin, the better able we are to asses local impact and craft national policies.

Conclusions and Recommendations

From our overview of Latino self-employment and entrepreneurship research, a consistent set of findings emerge that help explain both the accelerated growth of Latino entrepreneurial activity while capturing the barriers to successful small business life-cycle transitions. In particular, the literature suggests that (1) low educational attainment continues to be statistically significant and may be a driving force in creating the push into self-employment while contributing to the marginal existence of many Latino small businesses, (2) lack of financial resources (either personal wealth or access to capital) for operation and expansion purposes contributes to blocked business stage growth, and (3) Latino entrepreneurial activity continues to be concentrated in the service sector. The last finding is directly related to findings (1) and (2). These three persistent indicators have not changed significantly for the Latino population over the past twenty-five years. Policies crafted in a one-size-fits-all mold, however well intentioned, have contributed to the unchanging nature of the Latino business community indicators.

Research that continues uncovering the facets of the social and community links between the micro-entrepreneur and self-employed sector with the economic realities of community revitalization, gentrification, sustainable urbanism, transnational migration, ethnic biculturalism, and the permeable boundaries of the ethnic enclave would provide us with a deeper understanding of the role of the smallest entrepreneur in Latino communities and mainstream markets.

The growing college-educated pool of Latino entrepreneurs are becoming more visible and require researchers to recognize the bimodal nature of policy application for different entrepreneurial stakeholders within the Latino business community. Policy prescriptions aimed at the Latino college-educated entrepreneurial population anchored in university-business partnerships and collaborative programs that bring more entrepreneurship-skills programs and business leadership mentoring into the postgraduate, university, and community college environment could prove to have more permanent and positive outcomes. In addition, policies that include a pipeline component that creates linkages to community-based, Latino-serving organizations engaged in micro-enterprise lending and financial education outreach services would provide an upwardly mobile avenue for the less educated aspiring entrepreneur.

Notes

1. The latest Census data indicate the Latino population in the United States has the following characteristics by country of origin: 64 percent Mexican, 10 percent Puerto Rican, 3 percent Cuban, 3 percent Dominican, and 3 percent El Salvadoran, with the remaining percentages distributed among other Central and South American countries or other Hispanic or Latino origins.

2. The estimate was produced July 26, 2006, by the U.S. Census Bureau, Hispanic Heritage Month Facts, 2006 and does not include the 3.9 million residents of Puerto Rico (see http://www.census.gov/Press-Release/www/2006/cb06ff-14.pdf).

3. Bates (1997) reminded us that policies to promote minority business development in distressed local economies have a long history of repeating failed strategies.

4. Many of the studies focus on Mexican-origin populations, males in particular, given the larger sample sizes over time for this population.

References

Aldrich, H. E., and R. Waldinger. 1990. Ethnicity and entrepreneurship. *Annual Review of Sociology* 16:111-35.

Bates, T. 1987. Self-employed minorities: Traits and trends. *Social Science Quarterly* 68 (3): 539-51.

———. 1990. *Self-employment trends among Mexican-Americans.* Census Economic Studies Paper, No. 90-9. August. Washington, DC: U.S. Census Bureau, Center for Economic Studies.

———. 1997. *Race, self-employment and upward mobility: An illusive dream.* Baltimore: John Hopkins University Press; Washington, DC: Woodrow Wilson Center.

Bitler, M., A. Robb, and J. Wolken. 2001. Financial services used by small businesses: Evidence from the 1998 Survey of Small Business Finances. *Federal Reserve Bulletin*, April, 183-205.

Blanchflower, D., P. Levine, and D. Zimmerman. 2003. Discrimination in the small-business credit market. *Review of Economics and Statistics* 85 (4): 930-43.

Carvajal, M. 2004. Measuring economic discrimination of Hispanic-owned architecture and engineering firms in South Florida. *Hispanic Journal of Behavioral Sciences* 26 (1): 79-101.

Cavalluzzo, K., L. Cavalluzzo, and J. Wolken. 2002. Competition, small business financing, and discrimination: Evidence from a new survey. *Journal of Business* 75 (4): 641-79.

Cavalluzzo, K., and J. Wolken. 2005. Small business loan turndowns, personal wealth, and discrimination. *Journal of Business* 78 (6): 2153-77.

Cordero-Guzmán, H. 2005. Community-based organisations and migration in New York City. *Journal of Ethnic and Migration Studies* 31 (5): 889-909.

Cordero-Guzmán, H., and P. Auspos. 2006. Community economic development and community change. In *Community change: Theories, practice and evidence*, ed. K. Fulbright-Anderson and P. Auspos, 195-265. Washington, DC: Aspen Institute.

Cordero-Guzmán, H., and V. Q. Becerra. 2007. Transnational communities of the United States and Latin America. In *Reducing global poverty: The case for asset accumulation*, ed. C. Moser, chap. 15. Washington, DC: Brookings Institution Press.

Craig, B., W. Jackson, and J. Thomson. 2006. Small-firm credit markets, SBA-guaranteed lending and economic performance in low-income areas. Federal Reserve Bank of Cleveland, Working Paper no. 0601, Cleveland, OH.

Delgado, M. 1997. Role of Latina-owned beauty parlors in a Latino community. *Social Work* 42 (5): 445-53.

———. 1998. Puerto Rican elders and merchant establishments: Natural caregiving systems or simply business? *Journal of Gerontological Social Work* 30 (2): 33-45.

Edgcomb, Elaine, and Maria M. Armington. 2003. *The informal economy: Latino enterprises at the margin*. Washington, DC: FIELD, Aspen Institute.

Fairlie, R. W. 2004. Recent trends in ethnic and racial self-employment. *Small Business Economics* 23 (3): 203-18.

———. 2005. Entrepreneurship and earnings among young adults from disadvantaged families. *Small Business Economics* 25:223-36.

Fairlie, R. W., and B. D. Meyer. 1996. Ethnic and racial self-employment differences and possible explanations. *Journal of Human Resources* 31 (4): 756-93.

———. 2003. The effects of immigration on native self-employment. *Journal of Labor Economics* 21 (3): 619-50.

Flota, C., and M. Mora. 2001. The earnings of self-employed Mexican-Americans along the US-Mexico Border. *Annals of Regional Science* 35:483-99.

Johnson, J. 2002. A conceptual model for enhancing community competitiveness in the new economy. *Urban Affairs Review* 37 (6): 763-79.

Kasarda, D., and J. Johnson. 2006. *The economic impact of the Hispanic population on the state of North Carolina*. Frank Hawkins Kenan Institute of Private Enterprise, Kenan-Flagler Business School, University of North Carolina at Chapel Hill. http://www.kenan-flagler.unc.edu/assets/documents/2006_KenanInstitute_HispanicStudy.pdf.

Light, I., and S. Gold. 2000. *Ethnic economies*. San Diego, CA: Academic Press.

Lippard, C. 2005. Good-ole boy networks and racism: A comparison of white, black and Latino entrepreneurs in the Atlanta construction industry. Society for the Study of Social Problems, Conference Paper, Philadelphia.

Lofstrom, M. 2002. Labor market assimilation and the self-employment decision of immigrant entrepreneurs. *Journal of Population Economics* 15:83-114.

Logan, J., R. Alba, and T. McNulty. 1994. Ethnic economics in metropolitan regions: Miami and beyond. *Social Forces* 72 (3): 691-724.

Mora, M., and A. Davila. 2005. Ethnic group size, linguistic isolation, and immigrant entrepreneurship in the USA. *Entrepreneurship and Regional Development* 17 (5): 389-404.

———. 2006. Mexican immigrant self-employment along the US-Mexico border: An analysis of 2000 census data. *Social Science Quarterly* 87 (1): 91-109.

Morawska, E. 2004. Immigrant transnational entrepreneurs in New York. *International Journal of Entrepreneurial Behavior and Research* 10 (5): 325-48.

Olson, P., V. S. Zuiker, and C. P. Montalto. 2000. Self-employed Hispanics and Hispanic wage earners: Differences in earnings. *Hispanic Journal of Behavioral Sciences* 22 (1): 114-30.

Pearce, S. 2005. Today's immigrant woman entrepreneur. *Immigration Policy in Focus* 4 (1): 1-17.

Portes, A., W. Haller, and L. E. Guarnizo. 2002. Transnational entrepreneurs: The emergence and determinants of an alternative form of immigrant economic adaptation. *American Sociological Review* 67 (2): 278-98.

Raijman, R. 2001. Determinants of entrepreneurial intentions: Mexican immigrants in Chicago. *Journal of Socio-Economics* 30:393-411.

Raijman, R., and M. Tienda. 2000. Training functions of ethnic economies: Mexican entrepreneurs in Chicago. *Sociological Perspectives* 43 (3): 439-56.

Robles, B. 2002. Latino microenterprise and the US-Mexico border economy. *Estey Centre Journal of International Law and Trade Policy* 3 (2): 307-27.

———. 2004. Emergent entrepreneurs: Latina-owned businesses in the borderlands. *Texas Business Review*, October. Bureau of Business Research, McCombs School of Business, University of Texas–Austin.

———. 2006. *Asset accumulation and economic development in Latino communities: A national and border economy profile of Latino families*. Madison, WI: Filene Research Institute.

Rochin, R., R. Saenz, S. Hampton, and B. Calo. 1998. Colonias and Chicano/a entrepreneurs in rural California. Research Report no. 16, December, Julian Samora Research Institute, Michigan State University, East Lansing.

Rondinelli, D., J. Johnson, and J. Kasarda. 1998. The changing forces of urban economic development: Globalization and city competitiveness in the 21st century. *Cityscape: A Journal of Policy Development and Research* 3 (3): 71-105.

Ruiz-Vargas, Y. 2000. Small business financing sources between immigrants and natives in Puerto Rico. *Quarterly Review of Economics and Finance* 40:387-99.

Sanders, J. M., and V. Nee. 1996. Immigrant self-employment: The family as social capital and the value of human capital. *American Sociological Review* 61 (2): 231-49.

Sarason, Y., and C. Koberg. 1994. Hispanic women small business owners. *Hispanic Journal of Behavioral Sciences* 16 (3): 355-60.

Shim, S., and M. A. Eastlick. 1998. Characteristics of Hispanic female business owners: An exploratory study. *Journal of Small Business Management* 36 (3): 18-34.

Shim, S., M. A. Eastlick, and S. Lotz. 2000. Examination of U.S. Hispanic-owned, small retail and service businesses: An organizational life-cycle approach. *Journal of Retailing and Consumer Services* 7:19-32.

Toussaint-Comeau, M. 2005. Self-employed immigrants: An analysis of recent data. *Chicago Fed Letter*, No. 213, April.

U.S. Department of Commerce. 2006a. *Hispanic-owned firms: 2002*. Washington, DC: 2002 Economics Census, Survey of Business Owners, Department of Commerce. http://www.census.gov/prod/ec02/sb0200cshisp.pdf.

———. 2006b. *Survey of minority-owned business enterprises*. 1992 and 1997. Washington, DC: U.S. Census Bureau, U.S. Department of Commerce.

Valenzuela, A. 2001. Day labourers as entrepreneurs? *Journal of Ethnic and Migration Studies* 27 (2): 335-52.

Vincent, V. 1996. Decision-making policies among Mexican-American small business entrepreneurs. *Journal of Small Business Management* 34 (4): 1-13.

Zuiker, V. S., M. J. Katras, C. P. Montalto, and P. D. Olson. 2003. Hispanic self-employment: Does gender matter? *Hispanic Journal of Behavioral Sciences* 25:73-94.

This article examines causes of the low self-employment rates among Mexican-Hispanics by studying self-employment entry using the 1996 panel of the Survey of Income and Program Participation (SIPP). The data show that Mexican-Hispanics are less likely to be self-employed or enter self-employment, relative to non-Hispanic whites. The authors analyze self-employment by recognizing heterogeneity in business ownership across industries and show that a classification of firms by human and financial capital "intensiveness," or entry barriers, is effective in explaining differences in entrepreneurship across ethnic groups. The authors show that the lower self-employment entry rates among Mexican-Hispanics are due to lower entry rates into business ownership of firms in relatively high-barrier industries. In fact, Hispanics are more likely to start up a business in a low-barrier industry than whites.

Keywords: self-employment; entrepreneurship; Hispanic

Mexican-Hispanic Self-Employment Entry: The Role of Business Start-Up Constraints

By
MAGNUS LOFSTROM
and
CHUNBEI WANG

M exican-Hispanics are substantially less likely to be self-employed compared to non-Hispanic whites. Specifically, male Mexican-Hispanic self-employment rates are one-half of the self-employment rates of non-Hispanic whites, about 8 and 16 percent, respectively. This is similar to the difference in self-employment rates observed between whites and African Americans. Not surprisingly, the significantly lower minority self-employment rates are recognized by policymakers. The presence of a large number of government programs intended to increase

Magnus Lofstrom is an assistant professor of economics at the University of Texas at Dallas and a research fellow at the Institute for the Study of Labor (IZA). His research interests are in labor economics and applied microeconomics and covers topics in immigration, entrepreneurship, welfare, and education.

Chunbei Wang is a PhD candidate in economics at the University of Texas at Dallas. Her research interests include self-employment, immigration, and education.

NOTE: We thank Tim Bates, participants at the first Entrepreneurship Boot Camp, and the Conference on Entrepreneurship among Minorities and Women for helpful comments. Funding from the Ewing M. Kauffman Foundation is gratefully acknowledged.

DOI: 10.1177/0002716207303577

business ownership among minorities, such as set-asides and loans to minorities, shows policymakers' concern with the lower self-employment rates among minorities, including Hispanics, and suggests a perception of existing business ownership constraints that lead to some degree of economic inefficiency in the absence of market interventions (see, for example, Bates [1993] for a discussion of some of the programs and their success). Two potentially contributing factors to the low Mexican-Hispanic self-employment rates are their relatively low levels of educational attainment and limited access to financial capital. These constraints are likely to manifest themselves in differences across ethnic groups in the industries which minorities seek to enter. In this article, we address the role of industries and business start-up constraints faced by minorities in explaining the gap in self-employment rates between non-Hispanic whites and Mexican-Hispanics.

Up to now, research on Hispanic self-employment has not received nearly the same attention as African American entrepreneurship. Hispanics are of particular interest given the fact that this is the fastest-growing ethnic group in the United States. Primarily fueled by immigration from Mexico, Hispanics now represent almost 14 percent of the U.S. population, slightly greater than the proportion of non-Hispanic blacks (U.S. Census Bureau 2006). Like African Americans, Hispanics are a disadvantaged minority group, but there are a number of differences between the two groups, particularly regarding family composition, educational attainment, immigration status, and historical experiences in the United States. Given this, and the size and growth of Hispanics in the United States, this important ethnic group deserves separate attention. In this article, we focus our analysis on the largest Hispanic group in the United States, Mexican-Hispanics.

Our descriptive analysis shows that differences in industry composition across groups are significant in explaining business start-up differences between Mexican-Hispanics and non-Hispanic white males. We show that treating business ownership simply as a binary outcome (i.e., self-employment or not self-employment) hides significant complexities in entrepreneurship differences between Mexican-Hispanics and whites. Our data show that Mexican-Hispanic males are *more* likely than white males to start up new businesses in industries that require relatively low levels of educational attainment and that are not financially capital-intensive and that Mexican-Hispanic business start-ups are concentrated in these industries.

Previous Research

To identify possible determinants of the Mexican-Hispanic self-employment rate, we build on the entrepreneurship literature addressing business ownership choice. A major focus of the literature is on the role of access to financial capital: Do capital constraints shape self-employment entry and exit? This is often assessed by investigating whether exogenous changes in household net worth impact the decision to become a business owner, holding other factors constant. These studies typically find evidence of binding liquidity constraints in business start-ups (e.g., Evans and Leighton 1989; Evans and Jovanovic 1989; Lindh and Ohlsson 1996). An exception is Hurst and Lusardi (2004). Furthermore, Holtz-Eakin, Joulfaian, and Rosen (1994b) found that greater assets, measured as inheritances, lead to higher probability of business survival, again suggesting that liquidity constraints are binding. Furthermore, Bates (1990a, 1990b) found that an owner's educational background is a major determinant of both business survival and the financial capital structure of small business start-ups. Other factors linked to the self-employment entry decision include managerial ability (e.g., Jovanovic 1982); risk aversion (e.g., Kihlstrom and Laffont 1979); nonpecuniary benefits of owning one's business (e.g., Blanchflower and Oswald 1998); and intergenerational links, including parental wealth (Dunn and Holtz-Eakin 2000).

[T]reating business ownership simply as a binary outcome (i.e., self-employment or not self-employment) hides significant complexities in entrepreneurship differences between Mexican-Hispanics and whites.

These factors have also been linked to explaining low self-employment rates among African Americans and Hispanics, or Latinos. Although differences in household net worth, education, and family structure across groups have been found to partly explain differences in self-employment entry and exit rates (Fairlie 1999; Hout and Rosen 2000), differences in parental entrepreneurship appears to explain a significant proportion of the gap (Fairlie 1999; Hout and Rosen 2000). The fact that a substantial proportion of Hispanics are immigrants, and possess low levels of financial and human capital, as well as limited relevant business start-up information, is also a contributor to the self-employment gap (Fairlie and Meyer 1996).

Another aspect of financial capital constraints that may explain differences in business ownership is differential treatment in the credit market. Blanchflower, Levine, and Zimmerman (2003) found that black-owned small businesses are more likely to be denied credit and, if approved, pay a 1 percentage point higher interest rate than whites, even after controlling for differences in creditworthiness. Credit constraints are likely to impact the types of industries that minorities seek to enter and, hence, the industry composition of the minority business community (Bates 1995).

The only existing research, to our knowledge, directly addressing the lower self-employment rates among Hispanics by studying business entry and exits is by Fairlie and Woodruff (2005), who used matched Current Population Survey data and found that differences in education and wealth are key factors in explaining the low self-employment rates among Mexican Americans. Our nationally representative longitudinal data, the Survey of Income and Program Participation (SIPP), has the advantage of following individuals over a four-year period, as well as more detailed information regarding assets and business ownership. The SIPP data also contain information on the industry of the firm, which is important since we address the role of the industry that the entrepreneur chooses and operates in explaining the Mexican-Hispanic–white self-employment gap.

Data

Our data are derived from the 1996 panel of the SIPP and cover the four-year period from 1996 to 1999. The 1996 SIPP survey is a rotating panel made up of 12 waves of data collected every four months for approximately 36,700 U.S. households. The 1996 panel oversampled low-income households, and hence sampling weights are used throughout our analysis, making the data nationally representative. As with previous SIPP panels, each wave contains both core questions that are common to each wave and topical questions that are not updated in each wave. In addition to the core variables, we use information from two topical modules: immigration (which includes information on country of origin as well as year of arrival) and assets and liabilities (containing wealth and asset data, collected each year in waves 3, 6, 9, and 12).

The sample used is restricted to Mexican-Hispanic and non-Hispanic white males between the ages of twenty and sixty-four in the survey period. We do not restrict our sample to only full-time working individuals since a significant proportion of business entries are from nonemployment. Concentrating this specific research on males simplifies the analysis somewhat since male labor supply issues are arguably less complicated. Furthermore, we restrict our sample to males for whom immigration status and wealth information are available, as well as to individuals who are observed in at least two consecutive years. The sample restrictions yield a sample of 135,596 observations, or 19,756 individuals. Last, we define an individual to be self-employed if he reported owning a business in the sample wave and hence use the terms business start-up and self-employment entry interchangeably.

Self-Employment Entry

The number of individuals who are self-employed is determined by the number of individuals who enter and exit self-employment. In this article, we focus on differences in business start-ups between Mexican-Hispanics and whites.[1] We address the role of differences in the industry composition of entrepreneurs in explaining the relatively low Mexican-Hispanic self-employment rate.

Table 1 shows that the Mexican-Hispanic self-employment rate is 8.5 percent, more than half the self-employment rate among non-Hispanic whites, 16.1 percent.

TABLE 1
SELF-EMPLOYMENT RATES AND TRANSITIONS BY RACE/ETHNICITY

	Mexican-Hispanics		White (Non-Hispanics)	
	Percentage	N	Percentage	N
Self-employment rate	8.52	10,720	16.10	124,876
Self-employment entry	2.36	9,618	2.65	103,204
Entry from wage/salary	2.09	8,328	2.59	89,557
Entry from unemployment	6.01	316	9.41	1,520
Entry from NILF	5.16	1,008	4.73	12,760

SOURCE: 1996 Survey of Income and Program Participation.
NOTE: The self-employment entry rate sample size, N, refers to the number of observations where the person was not self-employed the previous year. NILF = not in the labor force.

The lower self-employment rates among Mexican-Hispanics, relative to whites, partially reflect lower Mexican-Hispanic self-employment entry rates. Table 1 also shows self-employment entry rates, defined as the probability of entering self-employment during a given year conditional on not being self-employed the previous year.[2] The table shows that Mexican-Hispanics have lower self-employment entry rates by about 0.3 percentage points, compared to non-Hispanic whites, 2.4 and 2.7 percent each. The table also indicates that slightly more than 10 percent of individuals who start their own business do so by coming from nonemployment. This suggests that it is of some importance to not restrict the sample to working individuals.

The relatively small differences in self-employment entry rates between Mexican-Hispanics and whites suggest that the main source of the observed Hispanic-white self-employment gap is the difference in self-employment exit rates. However, even though the differences in business entry rates are relatively small, this does not imply that they are unimportant and/or that minorities do not face additional business start-up constraints. We first demonstrate that the small self-employment entry rate difference helps explain a portion of the self-employment gap and then turn to examining potential start-up barriers.

One way to illustrate how small differences in entry rates have a meaningful impact on self-employment rates, and differences between groups, is to demonstrate what the self-employment gap would be if Mexican-Hispanics were as likely to enter self-employment as whites, that is, an increase in the Mexican-Hispanic self-employment entry rate by only 0.3 percentage points. Furthermore, we assume that self-employment is in steady-state and hence the self-employment rate can be expressed as the Entry Rate/(Entry Rate + Exit Rate), where we use the self-employment exit rates reported in Lofstrom and Wang (2006). In this hypothetical example, the Mexican-Hispanic self-employment rate would increase by slightly more than 1 percentage point and hence reduce the self-employment rate gap by that amount. In other words, this small difference in entry rates accounts for approximately 15 percent of the lower Mexican-Hispanic self-employment rate.

TABLE 2
SAMPLE STATISTICS BY ETHNICITY/RACE AND
SELF-EMPLOYMENT (CONDITIONAL ON EMPLOYMENT)

	Mexican-Hispanics		White (Non-Hispanics)	
	Wage/ Salary	Self- Employed	Wage/ Salary	Self- Employed
High school dropout	0.40	0.46	0.06	0.07
High school graduate	0.30	0.23	0.32	0.28
Some college	0.24	0.22	0.31	0.27
College graduate	0.06	0.09	0.31	0.38
Age	36.07	42.28	40.10	44.45
Married	0.69	0.79	0.69	0.76
Number of children	1.59	1.60	0.85	0.90
Number of persons in household	4.37	4.30	3.08	3.11
Urban resident	0.90	0.82	0.78	0.74
Immigrant	0.49	0.50	0.03	0.03
Years since immigration[a]	17.28	18.72	15.98	20.83
Total annual earnings				
Mean	23,040	22,246	39,023	46,866
Median	19,610	16,640	32,036	29,889
Hours work/week	41.32	46.24	43.44	50.49
Job tenure	6.42	N/A	8.79	N/A
Business tenure	N/A	6.81	N/A	9.63
Household wealth				
Mean	45,828	81,465	135,693	304,735
Median	15,050	36,537	57,141	135,096
Annual household asset income	125	151	632	1,452
Number of individuals	1,436	169	14,946	3,205
Sample size	8,133	913	87,775	20,102

SOURCE: 1996 Survey of Income and Program Participation.

a. Conditional on being an immigrant.

Industries and potential entry barriers

The self-employment entry difficulties Mexican-Hispanics may face are possibly due to low endowments of human capital, as well as limited access to financial resources. Table 2 shows that educational attainment of Mexican-Hispanics is substantially below that of whites. For example, close to one-half of self-employed Mexican-Hispanics have not completed high school, and only 9 percent are college graduates. The corresponding proportions among non-Hispanic white entrepreneurs are 7 percent high school dropouts and 38 percent college graduates. Table 2 also shows that household wealth among Mexican-Hispanics

TABLE 3
BUSINESS OWNERSHIP CHARACTERISTICS, PERCENTAGE OF BUSINESS
OWNERS AND SAMPLE MEANS, BY RACE/ETHNICITY

	Mexican-Hispanic	White (Non-Hispanic)
Business type (%)		
Incorporated	7.4	27.4
Unincorporated	69.1	49.2
Unincorporated with partner	10.3	11.1
Household business partner	6.2	11.6
Business equity ($)	25,037	89,537

SOURCE: 1996 Survey of Income and Program Participation.

is significantly below that of non-Hispanic whites.[3] Whether the latter should be interpreted as an indication of limited access to financial capital or as due to other factors, such as low schooling levels, is not clear. Nonetheless, there appear to be significant differences in human capital endowment, and possibly financial resources, between Mexican-Hispanics and whites. We will address some of the consequences of these differences on self-employment and, in particular, how small differences in self-employment entry rates may disguise business start-up barriers.

The type of business ownership is also of interest and related to potential barriers to entering self-employment. The SIPP data contain information on what type of business the individual owns, as well as business equity. These characteristics are shown in Table 3. The table shows that self-employed Mexican-Hispanics are substantially less likely to own an incorporated business than non-Hispanic whites. Furthermore, mean business equity is found to be lower among Hispanic-owned businesses than white-owned businesses. It is particularly low among Mexican-Hispanics, about $25,000, compared to close to $90,000 for the non-Hispanic whites. Although these observed characteristics may be the outcome of differences in the selection of types of business ownership between minorities and whites (see, e.g., Kawaguchi 2005), they are also consistent with Hispanics facing additional capital constraints, relative to whites, as well as group differences in educational attainment.

The relatively low educational attainment level of Mexican-Hispanics is likely to restrict access to certain industries (such as professional services, which includes physicians, dentists, and lawyers) and may "push" Mexican-Hispanic entrepreneurs into less selective, educationally speaking, industries. If industries that require relatively high schooling levels also have relatively high business survival rates, we may not observe large differences in business start-up rates, but average exit rates may be higher for Mexican-Hispanics. Furthermore, if Mexican-Hispanics enter certain types of less well-funded businesses or industries, because they face limited access to capital, it may reveal itself in higher business failure rates, even though the self-employment entry rates are not dramatically different. Clearly, it is quite challenging to address the latter issue, but the above discussion suggests that a closer look at industries is important to understand why Mexican-Hispanics are less likely to be business owners than non-Hispanic whites.

The relatively low educational attainment level of Mexican-Hispanics is likely to restrict access to certain industries (such as professional services, which includes physicians, dentists, and lawyers) and may "push" Mexican-Hispanic entrepreneurs into less selective, educationally speaking, industries.

Clearly, potential business ownership constraints faced by minorities are not directly observable. However, they may manifest themselves in the choice of industry, or types of business, as discussed above. For example, if minorities face additional lending constraints, as suggested by Blanchflower, Levine, and Zimmerman (2003) and Cavalluzzo, Cavalluzzo, and Wolken (2002), we would expect to see fewer minorities in financial capital-intensive industries. As discussed above, however, some barriers to self-employment are observable. For example, given the substantial observed differences in educational attainment between Mexican-Hispanics and whites, many Hispanics effectively do not have access to certain human capital–intensive industries. This can, at least partially, be addressed by simply controlling for schooling levels in regression models. However, Mexican-Hispanics' stock of human capital may be valued and/or perceived differently from non-Hispanics, suggesting that education may play different roles across ethnic/racial groups. Evidence of different roles of education in the U.S. labor market, in terms of schooling's impact on earnings, between immigrants and natives is found in Betts and Lofstrom (2000). Given the large proportion of immigrants among Mexican-Hispanics, this is relevant to the self-employment decision, which is at least partially based on expected earnings.

The distribution of industries in which entrepreneurs operate is substantially different between Mexican-Hispanics and whites. Table 4 shows the industry distribution for business owners, as well as mean years of schooling and business equity by these industries. The table shows that Mexican-Hispanic business owners are most

TABLE 4
BUSINESS OWNERSHIP–INDUSTRY CHARACTERISTICS AND DISTRIBUTION,
BY RACE/ETHNICITY

	Industry Characteristics: Sample Mean			
	Years of Schooling	Business Equity ($)	Mexican-Hispanic	White (Non-Hispanic)
Agriculture/forestry/fisheries	13.0	176,169	5.5	9.4
Construction	12.4	64,595	33.1	19.9
Manufacturing	13.8	106,813	3.9	5.6
Transportation/communications	12.3	59,313	6.6	4.6
Wholesale trade	14.0	139,648	1.1	5.4
Retail trade	13.3	71,833	13.9	10.0
Finance/insurance/real estate	15.0	112,720	3.0	5.9
Business services	14.5	63,265	3.0	8.5
Personal services	13.9	57,700	3.8	3.1
Entertainment/recreation services	14.6	20,587	2.0	4.2
Professional/related services	17.7	98,527	3.9	16.6
Gardening/landscaping	11.5	63,168	6.8	2.0
Repair services	11.7	26,275	13.5	4.4

SOURCE: 1996 Survey of Income and Program Participation.

likely to own a business in the construction industry, about 33 percent of Mexican-Hispanic entrepreneurs, which is also an industry with relatively low educational attainment and business equity. The construction industry is also the most common industry in which to own a business among whites, but by roughly 13 fewer percentage points. A large proportion of non-Hispanic whites own businesses in the professional services industry, slightly more than 16 percent. Only about 4 percent of Mexican-Hispanics own a business in this industry, where business owners have, on average, close to eighteen years of schooling, making them the most highly educated entrepreneurs. Overall, it appears that Mexican-Hispanics are overrepresented, relative to whites, in industries with lower educational attainment levels and business equity. The observed differences in the self-employed industry composition suggest that it is important to address the role of industries that vary in their human and financial capital requirements, as argued by Bates (1995), in analyzing self-employment differences between Mexican-Hispanics and whites.

Self-employment entry by industry groups

   In the analysis below, we attempt to tackle the above issues by analyzing self-employment entry into specific industry groups. The groups are defined based on industry human- and financial-capital requirements.

A practical restriction we face is that the number of individuals in the industries specified in Table 4 is in some cases small, particularly by ethnicity, making relatively precise inference difficult. Instead, we define three industry categories based on human and financial capital requirements, or barriers, to enter the industry. Clearly, any classification of industry categories, such as entry difficulty or barriers, is somewhat arbitrary.[4] Nonetheless, to determine whether an industry is a low-, medium-, or high-barrier industry, we use the 1997 Annual Capital Expenditure Survey (ACES) to determine average fixed private capital by the fourteen industries defined in Table 4, and the 2000 Census 5 percent Public Use Microdata Sample (PUMS) to determine entrepreneurs' educational attainment by industry. Based on the above data, we categorize gardening/landscaping, construction, retail trade, and repair services as low-barrier industries since all these industries display relatively low average educational attainment levels (roughly around high school graduate or below) and average capital expenditures rank among the lowest (all are in the bottom third). The medium-barrier category consists of firms in agriculture, manufacturing, transportation/communications, wholesale trade, business services, personal services, and entertainment/recreation services. These are industries in which entrepreneurs typically have at least some college education and/or average capital expenditures are in the midrange among our industries. The high-barrier industry category consists of firms in the finance/insurance/real estate and professional/related services industries. According to the 2000 Census, more than 85 percent of entrepreneurs in the finance/insurance/real estate and professional/related industries have some college education, while the 1997 ACES data show that businesses in the finance/insurance/real estate industries have the highest average capital expenditures.

Last, the increase in the number of categories, or choices, (no entry, entry into a low-barrier industry, entry into a medium-barrier industry, or entry into a high-barrier industry) also implies that the yearly probability of an individual choosing to enter self-employment in a specific industry group, or not, is rather small. Hence, for the analysis below, we focus on the four-year sample period entry probabilities, that is, the probability that an individual who was not self-employed during the first SIPP wave in 1996 becomes self-employed in the subsequent eleven waves.

We show the sample period self-employment entry rates by industry group separately for Mexican-Hispanics and whites in Table 5. The table reveals several interesting points. The probability a Mexican-Hispanic male will start up a business in the low-barrier industry group over the sample period is 4.4 percent, while it is only 2.9 percent for white males. That is, although Mexican-Hispanics are less likely to enter self-employment than whites, by approximately 1.8 percentage points, they are 1.5 percentage points *more* likely to start up a business in a low-barrier industry than whites. The picture is quite different when we analyze entry into medium- and high-barrier industry groups. The probability that a Mexican-Hispanic will start his own business during the 1996 to 1999 sample period in the medium-barrier industry group is 1.8 percent, almost one-half of the self-employment entry rate in this industry group among whites, 3.4 percent. The difference in the high-barrier industry self-employment entry rate is even

TABLE 5
SELF-EMPLOYMENT ENTRY PROBABILITIES BY INDUSTRY GROUP, FULL
SAMPLE PERIOD, BY RACE/ETHNICITY

	Mexican-Hispanic	White (Non-Hispanic)
Sample period transition probabilities		
No entry	93.7	91.9
Self-employment entry	6.3	8.1
Industry group entry probability		
Entry into low-barrier industry[a])	4.4	2.9
Entry into medium-barrier industry[b])	1.8	3.4
Entry into high-barrier industry[c])	0.2	1.9
Number of individuals	1,436	14,946

SOURCE: 1996 Survey of Income and Program Participation.
a. Gardening/landscaping, construction, retail trade or repair services.
b. Agriculture, manufacturing, transportation/communications, wholesale trade, business services, personal services, entertainment/recreation services.
c. Finance/insurance/real estate, professional/related services.

starker. Only 0.2 percent of our sample of Mexican-Hispanics started a business in this industry group, compared to 1.9 percent among whites.

[A]lthough Mexican-Hispanics are less likely to enter self-employment than whites, by approximately 1.8 percentage points, they are 1.5 percentage points more likely to start up a business in a low-barrier industry than whites.

The classification of self-employment entry by industry groups shows that the lower self-employment entry rate among Mexican-Hispanics is due to lower business start-up rates in the medium- and high-barrier industries. The self-employment entry rates by industry group also show that Mexican-Hispanics are quite likely to start their own businesses. However, the business start-ups are concentrated in the least difficult industries to enter, as measured by human capital and financial resource requirements. Table 5 shows that about two-thirds of Mexican-Hispanic business start-ups are in low-barrier industries, while only about one-third of white business entries are in these industries. Almost all of the other observed Mexican-Hispanic business start-ups are in the medium-barrier industry group, approximately one-third of all start-ups, while slightly more than 40 percent of white business start-ups are in this group. While only about 3 percent of newly entered Mexican-Hispanic self-employed males are in the high-barrier industry, almost one-fourth of white business start-ups are in this industry category. It is quite clear from Table 5 that the types of businesses started up are quite different for Mexican-Hispanics and non-Hispanic whites.

Summary and Conclusions

This article contributes to the minority entrepreneurship research by analyzing self-employment among Mexican-Hispanics, an important and growing minority group that has been relatively overlooked in the entrepreneurship literature. Our data reveal that Mexican-Hispanic males are substantially less likely to be business owners, relative to whites. We investigate the causes of the difference between Mexican-Hispanic–white differences in business ownership rates by analyzing self-employment entry rates, particularly the role of industries, and potential barriers to business start-ups.

Although these differences [in types of businesses owned] are partially due to differences in factors such as educational attainment, they are also consistent with existence of minority business start-up credit constraints that lead to less well-funded small business and/or selection into less capital-intensive industries.

We observe relatively small differences in self-employment entry rates across groups. We argue that this should not be interpreted to mean that Mexican-Hispanics do not face additional barriers to enter self-employment. We observe differences across groups in types of businesses owned, that is, incorporated or unincorporated, and industry composition. Although these differences are partially due to differences in factors such as educational attainment, they are also consistent with existence of minority business start-up credit constraints that lead to less well-funded small business and/or selection into less capital-intensive industries. Also, we show that relatively small differences in entry rates have a meaningful impact on the Mexican-Hispanic–white self-employment gap.

We discuss and examine the role of industries in further explaining differences in entrepreneurship between Hispanics and whites. Notably, we show that treating business ownership simply as a binary outcome (i.e., self-employment or not self-employment) hides significant complexities in self-employment differences across ethnic groups. We categorize firms into three industry groups based on human and financial capital requirements to enter the industry: low-, medium-, and high-barrier. This reveals that Mexican-Hispanics are more likely than whites to become business owners in the low-barrier industry group, the industry group where Mexican-Hispanic business start-ups are concentrated.

The observed lower self-employment entry rates among Mexican-Hispanics are due to lower entry rates into the relatively higher barrier industries. Although not addressed in this article, we investigate in more detail the role of educational attainment and household wealth in a separate work (see Lofstrom and Wang 2006). That analysis indicates that differences in industry group self-employment entry rates are primarily due to lower educational attainment levels among Mexican-Hispanics, although differences in financial wealth appear to contribute to some extent. It also shows that the industry grouping used in this article is very effective in explaining differences across ethnic groups in self-employment exit rates.

The findings in this article, and in Lofstrom and Wang (2006), are consistent with the hypothesis that the lower self-employment rate among Mexican-Hispanics, relative to whites, is at least partially due to human and financial capital start-up constraints. Particularly, the lower educational attainment levels among Mexican-Hispanics appear to restrict business start-ups to low-barrier industries. This points to the possibility that policies aimed at increasing the currently low average Mexican-Hispanic schooling levels may also succeed in increasing the Hispanic self-employment rate. Last, an important issue for future research is to assess whether there are differences in the success of self-employed Mexican-Hispanics and whites within industry groups. The entry barriers addressed in this article may also affect the success of Mexican-Hispanic entrepreneurs, which may be one of the mechanisms that leads to the observed low Mexican-Hispanic self-employment rate.

Notes

1. See Lofstrom and Wang (2006) for an analysis of self-employment exits among Hispanic males.

2. The entry rates shown in Table 1 appear to be consistent with previous research on self-employment entry. For example, Holtz-Eakin, Joulfaian, and Rosen (1994a, 1994b) reported four-year entry rates, 1981-1985, based on administrative data of 6.8 percent, quite similar to the sample period entry rate obtained with our definition of self-employment using the Survey of Income and Program Participation (SIPP) data with the above-specified sample, about 8 percent. Some of the differences are likely to be due to changes in self-employment since the 1980s and our sample selection.

3. Household wealth is defined as the sum of financial assets and equity in home, vehicle, and owned business.

4. We generated the results presented in Table 5 with two alternative definitions of the three industry groups as a robustness check of our definition. First, we define the highest of the low- and medium-barrier industries as medium and high, respectively. This puts retail trade in the medium-barrier industry and business services and transportations/communications in the high-barrier category. Our second alternative industry group definition puts the lowest of the medium- and high-barrier industries in the low and medium groups, respectively, which places agriculture in the low-barrier industry group while the real estate category is defined as a medium-barrier industry. Although the redefinitions change the reported entry rates and Hispanic-white gaps somewhat, the qualitative results and conclusions discussed in the article appear robust to these alternative industry groupings. The results and tables generated using the alternative definitions are not shown but are available upon request from the authors.

References

Bates, Timothy. 1990a. Entrepreneur human capital inputs and small business longevity. *Review of Economics and Statistics* 72 (4): 551-59.

———. 1990b. Self-employment trends among Mexican Americans. Working Paper, U.S. Census Economic Studies, Washington, DC.

———. 1993. *Assessment of state and local government minority business development programs.* Report to the U.S. Department of Commerce Minority Business Development Agency. Washington, DC: U.S. Department of Commerce.

———. 1995. Self-employment entry across groups. *Journal of Business Venturing* 10:143-56.

Betts, Julian R., and Magnus Lofstrom. 2000. The educational attainment of immigrants: Trends and implications. In *Issues in the economics of immigration*, ed. George J. Borjas, 51-115. Chicago: University of Chicago Press, for National Bureau of Economic Research.

Blanchflower, David G., P. Levine, and D. Zimmerman. 2003. Discrimination in the small business credit market. *Review of Economics and Statistics* 85 (4): 930-43.

Blanchflower, David G., and Andrew J. Oswald. 1998. What makes an entrepreneur? *Journal of Labor Economics* 16:26-60.

Cavalluzzo, Ken, Linda Cavalluzzo, and John Wolken. 2002. Competition, small business financing, and discrimination: Evidence from a new survey. *Journal of Business* 25 (4): 641-79.

Dunn, T., and D. Holtz-Eakin. 2000. Financial capital, human capital, and the transition to self-employment: Evidence from intergenerational links. *Journal of Labor Economics* 18:282-305.

Evans, David S., and Boyan Jovanovic. 1989. An estimated model of entrepreneurial choice under liquidity constraints. *Journal of Political Economy* 97:808-27.

Evans, David S., and Linda S. Leighton. 1989. Some empirical aspects of entrepreneurship. *American Economic Review* 79:519-35.

Fairlie, Robert W. 1999. The absence of the African-American owned business: An analysis of the dynamics of self-employment. *Journal of Labor Economics* 17 (1): 80-108.

Fairlie, Robert W., and Bruce D. Meyer. 1996. Ethnic and racial self-employment differences and possible explanations. *Journal of Human Resources* 31:757-93.

Fairlie, Robert W., and Christopher Woodruff. 2005. Mexican-American entrepreneurship. Paper presented at the 10th annual meeting of the Society of Labor Economists, San Francisco, June.

Holtz-Eakin, Douglas, David Joulfaian, and Harvey S. Rosen. 1994a. Entrepreneurial decisions and liquidity constraints. *Rand Journal of Economics* 25:334-47.

———. 1994b. Sticking it out: Entrepreneurial survival and liquidity constraints. *Journal of Political Economy* 102:53-75.

Hout, Michael, and Harvey Rosen. 2000. Self-employment, family background, and race. *Journal of Human Resources* 35 (4): 670-92.

Hurst, Erik, and Annamaria Lusardi. 2004. Liquidity constraints, household wealth, and entrepreneurship. *Journal of Political Economy* 112 (2): 319-47.

Jovanovic, Boyan. 1982. The selection and evolution of industry. *Econometrica* 50 (3): 649-70.

Kawaguchi, Daiji. 2005. Negative self selection into self-employment among African Americans. *Topics in Economic Analysis & Policy* 5 (1): article 9.

Kihlstrom, Richard E., and Jean-Jacques Laffont. 1979. A general equilibrium entrepreneurial theory of firm formation based on risk aversion. *Journal of Political Economy* 87 (4): 719-48.

Lindh, Thomas, and Henry Ohlsson. 1996. Self-employment and windfall gains. Evidence from the Swedish lottery. *The Economic Journal* 106:1515-26.

Lofstrom, Magnus, and Chunbei Wang. 2006. Hispanic self-employment: A dynamic analysis of business ownership. IZA Discussion Paper no. 2101, March, Institute for the Study of Labor (IZA), Bonn, Germany.

U.S. Census Bureau. 2006. *Statistical abstract of the United States*. Washington, DC: U.S. Department of Commerce.

Access to Financial Capital among U.S. Businesses: The Case of African American Firms

Using data from multiple sources, including the Characteristics of Business Owners Survey, the authors trace out the relationship between wealth and access to financial capital and the African American–owned business. African Americans are found to have levels of wealth that are one-eleventh those of whites. Starting with this disparity, blacks are much less likely to start businesses than are whites, which results in a substantially lower rate of business ownership. Even for those black entrepreneurs who are successful in starting businesses, the authors find that they invest much less capital at start-up on average than white entrepreneurs. Lower levels of start-up capital among black businesses appear to also limit their ability to grow and succeed. Racial disparities in start-up capital contribute to higher failure rates, lower sales and profits, less employment among black-owned businesses, and less survivability of the business.

Keywords: minority entrepreneurship; small business financing; African American businesses; business outcomes

By
ALICIA M. ROBB
and
ROBERT W. FAIRLIE

1. Introduction

The differences between African American business ownership rates and white business ownership rates are striking. Estimates from the 2000 Census indicate that 11.8 percent of white workers are self-employed business owners, compared with only 4.8 percent of black workers. Furthermore, black-white differences in business ownership rates have remained roughly constant over most of the twentieth century (Fairlie and Meyer 2000). In addition to lower rates of business ownership, black-owned businesses are less successful on average than are white or Asian firms. In particular, black-owned businesses have, on average, lower sales, hire fewer employees, and have smaller payrolls than white- or Asian-owned businesses (U.S. Census Bureau 2001; U.S. Small Business Administration 2001). Black firms also have

DOI: 10.1177/0002716207303578

lower profits and higher closure rates than white firms (U.S. Census Bureau 1997; U.S. Small Business Administration 1999). For most outcomes, the disparities are extremely large. For example, estimates from the 2002 Survey of Business Owners (SBO) indicate that white firms have average sales of $437,870 compared with only $74,018 for black firms.

The performance of black-owned businesses in the United States is a major concern among policymakers. Although controversial, there exist a large number of federal, state, and local government programs providing set-asides and loans to minorities, women, and other disadvantaged groups.[1] In addition, many states and the federal government are promoting self-employment as a way for families to leave the welfare and unemployment insurance rolls (Vroman 1997; Kosanovich et al. 2001; Guy, Doolittle, and Fink 1991; Raheim 1997). The interest in entrepreneurship and business development programs has been spurred by arguments from academicians and policymakers that entrepreneurship provides a route out of poverty and an alternative to unemployment.[2] It has been argued, for example, that the economic success of several immigrant groups in the United States is due, in part, to their ownership of small businesses (see Loewen 1971; Light 1972; Baron, Kahan, and Gross 1985; Bonacich and Modell 1980; Min 1996).

Stimulating minority business creation in sectors with high growth potential (e.g., construction, wholesale trade, and business services) may also represent an effective public policy for promoting economic development and job creation in

Alicia M. Robb is a research associate at the University of California, Santa Cruz. She is also the founder and president of the Foundation for Sustainable Development, an international grassroots community development organization. She previously worked as an economist for the Small Business Administration and the Federal Reserve Board of Governors. She received her PhD in economics from the University of North Carolina at Chapel Hill.

Robert W. Fairlie is an associate professor of economics and the director of the Masters Program in Applied Economics and Finance at the University of California, Santa Cruz. He was a visiting fellow at Yale University and is a research affiliate at RAND and the National Poverty Center at the University of Michigan.

NOTE: This research was partially funded by the Russell Sage Foundation and the Kauffman Foundation. The research in this article was conducted while the authors were special sworn status researchers of the U.S. Census Bureau at the Center for Economic Studies and California Research Data Center at the University of California, Berkeley. This article has been screened to ensure that no confidential data are revealed. The data can be obtained at a Census Research Data Center or at the Center for Economic Studies (CES) only after approval by the CES and IRS. See http://www.ces.census.gov/ for details on the application and approval process. The views expressed here are solely the responsibility of the authors and should not be interpreted as reflecting the views of the Russell Sage Foundation, the Kauffman Foundation, the U.S. Census Bureau, or the Board of Governors of the Federal Reserve System. We would like to thank Ken Brevoort, Tim Bates, Ken Couch, Tom Dunn, Kevin Moore, John Wolken, Will Jackson, and seminar participants at the Winter 2003 Meeting of the American Economic Association, the Board of Governors of the Federal Reserve System, the University of Maryland, the Urban Institute, Baruch College, Yale University, Dartmouth College, 2006 Kauffman/UNC Bootcamp, and the NBER Workshop on Entrepreneurship for their comments and suggestions. Bill Koch and Garima Vasishtha provided excellent research assistance.

poor neighborhoods (Bates 1993b). Past data show that minority firms have hired more than 4.2 million employees in the United States, with a disproportionate share of them being minorities (U.S. Census Bureau 1997, 2001). Self-employed business owners are also unique in that they create jobs for themselves. Business ownership is the main alternative to wage/salary employment for making a living and thus has important implications for earnings and wealth inequality. Both black and white entrepreneurs are found to have more upward mobility and less downward mobility in the wealth distribution than wage/salary workers (Bradford 2003).

Another important concern is that blacks are constrained in their choice to become business owners. For example, if liquidity constraints are present, which restrict access to financial capital, some blacks may not become entrepreneurs who otherwise would have become entrepreneurs given better access to capital. Limited access to financial capital may also result in undercapitalized businesses, limiting potential growth among black-owned businesses. These constraints not only hurt economic progress among blacks but also create more general efficiency loss in the economy. Many innovative products and services may never make it to the market because of these constraints.

Limited access to financial capital may . . .
result in undercapitalized businesses,
limiting potential growth among black-owned
businesses. These constraints not
only hurt economic progress among blacks,
but also create more general efficiency
loss in the economy.

Previous research on the low levels of business ownership and relative underperformance of black-owned businesses found that relatively low levels of education, assets, and parental self-employment were partly responsible (see Bates [1997], Fairlie [1999], and Hout and Rosen [2000] for a few recent examples). The lack of success among black-owned businesses relative to white-owned businesses in terms of higher rates of business closure, lower sales and profits, and less employment has been linked to low levels of start-up capital, education, and business human capital and disadvantaged family business backgrounds (Bates 1997; Fairlie and Robb 2007b). Although previous research provides explanations for low rates of black entrepreneurship and worse outcomes among black firms, previous studies have not traced out the relationship between wealth and access to financial capital and the life of the African American–owned business. The key questions addressed are as follows: First, do low levels of black personal wealth limit the formation of new businesses? Second, are blacks investing smaller amounts of capital in the new businesses that are created? Finally, among those businesses that are created, are lower levels of start-up capital resulting in less successful black-owned businesses relative to white-owned businesses?

To address these questions, we conduct a synthesis of the literature and an extensive analysis of data from several sources. These sources include the confidential and restricted-access Characteristics of Business Owners (CBO), Survey of Minority Owned Businesses (SMOBE), Survey of Business Owners (SBO), the Current Population Survey (CPS), the Panel Study of Income Dynamics (PSID), published estimates from the Survey of Income and Program Participation (SIPP), and published data from the CBO. The remainder of this article is organized as follows. In section 2, we provide a detailed discussion of these data. We discuss and analyze the black-white disparities in business ownership rates and business performance levels in section 3. Section 4 describes the racial disparities in wealth, while section 5 covers how personal wealth relates to business entry. We discuss racial differences in start-up capital in section 6. We discuss both racial differences in borrowing patterns and lending discrimination in section 7. Finally, in section 8 we provide some summary remarks and a few suggestions for future research in this area.

2. Data

The 1992 CBO survey was conducted by the U.S. Census Bureau to provide economic, demographic, and sociological data on business owners and their business activities (see U.S. Census Bureau [1997], Bates [1990a], Headd [1999], and Robb [2000] for more details on the CBO). The CBO is unique in that it contains detailed information on both the characteristics of business owners and the characteristics of their businesses. For example, owner characteristics include education, detailed work experience, hours worked in the business, and how the business was acquired; and business characteristics include profits, sales, employment, and industry. Most business characteristics refer to 1992, with the main exception being closure, which is measured over the period 1992 to 1996. Important for this analysis, the CBO contains information on business inheritances, business ownership among family members, and prior work experience in a family member's business and a large oversample of black-owned businesses.

The SBO is conducted by the U.S. Census Bureau every five years to collect statistics that describe the composition of U.S. businesses by gender, race, and ethnicity. This survey was previously conducted as the Survey of Minority- and

Women-Owned Business Enterprises (SMOBE/SWOBE). Data are compiled from several sources: IRS business tax returns, other Economic Census reports (e.g., Annual Survey of Manufacturers; Annual Retail Trade Survey), Social Security information on race and Hispanic or Latino origin, and a mailout/mail-back survey. The universe for the most recent survey is all firms operating during 2002 with receipts of $1,000 or more that filed tax forms as individual proprietorships, partnerships, or any type of corporation.[3] The SBO provides statistics that describe the composition of U.S. businesses by gender, race, and ethnicity. Additional statistics include owner's age, education level, veteran status, and primary function in the business; family- and home-based businesses; types of customers and workers; and sources of financing for expansion, capital improvements, or start-up. Economic policy makers in federal, state, and local governments use the SBO data to understand conditions of business success and failure by comparing census-to-census changes in business performances and by comparing minority-/nonminority- and women-/men-owned businesses.

The CPS is a monthly survey of about fifty thousand households conducted by the U.S. Census Bureau for the Bureau of Labor Statistics. Some of the items this survey covers are employment, unemployment, earnings, educational attainment, income, poverty, health insurance coverage, job experience and tenure, and school enrollment. Self-employed business owners can be identified from the class of worker information from their main job activity.

We also show results from other research that uses the PSID, which is a longitudinal study of a representative sample of U.S. individuals (men, women, and children) and the family units in which they reside and the SIPP, a continuous series of national panels that collects source and amount of income, labor force information, program participation and eligibility data, and general demographic characteristics.

3. Black-White Disparities in Business Ownership and Outcomes

We first report and discuss African American business ownership rates and business outcomes. We make comparisons to whites, non-Latinos, and additional major ethnic and racial groups for perspective. Microdata from the 2004 Outgoing Rotation Group File to the CPS are used for this analysis. These are the latest available national data on business ownership in the United States. Estimates of self-employed business ownership rates are reported in Table 1. The self-employment rate is defined as the percentage of nonagricultural workers that are self-employed business owners. Individuals working less than fifteen hours in the survey week are excluded to rule out weak attachment to the labor market and very small scale businesses.

A clear ordering of self-employment propensities across ethnic and racial groups emerges. Whites, non-Latinos, and Asians have the highest self-employment

TABLE 1
SELF-EMPLOYMENT RATES BY ETHNICITY/RACE: CURRENT POPULATION
SURVEY (CPS), OUTGOING ROTATION GROUP FILES (2004)

	Self-Employment Rate	Sample Size
White, non-Latino	11.2%	135,094
African American	5.1%	15,685
Latino	7.4%	17,133
Asian	11.0%	7,334
Total	10.0%	179,986

NOTE: (1) The sample consists of individuals ages sixteen and over who work fifteen or more hours during the survey week. (2) Self-employment status is based on the worker's main job activity and includes owners of both unincorporated and incorporated businesses. (3) Agricultural industries are defined using the North American Industry Classification System (NAICS) classifications and are excluded. (4) Estimates only include individuals reporting one race. (5) All estimates are calculated using sample weights provided by the CPS.

rates, whereas blacks have the lowest rates. The black self-employment rate of 5.1 percent is 46 percent of the white rate. Although there is evidence of improvement of black business ownership rates relative to white rates in recent years, disparities in business ownership rates have not declined substantially over time (see Fairlie and Meyer 2000).

Racial differences in business outcomes essentially follow the same patterns as business ownership rates. Black-owned businesses underperform white-owned firms, on average. We present results from the SBO, SMOBE, and CBO. Estimates from these sources are taken from published sources, special tabulations prepared for us by the Census Bureau, and generated from restricted-access microdata.

Estimates of sales and receipts by race from the 2002 SBO and prior SMOBE surveys (1982-1997) indicate that minority-owned businesses have lower total and average sales than white-owned businesses (see Table 2). Throughout the past two decades, black firms have substantially underperformed white-owned firms. For example, 2002 average sales and receipts are $74,018 for black-owned firms. In contrast, white-owned firms have average sales of $437,870.

Estimates from the 1992 CBO also indicate large racial disparities in business outcomes. Table 3 reports estimates of 1992 profits, employment, and sales, as well as closure rates between 1992 and 1996 from CBO microdata. For these estimates we use our sample of businesses with a substantial hours worked commitment by the owners. This restriction rules out the large number of very small businesses in the United States that are included in the SBO and SMOBE estimates. By restricting our sample to only include firms in which at least one owner worked at least twelve weeks during the year and at least ten hours per week, we reduce the number of firms in our sample by 22.1 percent. As expected, the

TABLE 2
SALES AND RECEIPTS BY RACE: SURVEY OF
MINORITY-OWNED BUSINESS ENTERPRISES (1982-1997)
AND SURVEY OF BUSINESS OWNERS (2002)

	All Firms	White-Owned Firms	Black-Owned Firms	Latino-Owned Firms	Asian- and Pacific Islander–Owned Firms
Total number of firms					
1982	12,059,950	11,284,494	308,260	248,141	204,211
1987	13,695,480	12,472,231	424,165	422,373	355,331
1992	17,253,143	15,154,826	620,912	771,708	603,426
1997	18,278,933	15,403,329	780,770	1,121,433	785,480
1997[a]	20,440,415	17,316,796	823,499	1,199,896	912,960
2002[a]	22,485,449	18,320,664	1,197,988	1,574,159	1,137,628
Total sales and receipts ($1,000s)					
1982	$967,450,721	$926,423,019	$9,619,055	$14,976,337	$15,785,561
1987	$1,994,808,000	$1,916,277,919	$19,762,876	$24,731,600	$33,124,326
1992	$3,324,200,000	$3,115,407,754	$32,197,361	$72,824,269	$95,713,613
1997	$4,239,708,305	$3,899,023,305	$42,671,000	$114,431,000	$161,142,000
1997[a]	$8,392,001,261	$7,763,010,611	$71,214,662	$186,274,581	$306,932,982
2002[a]	$8,844,543,267	$8,077,248,001	$92,681,562	$226,468,398	$348,542,296
Mean sales and receipts					
1982	$80,220	$82,097	$31,204	$60,354	$77,300
1987	$145,654	$153,644	$46,592	$58,554	$93,221
1992	$192,672	$205,572	$51,855	$94,368	$158,617
1997	$231,945	$253,129	$54,652	$102,040	$205,151
1997[a]	$410,559	$448,294	$86,478	$155,242	$336,195
2002[a]	$393,345	$440,882	$77,364	$143,866	$306,376

SOURCE: U.S. Census Bureau, Economic Census, Survey of Minority-Owned Business Enterprises (1982, 1987, 1992, 1997); U.S. Census Bureau, Survey of Business Owners (2002); and U.S. Census Bureau, Survey of Business Owners, special tabulations prepared by Valerie Strang (U.S. Census Bureau) using IRS data from Statistics of Income.
NOTE: (1) The white category for 1982, 1987, and 1992 is equal to the total minus all minority groups, and the white category for 2002 is equal to all white firms minus Latino-owned firms. (2) All firms excludes publicly held, foreign-owned, not for profit and other, which are not included in the estimates for ethnic/racial groups. (3) Asian estimates for 1992 are taken from the 1997 Census report.
a. Estimates for 1997 and 2002 include C corporations. Estimates for all other years exclude C corporations.

resulting sample has higher sales and employment on average than the SMOBE estimates for 1992, which is the underlying sample frame for the CBO.

We first discuss the results for black-owned businesses and make comparisons to white-owned businesses. The magnitude of the disparities in business outcomes found in our CBO sample is striking. For example, for 1992, only 13.9 percent of black-owned firms have annual profits of $10,000 or more, compared with

TABLE 3
SMALL BUSINESS OUTCOMES BY RACE: CHARACTERISTICS
OF BUSINESS OWNERS, 1992

	All Firms	White-Owned Firms	Black-Owned Firms
Percentage of firms in 1992 no longer operating in 1996 (closure)	22.5	22.6	26.9
Percentage of firms with a net profit of at least $10,000	30.1	30.4	13.9
Percentage of firms with a positive net profit	74.5	75.1	60.7
Percentage of firms with one or more paid employee(s)	21.3	21.4	11.3
Mean number of employees	1.77	1.80	0.63
Mean sales	$212,791	$219,190	$59,415
Mean log sales	10.10	10.10	9.43
Sample size	38,020	15,872	7,565

NOTE: (1) The sample includes businesses that are classified by the IRS as individual proprietorships or self-employed persons, partnerships and subchapter S corporations, have sales of $500 or more, and have at least one owner who worked at least twelve weeks and ten hours per week in the business. (2) All estimates are calculated using sample weights provided by the Characteristics of Business Owners.

30.4 percent of white-owned firms. In fact, the entire distribution of business net profits before taxes for black-owned firms is to the left of the distribution for white-owned firms (with the exception of the largest loss categories).[4] Surprisingly, nearly 40 percent of all black-owned firms have *negative* profits. Black-owned firms also have lower survival rates than white-owned firms. The average probability of business closure between 1992 and 1996 is 26.9 percent for black-owned firms compared with 22.6 percent for white-owned firms.[5]

Estimates from CBO microdata confirm the findings from SMOBE data on black-white differences in sales and employment. Black-owned firms are substantially smaller on average than are white-owned firms. Mean sales or total receipts among black-owned firms were $59,415 in 1992. Average sales among white-owned firms were nearly four times larger. The difference is not simply due to a few very large white firms influencing the mean. Median sales for black firms were one half that of white firms, and the percentage of black firms with sales of $100,000 or more was less than half the percentage of white firms. Estimates from the CBO also indicate that black-owned firms hire fewer employees than white-owned firms. In 1992, they averaged only 0.63 employees, whereas white-owned firms hired 1.80 employees. Interestingly, only 11.3 percent of black-owned firms hired *any* employees. In comparison, 21.4 percent of white-owned firms hired at least 1 employee. As we saw earlier, these trends have continued through the more recent surveys.

TABLE 4
HOUSEHOLD ASSETS BY RACE: U.S. CENSUS BUREAU ESTIMATES (1983-2000)

	Total	White	White, non-Latino	Black
Median net worth				
1983	$32,667	$39,135		$3,397
1988	$35,752	$43,279		$4,169
1991	$36,623	$44,408		$4,604
1993	$37,587	$45,740		$4,418
1995	$40,200	$49,030		$7,073
1998	$41,681	$52,301	$59,700	$5,490
2000	$46,506	$58,716	$67,000	$6,166
Percentage with own home, 2000	67.2		73.0	46.8
Median equity in own home among home owners, 2000	$59,000		$64,200	$35,000

SOURCE: U.S. Census Bureau estimates from various years of the Survey of Income and Program Participation (SIPP).

4. Wealth Inequality

Although earnings inequality continues to exist between blacks and whites (U.S. Bureau of Labor Statistics 2004), racial inequality in wealth is an order of magnitude larger in the United States. The median net worth of whites is nearly eleven times higher than the median net worth of blacks (see Table 4). The median level of net worth, defined as the current value of all assets minus all liabilities on those assets, for black households is only slightly more than $6,000. Remarkably, that estimate implies that if one adds home equity, the value of all savings, retirement and mutual fund accounts, and other assets, 50 percent of all black households have less than $6,166 in net worth. The median level of net worth among white households is $67,000. Large racial differences in net worth are also found using other datasets and within age groups, education levels, and marital statuses (for example, see Blau and Graham 1990; Oliver and Shapiro 1995; Scholz and Levine 2004; Altonji and Doraszelski 2005).

Examining the full distribution of wealth reveals even more inequality than revealed by a comparison of medians (Figure 1). Twenty-nine percent of blacks have net worth that is negative or zero. Forty-five percent of blacks have net worth of less than $5,000. Only about 11 percent of whites have net worth that is zero or negative. And less than one-fifth of all whites have net worth below $5,000. At the top of the distribution, only 2.7 percent of blacks have a value of net worth that is at least $250,000. Among whites, 22.2 percent have values of net worth in this range. Comparing asset distributions makes it strikingly clear— blacks are overwhelmingly more likely to have low asset levels and less likely to have high asset levels than are whites.

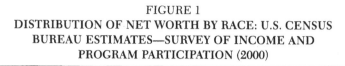

FIGURE 1
DISTRIBUTION OF NET WORTH BY RACE: U.S. CENSUS
BUREAU ESTIMATES—SURVEY OF INCOME AND
PROGRAM PARTICIPATION (2000)

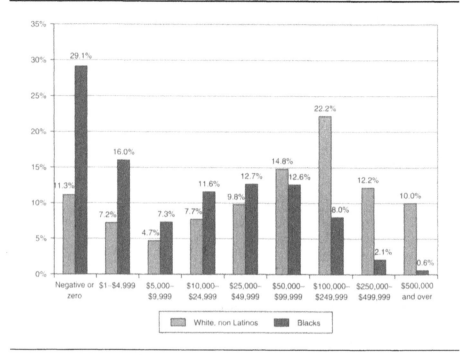

The single largest asset held by most households is their home. Estimates of
home ownership reported in Table 4 indicate that only 46.8 percent of all black
households own their own homes. For whites, 73.0 percent own their own home.
Blacks who own their home have much less home equity than whites. The
median home equity among black homeowners is $35,000, whereas the median
home equity among white homeowners is $64,200. Blacks are clearly less likely
to own their own homes and, among those who own homes, have less equity in
their homes. This is due to a combination of lower home values and having lower
equity/debt ratios in their homes.

Estimates from the SIPP also indicate that wealth inequality has decreased
only slightly in the past two decades. In 1983, the white/black ratio of median
asset levels was 11.5. By 2000, the ratio dropped to 9.5. However, some of this
decrease may have been due to the large increase in the white Latino population
in the 1980s and 1990s. Latinos have very low levels of net worth, which are only
slightly higher than the levels for blacks. If white, non-Latinos are used to
calculate the white/black ratio of median net worth, we find a ratio of 10.9. In
either case, racial wealth inequality is extremely large and does not appear to be
disappearing quickly.

Racial inequality in wealth is likely to have negative consequences for business formation and success through its effects on access to financial capital. Low levels of wealth and liquidity constraints may create a substantial barrier to entry for black entrepreneurs. Lower levels of wealth among blacks may translate into less access to start-up capital. Business creation is often funded by owner's equity and investors frequently require a substantial level of owner's investment of his or her own capital as an incentive and as collateral. Racial differences in home equity may be especially important in providing access to start-up capital. Homes provide collateral, and home equity loans provide relatively low-cost financing. Inadequate access to financial capital in turn limits business creation. Relatively low levels of human capital may limit the ability of black entrepreneurs to successfully run their businesses, and restricted access to financial capital may result in undercapitalized businesses and the inability of black firms to "weather" financial storms.

Relatively low levels of human capital may limit the ability of black entrepreneurs to successfully run their businesses, and restricted access to financial capital may result in undercapitalized businesses and the inability of black firms to "weather" financial storms.

---

5. Personal Wealth and Business Entry

The importance of personal wealth has taken center stage in the literature on the determinants of entrepreneurship and business ownership. Numerous studies using various methodologies, measures of wealth, and country microdata explore the relationship between wealth and self-employment. Most studies find that asset levels (e.g., net worth) measured in one-year increase the probability of entering self-employment by the following year.[6] The finding has generally been interpreted as providing evidence that entrepreneurs face liquidity constraints, although there is some recent evidence against this interpretation (Hurst and Lusardi 2004).[7]

These findings in the previous literature suggest that relatively low levels of assets among blacks may be a source of racial differences in rates of business ownership. Indeed, recent research using statistical decomposition techniques

TABLE 5
DECOMPOSITION OF BLACK/WHITE GAPS IN BUSINESS
ENTRY RATES: CURRENT POPULATION SURVEY (CPS), MATCHED
ANNUAL DEMOGRAPHIC SURVEYS (1998-2003) AND PANEL
STUDY OF INCOME DYNAMICS (PSID) (1968-1989)

	Specification		
	(1) CPS	(2) PSID	(3) PSID
Coefficient estimates	Pooled	White	Black
White/minority gap in entry rate	0.0144	0.0201	0.0201
Contributions from racial differences in:			
Sex	−.0002		
	−1.6%		
Education	.0009	.0012	.0001
	6.0%	5.8%	0.5%
Age	.0000		
	0.0%		
Marital status and children	.0007		
	5.0%		
Not-employed	−.0005		
	−3.4%		
Assets	.0022	.0028	.0031
	15.5%	13.9%	15.2%
Region	.0010		
	6.7%		
Central city status	.0008		
	5.4%		
Year effects	.0001		
	0.6%		
Father's education level		.0008	.0010
		4.2%	4.8%
Father's self-employment status		.0015	.0027
		7.5%	13.6%
Age, marital status, children, and other controls		−.0034	−.0010
		−17.1%	−5.0%
All included variables ("explained" part of the gap)	.0049	.0029	.0058
	34.0%	14.2%	29.1%

SOURCE: Fairlie (1999, 2007).
NOTE: (1) The CPS sample consists of individuals (ages twenty-five to fifty-five) who are not self-employed business owners in year t. The PSID sample consists of male nonagricultural workers (ages sixteen to fifty-four) who are heads of family units. (2) Contribution estimates are from nonlinear decompositions.

that estimate the explanatory effects of several potential factors provides evidence supporting this hypothesis. Table 5 reports estimates from two previous studies (Fairlie 1999, 2007). Estimates from matched CPS Annual Demographic

Files (ADF) data from 1998 to 2003 indicate that the largest single factor explaining racial disparities in business creation rates are differences in asset levels (specification 1). Assets are measured by home ownership, and dividend, interest, and rental income. Investment and rental income are not a direct measure of assets, but are roughly proportional to asset levels. These measures are included separately to allow for differential values on the underlying assets and liquidity. All measures of assets are measured prior to the self-employment decision. Estimates from the decompositions indicate that lower levels of assets among blacks account for 15.5 percent of the white/black gap in the probability of entry into self-employment.

The findings from the CPS data are very similar to estimates from Fairlie (1999) for men using the PSID. Estimates from the PSID indicate that 13.9 to 15.2 percent of the black-white gap in the transition rate into self-employment can be explained by differences in assets, which are statistically significant (see specifications 2 and 3 in Table 5).

These findings from the CPS and PSID are consistent with the presence of liquidity constraints and low levels of assets limiting opportunities for black entrepreneurs to start businesses. In turn, these lower rates of business entry contribute to the lower rates of business ownership discussed above (Fairlie 1999, 2007).

6. Racial Differences in Start-Up Capital

Although previous research provides evidence that is consistent with low levels of personal wealth resulting in lower rates of business creation among blacks, very little research has focused on the related question of whether low levels of personal wealth and liquidity constraints also limit the ability of black entrepreneurs to raise start-up capital, resulting in undercapitalized businesses. The consequence is that these undercapitalized businesses will likely have lower sales, profits, and employment and will be more likely to fail than businesses receiving the optimal amount of start-up capital, which we investigate further in the next section.

To investigate this question, we analyze data from the CBO. The CBO contains categorical information on "the total amount of capital required to start/acquire the business" (U.S. Census Bureau 1997, C-15).[8] Some caution is warranted, however, in interpreting racial differences in this measure and their contribution to racial differences in business outcomes. The amount of required start-up capital is potentially endogenous to business success (Bates 1990b). The problem is that potentially successful business ventures are likely to generate more start-up capital than business ventures that are viewed as being potentially less successful. Thus, we cannot determine with certainty that lower levels of start-up capital are primarily driven by constraints in obtaining financing. In support of the use of this measure, however, there is evidence suggesting that the size of inheritances received by individuals increases the amount of capital invested in the business (Holtz-Eakin, Joulfaian, and Rosen 1994a). This finding suggests that the receipt of inheritances might relieve liquidity constraints, and thus lower levels of start-up capital, which at least partly reflect barriers to access to financial capital.

Additional evidence on the link between start-up capital and owner's wealth is provided by examining the relationship between business loans and personal commitments, such as using personal assets for collateral for business liabilities and guarantees that make owners personally liable for business debts. Using data from the Survey of Small Business Finances (SSBF) and Survey of Consumer Finances (SCF), Avery, Bostic, and Samolyk (1998) found that the majority of all small business loans have personal commitments. The common use of personal commitments to obtain business loans suggests that wealthier entrepreneurs may be able to negotiate better credit terms and obtain larger loans for their new businesses, possibly leading to more successful firms.[9] Cavalluzzo and Wolken (2005) found that personal wealth, primarily through home ownership, decreases the probability of loan denials among existing business owners. If personal wealth is important for existing business owners in acquiring business loans, then it may be even more important for entrepreneurs in acquiring start-up loans. Interestingly, however, Avery, Bostic, and Samolyk (1998) did not find evidence of a consistent relationship between personal commitments and owner's wealth across specifications.

Estimates from the 1992 CBO microdata indicate that black-owned businesses have very low levels of start-up capital relative to white-owned businesses (Figure 2). Less than 2 percent of black firms start with $100,000 or more of capital and 6.5 percent have between $25,000 and $100,000 in start-up capital. Nearly two-thirds of black businesses have less than $5,000 in start-up capital. Although a large percentage of white firms also start with little capital, a higher percentage start with large amounts of capital than black firms. Nearly 5 percent of white firms start with $100,000 or more in capital, and 11.1 percent start with between $25,000 and $100,000.

Racial disparities in start-up capital may reflect differences in the perceived potential success of firms, and thus ability to raise capital by firms. In other words, black entrepreneurs have difficulty raising capital because their businesses are predicted to be less likely to succeed. If so, banks and other investors will rationally decline to invest in these businesses. Of course, an alternative explanation is that black business owners invest less start-up capital in their businesses because they have less access to capital. This may be due to having lower levels of personal and family wealth to borrow against or use as equity financing and may also be due to lending discrimination. Evidence favoring these explanations over the alternative explanations that black businesses are predicted to be less successful by potential investors is provided by the finding that black-owned firms have lower levels of start-up capital across all major industries (U.S. Census Bureau 1997). Thus, racial disparities in start-up capital do not simply reflect racial differences in the industries of these firms. In addition, the finding that personal wealth decreases the probability that an existing firm is denied a loan is consistent with racial disparities in wealth contributing to racial differences in start-up capital.

FIGURE 2
START-UP CAPITAL BY RACE: CHARACTERISTICS OF
BUSINESS OWNERS, 1992

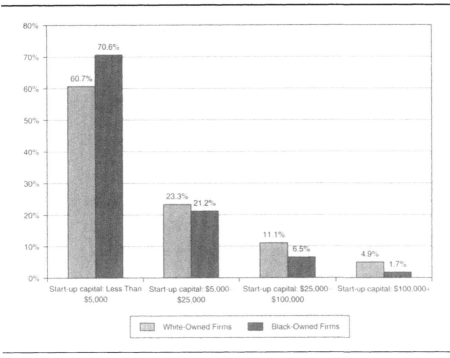

What are the likely consequences of these racial disparities in start-up capital? In particular, do low levels of personal wealth and liquidity constraints limit the ability of black entrepreneurs to raise start-up capital, resulting in undercapitalized businesses? These undercapitalized businesses will likely have lower sales, profits, and employment and will be more likely to fail than businesses receiving the optimal amount of start-up capital. Indeed, previous research indicates that the level of start-up capital is a strong predictor of business success (see, for example, Bates 1997; Fairlie and Robb 2007a). Although it is difficult to measure the magnitude of the causal effect, theoretically we expect it to be large. If start-up capital levels are influenced by entrepreneurial wealth, a strong link between racial inequality in wealth and racial disparities in business outcomes is expected. Related to this issue, and potentially exacerbating the problem, is that black entrepreneurs may face discrimination in the lending market, which will also limit their ability to invest in their businesses.

The literature on minority business ownership provides evidence that access to financial capital limits opportunities for blacks to start businesses as discussed above. A much smaller literature indicates that racial differences in wealth or start-up capital affect business success. Using earlier CBO data, Bates (1989, 1994,

1997) found evidence that racial differences in business outcomes are associated with disparities in levels of start-up capital. Estimates from the 1987 CBO indicate that black-owned businesses have substantially lower levels of start-up capital than white-owned businesses. Bates also found that start-up capital levels are strongly positively associated with business survival. These two findings indicate that racial disparities in start-up capital contribute to racial differences in survival.

[R]acial disparities in start-up capital do not simply reflect racial differences in the industries of these firms . . . the finding that personal wealth decreases the probability that an existing firm is denied a loan is consistent with racial disparities in wealth contributing to racial differences in start-up capital.

Robb (2000) provided additional evidence on the importance of start-up capital using employer firms from the 1992 CBO linked to the 1992 to 1996 Business Information Tracking Series. Estimates from regression models indicate that the level of start-up capital has a negative and statistically significant effect on the probability of business closure. Black employer firms are also found to have substantially lower levels of start-up capital than white employer firms. Thus, racial disparities in the amount of capital used to start the business result in higher closure rates among black employer firms relative to white employer firms.

Estimates from the 1992 CBO microdata also provide evidence suggesting that racial disparities in start-up capital contribute to worse outcomes among black-owned businesses. There is a strong positive relationship between start-up capital and business success. Higher levels of start-up capital are associated with lower closure probabilities, higher profits, more employment and higher sales (Fairlie and Robb forthcoming-a). In addition, estimates from the 1992 CBO indicate that blacks have substantially lower levels of start-up capital, which are likely due in part to low levels of personal wealth and may also be due to lending discrimination. Thus, black-white differences in start-up capital appear to contribute to racial disparities in business outcomes. What we do not know from these findings, however, is how much these differences contribute to racial disparities in business outcomes. We also do not know how much racial differences in start-up capital contribute to business outcomes relative to other factors such as education, business human capital, family business background, and other owner and firm differences.[10]

Table 6 reports estimates from a procedure that decomposes black-white gaps in small business outcomes into contributions from racial differences in owner and business characteristics, and from racial differences in the determinants and unexplained part of business outcomes.[11] The separate contributions from racial differences in each set of independent variables are reported. These variables are potential determinants of small business outcomes. Their effects on small business outcomes are estimated from separate regression models (see Fairlie and Robb 2007b). As noted above, the black-white gaps in small business outcomes are large. We focus on the contributions from racial differences in start-up capital and industry. The contributions from racial differences in other owner and business characteristics are discussed in Fairlie and Robb (2007b). Black-owned firms clearly have less start-up capital than white-owned firms. For example, 8.1 percent of black-owned businesses required at least $25,000 in start-up capital compared with 15.7 percent of white-owned businesses. These racial differences in start-up capital explain a substantial portion of the black-white gaps in small business outcomes, and, in fact, are the most important explanatory factor. The contribution estimates range from 14.5 to 43.2 percent. Clearly, lower levels of start-up capital among black-owned firms are associated with less successful businesses. These lower levels of start-up capital may be related to difficulty in obtaining funding because of low levels of personal wealth or lending discrimination.

7. Borrowing Patterns and Discrimination in Lending

Black and white entrepreneurs differ in the types of financing they use for their businesses. Although these differences are likely to be caused by many factors, they may be partly due to differences in personal wealth and lending discrimination. Focusing on start-up capital differences, evidence suggests black entrepreneurs rely less on banks than whites for start-up capital. Published estimates from the 1992 CBO indicate that only 6.6 percent of black firms received business loans from banking or commercial lending institutions. Nearly twice that percentage of white firms received bank loans for start-up capital. Blacks are also less likely to use a home equity line for start-up capital than are whites, which may be partly due to the lower rates of home ownership reported above. They are also less likely to use equity or nonborrowed sources of start-up capital and are less likely to have loans from other sources (except government-backed loans). On the other hand, black business owners are more likely to rely on credit cards for start-up funds than are white business owners.

In a few studies using the 1987 CBO, Bates (1997, 1999, 2005) conducted a thorough comparison of differences between black and white firms in their use

TABLE 6
DECOMPOSITIONS OF BLACK/WHITE GAPS IN SMALL BUSINESS
OUTCOMES: CHARACTERISTICS OF BUSINESS OWNERS, 1992

	Specification			
	(1)	(2)	(3)	(4)
Dependent variable	Closure	Profits	Employer	Ln sales
Black mean	.2692	.1414	.1116	9.4221
White mean	.2288	.3003	.2065	1.0615
Black/white gap	−.0404	.1590	.0948	.6394
Contributions from racial differences in:				
Sex	−.0019	.0231	.0060	.0562
	4.7%	14.6%	6.3%	8.8%
Marital status	−.0030	.0055	.0041	.0118
	7.5%	3.5%	4.3%	1.8%
Education	−.0031	.0045	.0013	.0066
	7.8%	2.8%	1.4%	1.0%
Region	−.0031	.0035	.0010	.0160
	7.6%	2.2%	1.0%	2.5%
Urban	−.0012	−.0078	.0021	−.0277
	2.9%	−4.9%	2.2%	−4.3%
Prior work experience	.0014	−.0021	−.0010	−.0032
	−3.5%	−1.3%	−1.1%	−0.5%
Prior work experience in a managerial capacity	.0065	.0005	.0018	.0035
	−16.1%	0.3%	1.9%	0.5%
Prior work experience in a similar business	−.0029	.0042	.0022	.0277
	7.1%	2.6%	2.3%	4.3%
Have a self-employed family member	−.0032	.0001	.0009	−.0128
	7.8%	0.0%	1.0%	−2.0%
Prior work experience in a family member's business	−.0032	.0019	.0033	.0246
	7.9%	1.2%	3.4%	3.8%
Inherited business	−.0001	.0005	.0000	.0007
	0.1%	0.3%	0.0%	0.1%
Start-up capital	−.0175	.0231	.0350	.1512
	43.2%	14.5%	36.9%	23.6%
Industry	−.0083	.0112	.0092	.0633
	2.5%	7.0%	9.7%	9.9%
All included variables	−.0395	.0683	.0658	.3179
	97.7%	42.9%	69.4%	49.7%

NOTE: (1) The sample and regression specifications are described in the text. (2) Contribution estimates are mean values of the decomposition using one thousand subsamples of whites. See text for more details.

of start-up capital. Bates found that black firms were more likely to start with no capital, less likely to borrow start-up capital, and more likely to rely solely on equity capital than white firms. In his sample of male-owned firms started in the past ten years, he found that 28.8 percent of black firms used borrowed funds for start-up capital compared to 37.2 percent of white firms. Focusing on start-up funding from financial institutions, he also found that black-owned firms receive less in start-up capital from banks on average than white-owned firms. Among firms borrowing start-up capital, he estimated that the average black firm borrowed $31,958 from financial institutions compared to $56,784 for white firms.

Bates (1997, 1999, 2005) also explored where the disparities in levels of start-up capital are partly due to differences in equity start-up capital. He found that black firms receive $2.69 per dollar of equity capital invested in loans from financial institutions. This is lower than the $3.10 per dollar of equity investment for white firms. After controlling for other owner and business characteristics, he found a roughly similar sized difference between black and white debt per equity dollar invested. These differences are not large, however, suggesting that an important hurdle to obtaining loans from financial institutions for black entrepreneurs is low levels of equity financing in addition to differential treatment by financial institutions (Bates 2005). In fact, using a pooled sample of black and white firms, Bates (2005) found that loans received by black firms borrowing start-up capital are significantly smaller than those received by white firms even after controlling for equity capital and owner and business characteristics such as education and industry. Racial differences in personal wealth, which are not measured in the CBO, may be a key factor in explaining the remaining black-white differences in business loans.

Racial inequality in wealth may also have an effect on the continuing success of businesses. If business owners cannot freely borrow to offset periods of low sales, then those owners with fewer financial resources may be more likely to close. In addition, access to personal or family wealth may allow owners to avoid potential liquidity constraints in expanding existing businesses. Even if black business owners were able to obtain adequate start-up capital, future limitations to access to financial capital may result in higher closure rates and underperformance.

Some suggestive evidence on racial differences in access to financial capital is provided by published estimates from the CBO (U.S. Census Bureau 1997). The CBO questionnaire asks owners with unsuccessful businesses from 1992 to 1996 why their businesses were unsuccessful. Black business owners were twice as likely as all business owners to report "lack of access to business loans/credit" as a reason for closure (16.2 percent compared with 8.3 percent). They were also nearly three times more likely than all business owners to report "lack of access to personal loans/credit" as a reason for closure (8.8 percent compared to 3.3 percent). Although this information is subjective and open to several different interpretations, it suggests that capital constraints are important for black entrepreneurs.

A factor that may pose a barrier to obtaining financial capital for black-owned businesses is lending discrimination. Much of the recent research on the issue of discrimination in business lending uses data from the 1998 SSBF.[12] The main finding from this literature is that minority-owned businesses experience higher loan denial probabilities and pay higher interest rates than white-owned businesses even after controlling for differences in creditworthiness and other factors (Blanchard, Yinger, and Zhao 2004; Blanchflower, Levine, and Zimmerman 2003; Cavalluzzo, Cavalluzzo, and Wolken 2002; Cavalluzzo and Wolken 2005; Coleman 2002, 2003; Mitchell and Pearce 2004).

Cavalluzzo and Wolken (2005) found that while greater personal wealth is associated with a lower probability of denial, even after controlling for personal wealth, there remained a large difference in denial rates across demographic groups. They estimated the magnitude of contributions from group differences in characteristics to racial gaps in loan denial rates. They found that group differences in personal wealth account for only a modest role in explaining black-white differences in denial rates. Credit history differences are found to explain most of the difference. They also found that denial rates for blacks increased with lender market concentration, a finding consistent with Becker's (1957/1971) classic theories of discrimination.

Using the 1993 SSBF, Cavalluzzo, Cavalluzzo, and Wolken (2002) found that all minority groups were more likely than whites to have unmet credit needs. Blacks were more likely to have been denied credit, even after controlling for many factors related to creditworthiness. In fact, denial rates and unmet credit needs for blacks widened with an increase in lender market concentration. The fear of denial often prevented some individuals from applying for a loan, even when they had credit needs. Blacks and Hispanics most notably had these fears. Blanchflower, Levine, and Zimmerman (2003) conducted a similar analysis with similar results but did not have access to some of the proprietary information available to researchers from the Federal Reserve. However, they did find black-owned businesses were more likely to have a loan application denied, even after controlling for differences in creditworthiness, and that blacks paid a higher interest rate on loans obtained. They also found that concerns over whether a loan application would be denied prevented some prospective borrowers from applying for a loan in the first place. The disparities between the denial rates between whites and blacks grew when taking these individuals into consideration along with those that actually applied for a loan. Bostic and Lampani (1999) brought in additional geographic controls but also found a statistically significant difference in approval rates between blacks and whites.

Although it is difficult to prove without a doubt that lending discrimination exists against black businesses, the evidence from the literature is consistent with the existence of lending discrimination against black-owned firms. Black firms are more likely to be denied loans, pay higher interest rates, and are less likely to borrow from banks for start-up or continuing capital. Lending discrimination may have a direct effect on business outcomes because it limits access to loans that can help a business "weather a storm" or limits the ability of firms to expand or diversify into new products or markets.

Although the evidence from the literature focuses on existing black businesses, lending discrimination may also severely limit access to start-up capital, potentially discouraging would-be minority entrepreneurs and reducing the success and longevity of minority-owned businesses.

8. Conclusions

African Americans are found to have levels of wealth that are one-eleventh those of whites. The median level of net worth, defined as the current value of all assets minus all liabilities on those assets, for black households is only $6,166. Starting with this disparity, blacks are much less likely to start businesses than are whites, resulting in a substantially lower rate of business ownership. Even for those black entrepreneurs that are successful in starting businesses, we find that they invest much less capital at start-up on average than white entrepreneurs. Lower levels of start-up capital among black businesses appear to also limit their ability to grow and succeed. Racial disparities in start-up capital contribute to higher failure rates, lower sales and profits, and less employment among black-owned businesses. Evidence from the SSBF also suggests black-owned businesses face significant barriers to access to capital, which are possibly due to lending discrimination. Even after controlling for detailed owner and firm characteristics and credit histories, black businesses are less likely to have loans approved and are more likely to not apply for loans because of fear of denial.

Minority-owned businesses lag behind non-minority-owned businesses in terms of sales, profits, survivability, and employment; facing greater obstacles in obtaining financing for their businesses implies that an already difficult situation is growing worse.

Given the importance of financial capital in a firm's formation and ability to survive, credit market imperfections can have profound implications for business performance and viability. Minority-owned businesses lag behind nonminority-owned businesses in terms of sales, profits, survivability, and employment; facing greater obstacles in obtaining financing for their businesses implies that an already difficult situation is growing worse.

Several important policy implications evolve from this research. The most obvious implication is addressing discrimination in the lending market. This may be accomplished through additional oversight by the lending community. This could entail improved training for internal loan review practices in financial institutions. Technical assistance programs to assist minority-owned businesses with starting and operating a business, applying for a loan, and financial literacy and accounting training are some other types of programs that could benefit minority-owned businesses and help them access credit markets for their business ventures. Finally, programs like individual development accounts (IDAs) and first-time homeowner programs that help low-income people build assets and human capital could help these individuals build the financial and human capital needed to start and succeed in entrepreneurship.

There are two clear areas for future research. The first is access to capital among established black firms. Do larger, more established black-owned businesses also face barriers to obtaining financial capital or are the barriers limited to minority start-ups? In future research, we plan to use data from the SSBF to investigate this question. The second is a study that can make the direct link between black net worth and levels of start-up capital used. There is evidence of a positive relationship between personal wealth and entrepreneurship and a positive relationship between start-up capital and business success, but there is little evidence on the relationship between the owner's wealth and how much is invested in the business at start-up because of data limitations. Evidence on this question would be useful for a more complete understanding of the processes by which wealth inequality leads to racial disparities in business success.

Notes

1. See Bates (1993a) for a description of programs promoting self-employment among minorities.

2. See Glazer and Moynihan (1970), Light (1972, 1979), Sowell (1981), and Moore (1983).

3. Sole proprietorships complete a 1040C form, partnerships complete a 1065 form, S corporations complete a 1120S form, and C corporations complete a 1120 form.

4. The Characteristics of Business Owners (CBO) only includes a categorical measure for profits.

5. Although sample weights are used that correct for nonresponse, there is some concern that closure rates are underestimated for the period from 1992 to 1996. Many businesses closed or moved over this period and did not respond to the survey that was sent out at the end of the period. Indeed, Robb (2000) showed, through matching administrative records, that nonrespondents had a much higher rate of closure than respondents. Racial differences in closure rates, however, were similar across the respondents and nonrespondents.

6. For example, see Evans and Jovanovic (1989); Evans and Leighton (1989); Meyer (1990); Holtz-Eakin, Joulfaian, and Rosen (1994a, 1994b); Lindh and Ohlsson (1996); Black, de Meza, and Jeffreys (1996); Blanchflower and Oswald (1998); Dunn and Holtz-Eakin (2000); Fairlie (1999, 2002); Earle and Sakova (2000); Johansson (2000); Taylor (2001); and Holtz-Eakin and Rosen (2004).

7. Hurst and Lusardi (2004) found a flat relationship between wealth and entrepreneurship through most of the wealth distribution.

8. Unfortunately, the CBO does not contain a measure of the owner's net worth prior to starting the business. Using the 1987 CBO, Astebro and Bernhardt (2004) instead used instrumented household income as a proxy for household wealth and find a positive relationship between this variable and start-up capital controlling for other owner and business characteristics.

9. Astebro and Berhardt (2003) found a positive relationship between business survival and having a bank loan at start-up after controlling for owner and business characteristics.

10. Using individual-level data, Fairlie (1999, 2007) provided some evidence on this question. Focusing on the causes of the higher annual rate of exit from self-employment for blacks than whites, estimates from the Current Population Survey (CPS) indicate that racial differences in personal wealth explain 7.3 percent of the gap. Estimates from the Panel Study of Income Dynamics (PSID) indicate that 1.8 to 11.1 percent of the male black-white gap in exit rates from self-employment is explained by differences in asset levels. The use of individual-level data, the focus on transitions out of self-employment, and the inclusion of personal wealth, however, make it difficult to draw conclusions about whether racial disparities in access to start-up capital contribute to racial differences in business outcomes.

11. See Blinder (1973) and Oaxaca (1973) for more details of the decomposition technique for linear outcomes and Fairlie (1999, 2005) for more details of the nonlinear decomposition technique used for binary outcomes and logit regressions. SAS programs are available for the nonlinear decomposition technique at econ.ucsc.edu/~fairlie/decomposition, and a Stata program and help file is available by entering "ssc install fairlie" in Stata.

12. The Survey of Small Business Finances (SSBF) is a survey of small businesses in the United States, which is conducted roughly every five years. The 1998 SSBF includes a nationally representative sample of more than thirty-five hundred for-profit, nongovernmental, nonagricultural businesses with fewer than five hundred employees. It includes detailed information on many firm and owner characteristics, including firm and owner credit histories, the firm's recent borrowing experiences, balance sheet data, and the frequency and sources of financial products and services used. See Bitler, Robb, and Wolken (2001) for more information.

References

Altonji, Joseph G., and Ulrich Doraszelski. 2005. The role of permanent income and demographics in black/white differences in wealth. *Journal of Human Resources* 40 (1): 1-30.

Astebro T., and I. Bernhardt. 2003. Start-up financing, owner characteristics and survival. *Journal of Economics and Business* 55 (4): 303-20.

———. 2004. The winners curse of human capital. *Small Business Economics* 24 (1): 63-78.

Avery, Robert B., Raphael W. Bostic, and Katherine A. Samolyk. 1998. The role of personal wealth in small business finance. *Journal of Banking and Finance* 22:1019-61.

Baron, Salo W., Arcadius Kahan, and Nachum Gross. 1985. *Economic history of the Jews*. New York: Schocken Books.

Bates, Timothy. 1989. The changing nature of minority business: A comparative analysis of Asian, nonminority, and black-owned businesses. *Review of Black Political Economy* 18 (Fall): 25-42.

———. 1990a. The characteristics of business owners data base. *Journal of Human Resources* 25 (4): 752-56.

———. 1990b. Entrepreneur human capital inputs and small business longevity. *Review of Economics and Statistics* 72 (4): 551-59.

———. 1993a. *Assessment of state and local government minority business development programs*. Report to the U.S. Department of Commerce Minority Business Development Agency. Washington, DC: U.S. Department of Commerce.

———. 1993b. *Banking on black enterprise*. Washington, DC: Joint Center for Political and Economic Studies.

———. 1994. An analysis of Korean-immigrant-owned small-business start-ups with comparisons to African-American and nonminority-owned firms. *Urban Affairs Quarterly* 30 (2): 227-48.

———. 1997. *Race, self-employment & upward mobility: An illusive American dream*. Washington, DC: Woodrow Wilson Center Press; Baltimore: Johns Hopkins University Press.

————. 1999. Available evidence indicates that black-owned firms are often denied equal access to credit: Discussion comments. *Business Access to Capital and Credit: A Federal Reserve System Research Conference, Conference Proceedings*. Washington, DC: Federal Reserve.

————. 2005. *Financing disadvantaged firms. Credit markets for the poor*. Edited by Patrick Bolton and Howard Rosenthal, 149-78. New York: Russell Sage Foundation.

Becker, G. 1957/1971. *The economics of discrimination*. Chicago: University of Chicago Press.

Bitler, Marianne, Alicia Robb, and John Wolken, 2001. Financial services used by small businesses: Evidence from the 1998 Survey of Small Business Finances. *Federal Reserve Bulletin* 87 (April).

Black, Jane, David de Meza, and David Jeffreys. 1996. House prices, the supply of collateral and the enterprise economy. *The Economic Journal* 106 (434): 60-75.

Blanchard, Lloyd, John Yinger, and Bo Zhao. 2004. Do credit market barriers exist for minority and women entrepreneurs? Syracuse University Working Paper, Syracuse, NY.

Blanchflower, David G., P. Levine, and D. Zimmerman. 2003. Discrimination in the small business credit market. *Review of Economics and Statistics* 85 (4): 930-43.

Blanchflower, David G., and Andrew J. Oswald. 1998. What makes an entrepreneur? *Journal of Labor Economics* 16 (1): 26-60.

Blau, Francine, and David Graham. 1990. Black-white differences in wealth and asset composition. *Quarterly Journal of Economics* 105 (2): 321-39.

Blinder, Alan S. 1973. Wage discrimination: Reduced form and structural variables. *Journal of Human Resources* 8:436-55.

Bonacich, Edna, and John Modell. 1980. *The economic basis of ethnic solidarity in the Japanese American community*. Berkeley: University of California Press.

Bostic, R., and K. P. Lampani. 1999. Racial differences in patterns of small business finance: The importance of local geography. Working Paper.

Bradford, William D. 2003. The wealth dynamics of entrepreneurship for black and white families in the U.S. *Review of Income and Wealth* 49 (1): 89-116.

Cavalluzzo, Ken, Linda Cavalluzzo, and John Wolken. 2002. Competition, small business financing, and discrimination: Evidence from a new survey. *Journal of Business* 75 (4). 641-79.

Cavalluzzo, Ken, and John Wolken. 2005. Small business loan turndowns, personal wealth and discrimination. *Journal of Business* 78 (6): 2153-77.

Coleman, Susan. 2002. The borrowing experience of black and Hispanic-owned small firms: Evidence from the 1998 Survey of Small Business Finances. *Academy of Entrepreneurship Journal* 8 (1): 1-20.

————. 2003. Borrowing patterns for small firms: A comparison by race and ethnicity. *Journal of Entrepreneurial Finance & Business Ventures* 7 (3): 87-108.

Dunn, Thomas A., and Douglas J. Holtz-Eakin. 2000. Financial capital, human capital, and the transition to self-employment: Evidence from intergenerational links. *Journal of Labor Economics* 18 (2): 282-305.

Earle, John S., and Zuzana Sakova. 2000. Business start-ups or disguised unemployment? Evidence on the character of self-employment from transition economies. *Labour Economics* 7 (5): 575-601.

Evans, David, and Boyan Jovanovic. 1989. An estimated model of entrepreneurial choice under liquidity constraints. *Journal of Political Economy* 97 (4): 808-27.

Evans, David, and Linda Leighton. 1989. Some empirical aspects of entrepreneurship. *American Economic Review* 79:519-35.

Fairlie, Robert W. 1999. The absence of the African-American owned business: An analysis of the dynamics of self-employment. *Journal of Labor Economics* 17 (1): 80-108.

————. 2002. Drug dealing and legitimate self-employment. *Journal of Labor Economics* 20 (3): 538-67.

————. 2005. An extension of the Blinder-Oaxaca decomposition technique to logit and probit models. *Journal of Economic and Social Measurement* 30 (4): 305-16.

————. 2007. Entrepreneurship among disadvantaged groups: An analysis of the dynamics of self-employment by gender, race and education. In Women, minorities and the less educated. In *International handbook series on entrepreneurship*, vol. 3, *The life cycle of entrepreneurial ventures*, ed. Simon Parker. New York: Springer.

Fairlie, Robert W., and Bruce D. Meyer. 2000. Trends in self-employment among black and white men: 1910-1990. *Journal of Human Resources* 35 (4): 643-69.

Fairlie, Robert W., and Alicia Robb. 2007a. Families, human capital, and small businesses: Evidence from the characteristics of business owners survey. *Industrial and Labor Relations Review* 60 (2): 225-245.

———. 2007b. Why are black-owned businesses less successful than white-owned businesses: The role of families, inheritances, and business human capital. *Journal of Labor Economics* 25 (2): 289-324.

Glazer, Nathan, and Daniel P. Moynihan. 1970. *Beyond the melting pot: The Negroes, Puerto Ricans, Jews, Italians, and Irish of New York City.* 2nd ed. Cambridge, MA: MIT Press.

Guy, Cynthia, Fred Doolittle, and Barbara Fink. 1991. *Self-employment for welfare recipients: Implementation of the SEID program.* New York: Manpower Demonstration Research Corporation.

Headd, Brian. 1999. The characteristics of business owners database, 1992. Census Bureau, Center for Economic Studies, Working Paper Series, CES-WP-99-8, U.S. Census Bureau, Washington, DC.

Holtz-Eakin, Douglas, David Joulfaian, and Harvey Rosen. 1994a. Entrepreneurial decisions and liquidity constraints. *Rand Journal of Economics* 23:334-47.

———. 1994b. Sticking it out: Entrepreneurial survival and liquidity constraints. *Journal of Political Economy* 102 (1): 53-75.

Holtz-Eakin, Douglas, and Harvey Rosen. 2004. Cash constraints and business start-ups: Deutschmarks versus dollars. Syracuse University Working Paper, Syracuse, New York.

Hout, Michael, and Harvey S. Rosen. 2000. Self-employment, family background, and race. *Journal of Human Resources* 35 (4): 670-92.

Hurst, Erik, and Annamaria Lusardi. 2004. Liquidity constraints, household wealth, and entrepreneurship. *Journal of Political Economy* 112 (2): 319-47.

Johansson, Edvard. 2000. Self-employment and liquidity constraints: Evidence from Finland. *Scandinavian Journal of Economics* 102 (1): 123-34.

Kosanovich, William T., Heather Fleck, Berwood Yost, Wendy Armon, and Sandra Siliezar. 2001. *Comprehensive assessment of self-employment assistance programs.* U.S. Department of Labor Report. Washington, DC: U.S. Department of Labor.

Light, Ivan. 1972. *Ethnic enterprise in America.* Berkeley: University of California Press.

———. 1979. Disadvantaged minorities in self employment. *International Journal of Comparative Sociology* 20 (1-2): 31-45.

Lindh T., and H. Ohlsson. 1996. Self-employment and windfall gains: Evidence from the Swedish lottery. *Economic Journal* 106 (439): 1515-26.

Loewen, James W. 1971. *The Mississippi Chinese: Between black and white.* Cambridge, MA: Harvard University Press.

Meyer, Bruce. 1990. Why are there so few black entrepreneurs? NBER Working Paper no. 3537, National Bureau of Economic Research, Cambridge, MA.

Min, Pyong Gap. 1996. *Caught in the middle: Korean merchants in America's multiethnic cities.* Berkeley: University of California Press.

Mitchell, K., and D. K. Pearce. 2004. Availability of financing to small firms using the Survey of Small Business Finances. Washington, DC:. U.S. Small Business Administration, Office of Advocacy.

Moore, Robert L. 1983. Employer discrimination: Evidence form self-employed workers. *Review of Economics and Statistics* 65:496-501.

Oaxaca, Ronald. 1973. Male-female wage differentials in urban labor markets. *International Economic Review* 14:693-709.

Oliver, Melvin L., and Thomas M. Shapiro. 1995. *Black wealth/white wealth: A new perspective on racial inequality.* New York: Routledge.

Raheim, Salome. 1997. Problems and prospects of self-employment as an economic independence option for welfare recipients. *Social Work* 42 (1): 44-53.

Robb, Alicia. 2000. The role of race, gender, and discrimination in business survival. Doctoral diss., University of Michigan, Ann Arbor.

Scholz, John Karl, and Kara Levine. 2004. U.S. black-white wealth inequality. In *Social inequality*, ed. K. Neckerman, 895-929. New York: Russell Sage Foundation.

Sowell, Thomas. 1981. *Markets and minorities.* New York: Basic Books.

Taylor, Mark. 2001. Self-employment and windfall gains in Britain: Evidence from panel data. *Economica* 63:539-65.

U.S. Bureau of Labor Statistics. 2004. Median weekly earnings of full-time wage and salary workers by selected characteristics. Labor Force Statistics from the Current Population Survey. http://www.bls.gov/cps/cpsaat37.pdf.

U.S. Census Bureau. 1997. *1992 economic census: Characteristics of business owners*. Washington, DC: Government Printing Office.

———. 2001. America's families and living arrangements: March 2000. Current Population Reports, P20-537. Washington, DC: U.S. Census Bureau.

U.S. Small Business Administration. 1999. *Minorities in business*. Washington, DC: U.S. Small Business Administration, Office of Advocacy.

———. 2001. *Minorities in business*. Washington, DC: U.S. Small Business Administration, Office of Advocacy.

Vroman, Wayne. 1997. *Self-employment assistance: Revised report*. Washington, DC: Urban Institute.

Small Firm Credit Market Discrimination, Small Business Administration Guaranteed Lending, and Local Market Economic Performance

By
BEN R. CRAIG,
WILLIAM E. JACKSON III,
and
JAMES B. THOMSON

In this article, the authors empirically test whether Small Business Administration (SBA) guaranteed lending has a greater impact on economic performance in markets with a high percentage of potential minority small businesses. This hypothesis is based on the assumptions that (1) credit rationing is more likely to occur in markets with a higher percentage of minority small businesses; and (2) SBA guaranteed lending is likely to reduce these credit rationing problems, thus improving economic performance in the local market. Using local market employment rates as the measure of economic performance, the authors find evidence consistent with this proposition. Specifically, the authors find a positive and significant impact of SBA guaranteed lending on the average employment rate in a local market. And, this impact is 200 percent larger in markets with a high percentage of potential minority small businesses. This result has important implications for public policy in general and SBA guaranteed lending in particular.

Keywords: discrimination; employment rates; small firm credit markets; loan guarantees; credit rationing

Minority entrepreneurs more often report that access to adequate capital is a major problem than do their majority counterparts. For example, in a recent study, Blanchflower, Levine, and Zimmerman (2003) reported that black small business owners are three times as likely as white small business owners to list access to sufficient capital at reasonable rates as a major problem faced by their firm.

This reported disparity in access to capital between minority and majority small business owners may stem from one or two possible sources, or some combination of these sources. Minority small business owners may not offer capital providers as many positive net present value (NPV) projects, on average, as majority small business owners. Or, minority small business owners are subject to certain constraints on the flow of capital to their operations that majority small business owners do not encounter.

The former is simply a perception of capital access disparities. However, the latter represents

DOI: 10.1177/0002716207303579

real economic effects that serve to distort capital markets and reduce the efficiency of our overall financial system. Most of the existing literature concludes that the latter description paints the more accurate picture of the current market conditions faced by minority owners of small firms. For example, Cavalluzzo, Cavalluzzo, and Wolken (2002) reported that minority-owned small businesses are not significantly less profitable than majority-owned small businesses. Thus, the data do not support the hypothesis that minority-owned small business owners on average have fewer NPV projects.

What, then, are the likely sources of capital access constraints on minority-owned small businesses? The current literature usually points to discrimination as the likely culprit. For example, Blanchflower, Levine, and Zimmerman (2003) concluded that their analysis (which considers a very rich set of explanatory variables) strongly points to severe levels of discrimination in small business credit markets.

There are at least two reasons why discrimination against minority-owned firms might be observed in small business credit markets. The first is simply prejudicial type discrimination behavior as examined by Becker (1971). The second is related to differential levels of asymmetric information and credit rationing. If minority-owned firms are more likely to be credit rationed because of relatively larger asymmetric information problems, then it is possible to observe capital allocation outcomes in the small firm credit market that coincide with outcomes based on prejudicial discriminatory behavior. However, if the source of the disparity is credit rationing, then this type of behavior is more accurately described as statistical discrimination and does not carry the nefarious connotations associated with prejudicial discrimination. Nevertheless, it is still discrimination, and more important, it places a real cost on our economic system.

Ben R. Craig is an economic advisor in the Research Department of the Federal Reserve Bank of Cleveland. His principal fields of activity are the economics of banking and international finance and econometrics. He received his Ph.D. in economics from Stanford University.

William E. Jackson III is a professor of finance, professor of management, and the Smith Foundation Endowed Chair of Business Integrity in the Culverhouse College of Commerce at the University of Alabama. His research interests focus on financial markets and institutions, corporate governance, small firm finance, and political economy. He received his Ph.D. in economics from the University of Chicago.

James B. Thomson is vice president and economist in the Research Department of the Federal Reserve Bank of Cleveland. His research interests focus on financial markets and institutions, historical banking, and government-sponsored enterprises. He received his Ph.D. in economics from The Ohio State University.

NOTE: The views expressed are those of the authors and not those of the Federal Reserve Banks of Atlanta or Cleveland or the Board of Governors of the Federal Reserve System. We thank Timothy Bates and seminar participants at the 2006 University of North Carolina at Chapel Hill Conference on Minority Entrepreneurship for providing helpful comments on this manuscript. We also thank the Small Business Administration (SBA) for providing the SBA loan-guarantee data and Pat Higgins for providing outstanding research support. Additionally, William E. Jackson III thanks the E. M. Kauffman Foundation for providing financial support for this research project. Questions or comments on this article should be directed to William E. Jackson III at wjackson@cba.ua.edu.

One method likely to reduce these costs of asymmetric information-based discrimination is to reduce the amount of asymmetric information in these credit markets, especially for minority-owned firms. One very practical method for doing this is to encourage lenders to make profitable loans that they would not otherwise make. In so doing, the lender develops a relationship with the borrower; such a relationship allows for the collection of borrower-specific information at a relatively low cost through basic monitoring of the loan. This reduces future levels of asymmetric information and reduces observed statistical discrimination by fostering a relationship between the minority-owned small business and the lending entity.

One program designed to ameliorate the asymmetric information problem in small business credit markets is the Small Business Administration (SBA) guaranteed lending program. There is some evidence that this program helps to reduce credit rationing problems in small firm credit markets (Craig, Jackson, and Thomson 2007). Because the financial contracting problems that lead to credit rationing are basically the same types of problems that lead to statistical discrimination, it is reasonable to investigate whether a government intervention that reduces credit rationing reduces observed disparate treatment or observed discrimination as well.

Because the financial contracting problems that lead to credit rationing are basically the same types of problems that lead to statistical discrimination, it is reasonable to investigate whether a government intervention that reduces credit rationing also reduces observed disparate treatment or observed discrimination.

The primary research question addressed in this article is, Does SBA guaranteed lending lessen the negative impacts of discrimination on minority entrepreneurs and their communities? In the second section, we provide some background on economic performance and financial market development. In the third section, we present a discussion of public policy and small business credit markets. In the fourth, we provide a brief review of the academic literature on credit rationing and relationship lending, which is consistent with the hypothesis that information problems in lending markets are particularly severe in the small firm credit market and hence provides a rationale for SBA loan guarantees. An overview of SBA lending programs is presented in the fifth section; and the sixth outlines the data, our hypotheses, and our empirical strategy. The results appear in the seventh section. Finally, our conclusions and future research questions are outlined in the eighth section.

Background on Economic Performance and Financial Market Development

It is a well-documented finding in the economics literature that economic growth and financial market development tend to be positively correlated. However, whether relatively higher levels of financial development actually cause higher levels of economic performance, or higher levels of economic performance cause higher levels of financial development, is an issue of debate that dates at least to the studies of Schumpeter (1911) and Robinson (1952).

Three important recent studies provide evidence that relatively higher levels of financial market development do indeed lead to higher levels of economic performance or growth. Jayaratne and Strahan (1996); Rajan and Zingales (1998); and Guiso, Sapienza, and Zingales (2004) all reported significant evidence supporting the proposition that the causal relationship runs from more financial market development to more economic growth. All of these papers are very careful to develop reasonable arguments to compensate for the relative amount of local financial market development.

In this article, we focused on a particular rationale for such a relationship to investigate whether local financial market development helps to promote economic performance. Our rationale is that financial market development may increase the amount of external finance available to minority-owned small firms. Specifically, we examine whether a government intervention aimed at increasing small firms' access to bank credit has a relatively greater impact in high-minority areas. We use SBA guaranteed lending as our government invention method. We choose the minority-owned small firm credit market because of the high degree of information asymmetry that may be associated with it, and because this information asymmetry may lead to a credit rationing problem as explained in Stiglitz and Weiss (1981). This may be especially important in high-minority areas where the per capita number of minority-owned small businesses is likely to be higher.

We choose the SBA guaranteed lending program because our previous research (Craig, Jackson, and Thomson 2007) suggests that SBA guaranteed lending has a small positive influence on the rate of economic growth in local geographic markets. Our previous research used metropolitan statistical areas (MSAs) and non-MSA counties to represent local geographic financial markets. However, we did not investigate whether a positive relationship between SBA guaranteed lending and other measures of economic performance existed. Nor did we investigate whether these relationships were different for areas with a relatively high proportion of minorities in the local market (Craig, Jackson, and Thomson 2007). We refer to these markets as high-minority markets. And we use the level of labor market employment, or the employment rate, as our measure of economic performance. Accordingly, we test whether SBA guaranteed lending has a differential impact for high-minority markets.

In this article, our null hypothesis is that SBA guaranteed lending does not impact high-minority markets differently than low-minority markets. And our primary alternative hypothesis is that SBA guaranteed lending has a greater impact on the employment rate in high-minority markets. This alternative hypothesis is predicated on priors related to three assumptions. First, less developed financial markets are more likely to experience severe information asymmetry problems, and as Stiglitz and Weiss (1981) pointed out, that could lead to credit rationing. Second, SBA guaranteed lending is likely to reduce these credit rationing problems. This will improve the level of development of that local financial market. And third, this increased financial market development will help to lubricate the wheels of economic performance, especially in high-minority markets, and increase the effective level of labor utilization, or the employment rate (Rajan and Zingales 1998).

Our results suggest that high-minority markets are positively impacted by SBA guaranteed lending. Moreover, the impact for high-minority markets is three times as large as it is for low-minority markets. This result has important implications for public policy in general and SBA guaranteed lending in particular.

Public Policy and Small Business Credit Markets

The promotion of small businesses is a cornerstone of economic policy for a large number of industrialized countries. Public support for small enterprise appears to be based on the widely held perception that the small business sector is an incubator of economic growth, a place where innovation takes place and new ideas become economically viable business enterprises. In addition, policy makers routinely point to small businesses as important sources of employment growth. It is not surprising, then, that there is widespread political support for government programs, tax breaks, and other subsidies aimed at encouraging the growth and development of small business in the United States and increasingly around the world.

A particular area of concern for policy makers is whether small businesses have access to adequate credit. After all, a lot of small firms are relatively young and have little or no credit history. Lenders may be reluctant to fund small firms with new and innovative products because of the difficulty associated with evaluating the risk of such products. These difficulties are classic *information* problems—problems obtaining sufficient information about the parties involved in a transaction—and they may prevent otherwise creditworthy firms from obtaining credit. If information problems are substantial, they can lead to credit rationing, that is, loans are allocated by some mechanism other than price. If small businesses face credit rationing, the next Google, Microsoft, or Starbucks might wither on the vine for want of funding. To the extent that credit rationing significantly affects small business credit markets, a rationale exists for supporting small enterprises through government programs aimed at improving small business access to credit. This rationale may be even stronger when applied to high-minority markets.

If small businesses face credit rationing, the next Google, Microsoft, or Starbucks might wither on the vine for want of funding.

One specific government intervention aimed at improving the private market's allocation of credit to small enterprises is the SBA guaranteed lending program. SBA loan guarantees are well established, and their volume has grown over the past decade. Nearly 20 million small businesses have received direct or indirect help from one or another of the SBA's programs since 1953. The SBA's business loan portfolio of roughly 240,000 loans was worth about $60 billion in 2004, making it the largest single financial backer of small businesses in the United States. To place this amount in perspective, consider that in June 2004 commercial banks reported a total of about $522 billion of small business loans outstanding (SBA 2005). SBA guaranteed loans represented more than 10 percent of total commercial bank small business loans outstanding at that time. And commercial banks provide the majority of small business loans supplied in the United States.

The rationale for SBA guarantees appears to be that credit market imperfections can result in small enterprises being credit rationed—particularly for longer-term loans for purposes such as capital expansion. If SBA loan guarantees indeed reduce credit rationing in the markets for small business loans, then there should be a relationship between measures of SBA guaranteed lending activities and economic performance; this is what we found in Craig, Jackson, and Thomson (2007). In particular, we found a positive and significant relationship, albeit small, between the level of SBA lending in a local market and future per capita income growth in that market. Overall, our empirical results were consistent with a positive impact on social welfare of SBA guaranteed lending.

In this article, we use a simplified version of the analysis in Craig, Jackson, and Thomson (2007) to evaluate a potential determinant of economic performance in high-minority communities. Specifically, we test whether SBA guaranteed lending to small firms has a relatively greater impact on the average level of labor employment in high-minority local markets. We find that it does.

In the next section, we provide a brief discussion of the economics of small firm credit markets. This discussion focuses on a highly select group of theoretical and empirical articles that help explain the severe credit allocation problems caused by imperfect information in small firm credit markets. These articles provide insight into the mechanism that allow a government intervention, such as the SBA guaranteed lending program, to result in higher economic performance in high-minority markets.

The Economics of Small Firm Credit Markets

The economic justification for any government-sponsored small business lending program or loan guarantee program must rest on a generally acknowledged failure of the private sector to allocate loans efficiently. Absent such a clearly identified problem with private sector lending to small businesses, the SBA's activities would simply seem a wasteful, politically motivated subsidy to this sector of the economy.

Many economists, most notably Joseph Stiglitz and Andrew Weiss (1981), contend that private lending institutions may indeed fail to allocate loans efficiently because of fundamental information problems in the market for small business loans. These information problems may be so severe that they lead to credit rationing and constitute the failure of the credit market. Stiglitz and Weiss argued that banks consider both the interest rate they receive on the loan and the risk of the loan when deciding to make a loan. But the lack of perfect information in loan markets may cause two effects that allow the interest rate itself to affect the riskiness of the bank's loan portfolio. When the price (here, the interest rate) affects the nature of the transaction, it is unlikely that a price will emerge that suits either the available buyers or sellers; that is, no price will "clear the market." The first effect, adverse selection, impedes the ability of markets to allocate credit using price by increasing the proportion of high-risk borrowers in the set of likely borrowers. The second effect, moral hazard, reduces the ability of prices to clear lending markets because it influences the ex post actions of borrowers.

The adverse selection effect is a consequence of different borrowers having different probabilities of repaying their loans. The expected return to the bank on a loan obviously depends on the probability of repayment, so the bank would like to be able to identify borrowers who are more likely to repay. But it is difficult to identify such borrowers. Typically, the bank will use a variety of screening devices to do so. The interest rate that a borrower is willing to pay may act as one such screening device. For example, those who are willing to pay a higher interest rate are likely to be, on average, worse risks. These borrowers are willing to borrow at a higher interest rate because they perceive their probability of repaying the loan to be lower. So as the interest rate rises, the average risk of those who are willing to borrow increases, and this may actually result in lowering the bank's expected profits from lending.

Similarly, as the interest rate and other terms of the contract change, the behavior of the borrower is likely to change, too. For instance, raising the interest rate decreases the profitability of projects that succeed. Higher interest rates may thus induce firms to undertake riskier projects—projects with lower probabilities of success but higher payoffs when successful. In other words, the price a firm pays for credit may affect its investment decisions. This is the moral hazard problem.

As a result of these two effects, a bank's expected return may increase less for an additional increase in the interest rate; and beyond a certain point, it may actually decrease as the interest rate is increased. Clearly, under these conditions, it is conceivable that the demand for credit may exceed the supply of credit in equilibrium. Although traditional analysis would argue that in the presence of an excess demand for credit, unsatisfied borrowers would offer to pay a higher interest rate to the bank, thus bidding up the interest rate until demand equals supply, it does not happen in this case. This is because the bank would not lend to someone who offered to pay the higher interest rate, as such a borrower is likely to be a worse risk than the average current borrower. The expected return on a loan to this borrower at the higher interest rate may be actually lower than the expected return on the loans the bank is currently making. Hence, there are no competitive forces leading supply to equal demand, and credit is rationed.

Stiglitz and Weiss (1981) argued that when borrowers are distinguishable, the lender may decide to deny credit to an entire group. This is the classic redlining argument. We expect the likelihood of this type of credit rationing to be higher in high-minority communities. Furthermore, because the value of collecting information on borrowers may be less in high-minority markets (because of expectations of less aggregate per capita lending), the levels of imperfect information may be higher, in equilibrium, in high-minority markets.

Importance of Lending Relationships

Kane and Malkiel (1965) came to a similar conclusion about the possibility of banks rationing credit. But they also suggested that the extent of credit rationing depends on the strength of existing customer relationships; the size, stability, and prospects for future growth of deposits; and the existence of profitable future lending opportunities. Loans may be rationed to current and prospective borrowers in accordance with the cohesion of the existing relationships along with expectations about the future profitability of those relationships. In our empirical analysis, we use the notion from Kane and Malkiel that differences in the relative size of the bank deposit base across markets may provide an indicator of the relative degree of credit rationing in that local market.

Petersen and Rajan (1994) extended the theory that relationships are important factors in determining credit rationing. They suggested that the causes of credit rationing, adverse selection and moral hazard, may be more prominent when firms are young or small. However, through close and continued interaction, a firm may provide a lender with sufficient information about, and a voice in, the firm's affairs to lower the cost and increase the availability of credit. In addition, these authors suggested that an important dimension of a relationship is its duration. Conditional on its positive past experience with the borrower, the bank may expect future loans to be less risky. This should reduce its expected cost of lending and increase its willingness to provide funds.

Petersen and Rajan (1994) suggested that in addition to interaction over time, relationships can be built through interaction over multiple products. Borrowers may obtain more than just loans from a bank. Borrowers may purchase a variety of financial services and maintain checking and savings accounts with the bank. These added dimensions of a relationship can affect the firm's borrowing cost in two ways. First, they increase the precision of the lender's information about the borrower. For example, the lender can learn about the firm's sales by monitoring the cash flowing through its checking account or by factoring the firm's accounts receivables. Second, the lender can spread any fixed costs of producing information about the firm over multiple products. Petersen and Rajan reported that both effects reduce the lender's costs of providing loans and services, and the former effect increases the availability of funds to the firm.

Berger and Udell (1995) also studied the importance of relationships in the extension of credit to small firms. They found that small firms with longer banking relationships borrow at lower rates and are less likely to pledge collateral than are other small firms. These effects appear to be both economically and statistically significant. According to Berger and Udell (1996), these results suggest that banks accumulate increasing amounts of this private information over the duration of the bank-borrower relationship and use this information to refine their loan contract terms.

Small Business Administration Loan Guarantee Programs

SBA loan guarantees may improve credit allocation by providing a mechanism for pricing loans that is independent of borrower behavior. By reducing the expected loss associated with a loan default, the guarantee increases the expected return to the lender—without increasing the lending rate. In the absence of adverse selection, lenders could simply offer loan rates to borrowers that reflected the average risk of the pool of borrowers.[1]

With the guarantee in place, the lender could profitably extend credit at loan rates below what would be dictated by the risk of the average borrower. The reason for this is that the guarantee increases the profitability of the loan by reducing the losses to the bank in those instances when the borrower defaults. To the extent that the loan guarantees reduce the rate of interest at which banks are willing to lend, external loan guarantees will help mitigate the moral hazard problem. The lower lending rates afforded by external guarantees reduce the bankruptcy threshold and thereby increase the expected return of safe projects vis-à-vis riskier ones. Additionally, lowering the lending rate increases the number of low-risk borrowers applying for credit, which, in turn, increases the likelihood that the average risk of firms applying for loans is representative of the pool of borrowers. Hence, external loan guarantees help mitigate the adverse selection problem. In theory, SBA loan guarantees should reduce the probability that a viable minority-owned small business is credit rationed.

Because relationships may be more costly for small businesses to establish relative to large businesses, and because lack of relationships may lead to severe credit rationing in the small business credit market, some form of government intervention to assist small businesses in establishing relationships with lenders may be appropriate. However, the nature of intervention must be carefully evaluated. The SBA's guaranteed lending programs may well be a reasonable intervention as they serve as a substitute for small business collateral. The program also reduces the risk to the lender of establishing a relationship with informationally opaque small business borrowers. Finally, the SBA loan guarantee programs may improve the intermediation process by lowering the risk to the lender of extending longer-term loans, ones that more closely meet the needs of small businesses for capital investment. It is interesting to note that the problem of long-term credit for small businesses was one of the primary reasons stated by Congress for establishing the SBA.

The legislation that created the SBA was enacted on July 30, 1953.[2] The following year, the SBA began making direct loans and guaranteeing bank loans to small businesses. In addition, Congress assigned to the SBA the function of making loans to victims of natural disasters. This was a continuation of one of the functions of the Reconstruction Finance Corporation, an organization dissolved by Congress when it created the SBA. Congress also directed the SBA to continue some of the functions of the dissolved Small Defense Plants Administration. These functions included working to help small businesses procure government contracts, helping small business owners with managerial and technical assistance, and assisting small businesses in developing employee training programs.

Recognizing that private financial institutions are typically better than government agencies at deciding on which small business loans to underwrite, the SBA began moving away from making direct loans and toward guaranteeing private loans in the early 1970s. Currently, the SBA makes direct loans only under very special circumstances. Guaranteed lending through the SBA's 7(a) guaranteed loan program and the 504 loan program are the main form of SBA activity in lending markets (see www.sba.gov).

The 7(a) loan program is the more basic and more significant of these two programs. The name of the program originates from the section of the Small

Business Administration Act that authorizes the agency to provide business loans to American small businesses (Section 7[a]).

7(a) loans are available only on a guaranty basis. This means that they are provided by lenders who choose to structure their own loans according to SBA's requirements and who apply for and receive a guaranty from SBA on a portion of this loan. The SBA does not fully guarantee 7(a) loans. The SBA guaranty is usually in the range of 50 to 85 percent of the loan amount. Currently, the maximum guarantee is $1,500,000, and the maximum loan amount under the 7(a) program is $2,000,000. The maximum guarantee is 75 percent of the maximum loan amount (see www.sba.gov).

The lender and SBA share the risk that a borrower will not be able to repay the loan in full. The guaranty is a warranty against payment default and does not cover other contingencies such as imprudent decisions by the lender (such as underpricing of the loan, failure to enforce loan covenants, or failure to perfect a lien on collateral) or misrepresentation by the borrower (see www.sba.gov).

The 504 loan program is a long-term financing tool for economic development within a community. The 504 program provides growing businesses with long-term, fixed-rate financing for major fixed assets, such as land or buildings, through a certified development company (CDC). A CDC is a nonprofit corporation set up to contribute to the economic development of its community. CDCs work with the SBA and private sector lenders to provide financing to small businesses. There are about 270 CDCs nationwide. Each CDC covers a specific geographic area (see www.sba.gov).

Typically, a 504 project includes a loan from a private sector lender covering up to 50 percent of the project cost, a loan from the CDC (backed by a 100 percent SBA guaranteed debenture) covering up to 40 percent of the cost, and a contribution of at least 10 percent equity from the borrower. The SBA-backed loan from the CDC is usually subordinate to the private loan, which has the effect of insulating the private lender from loss in the event of default (see www.sba.gov for more on the 504 program).

The Hypotheses, Data, and Empirical Strategy

One method likely to reduce the costs of asymmetric information based credit rationing is to reduce the amount of asymmetric information in these credit markets, especially for firms in high-minority areas. One very practical method for doing this is to encourage lenders to make (profitable) loans that they would not otherwise make. And in so doing, the lender develops a "relationship" with the borrower. This relationship allows for the collection of borrower-specific information at a relatively low cost through basic monitoring of the loan. This reduces future levels of asymmetric information and reduces credit rationing by fostering a relationship between the high-minority area small business and the lending entity.

It also encourages the lender to learn more about the high-minority area in general and increases the likelihood of the lending bank making additional loans in that area. This is the positive information externality effect discussed in Lang and Nakamura (1993). SBA guaranteed lending may increase the level of local bank credit available to small firms in high-minority markets by decreasing the amount of firm specific asymmetric information in the local financial market and by increasing the positive information externality associated with learning about the high-minority area.

Our empirical research focuses on SBA guaranteed lending because this is where the empirical evidence is likely to be strongest concerning the impact of government intervention in small firm credit markets. This conclusion is based on two observations: first, SBA guaranteed lending programs encompass all types of small business lenders, from community banks and thrifts to bigger banks; and second, the SBA guaranteed lending programs are relatively large and have operated for more than a half a century.

To the extent that SBA [Small Business Administration] guaranteed lending programs mitigate credit market frictions, there should be a positive relationship between SBA guaranteed lending and the level of employment.

We take as our maintained hypothesis that credit market frictions—primarily in the form of costly information and verification of a small firm's projects—can lead to a socially suboptimal credit allocation that negatively impacts the labor employment rate in the local market. The implicit assumption here is that labor and capital are complements for small firms. To the extent that SBA guaranteed lending programs mitigate credit market frictions, there should be a positive relationship between SBA guaranteed lending and the level of employment, especially across less developed (e.g., high-minority) financial markets. Therefore, we test for whether SBA loan guarantees lessen credit market frictions by testing whether a measure of the normalized amount of SBA guaranteed lending in a local market correlates with relatively higher levels of employment in high-minority areas. Our null hypothesis is that there are no discernible differences in the impact of SBA guaranteed lending on employment rates in high-minority markets relative to low-minority markets.

Data

To examine this SBA guaranteed lending and employment rates in high-minority areas hypothesis, we utilize data from three sources. Our first source is loan-specific data—including borrower and lender information—on SBA guaranteed 7(a) and 504 loans from January 2, 1991, through December 31, 1999. In 2000, the Census Bureau reclassified its racial categories. Because of this change, we do not include data after 1999. A breakdown of loan size, total credit, and number of loans reveals that we have more than three hundred thousand loans in our sample. The average size of these loans was about $225,000, suggesting that about $68 billion of credit was extended over our sample period.

Our second source of data, on economic conditions, is from the National Bureau of Economic Research (NBER), the Bureau of Labor Statistics (BLS), and the Bureau of Economic Analysis (BEA) from 1991 through 1999. Our third source is data from the Federal Deposit Insurance Corporation's annual summary of deposit data (SUMD) files.

All of our individual loan data are aggregated to the local market level. For this study, we aggregate over time to produce cross-sectional observations for our local markets. As in studies by Berger and Hannon (1989), Calem and Carlino (1991), Jackson (1992a, 1992b), Shaffer (1994, 2004), and Berger (1995), we use MSAs to define the relevant local market for urban areas and non-MSA counties as the local market for rural areas.

Empirical strategy

To test our null hypothesis we simplify our previous analysis from Craig, Jackson, and Thomson (2007). We estimated our models using classic Arellano and Bond panel regression estimation techniques. In this study, we estimate a simple cross-sectional ordinary least squares (OLS) fixed effects regression model that incorporates measures of employment levels over our sample period. Our basic model is as follows:

$$EMPR_i = \alpha_0 + \alpha_1 PICAP_i + \alpha_2 HERF_i + \alpha_3 MSADUM_i + \alpha_4 DEPPOP_i$$
$$+ \alpha_5 SBAPOP_i + \alpha_6 SBADEP_i + \varepsilon_i. \tag{1}$$

Equation (1) uses the average annual employment rate over our sample period ($EMPR$) at the local market level to proxy for economic performance. We are interested in how SBA guaranteed lending affects cross-sectional changes in $EMPR$. The primary variables of interest on the right side of equation (1) are $DEPPOP$ (the inflation-adjusted deposits per capita in a local market), $SBAPOP$ (the inflation-adjusted total dollar amount of SBA-guaranteed loans per capita in the local market), and $SBADEP$. The variable $SBADEP$ is equal to $DEPPOP$ times $SBAPOP$. It is a measure of the cross-partial derivative, or interaction term, for the impact on $EMPR$ of higher (or lower) amounts of SBA guaranteed lending at higher (or lower) levels of inflation-adjusted deposits per capita in a local market (*DEPPOP*). *SBADEP* is of interest because it provides an indication of whether SBA guaranteed lending has a different impact in less developed local financial markets. For example, a negative coefficient on *SBADEP* would imply that the impact of *SBAPOP* is less at higher levels of *DEPPOP*. Or, stated differently, SBA guaranteed lending has less impact in more developed local financial markets.

The analysis described above is used to introduce the general relationship between SBA guaranteed lending and local financial market development. Next, we consider the relationship between SBA guaranteed lending and local financial market development in high-minority areas. We use equation (2) to conduct this analysis. Equation (2) is designed to specifically test whether SBA guaranteed lending has a differential impact on local market employment rates in high-minority areas. Two interactive variables are included in equation (2) to accomplish this test. The two variables are *SBAMIN and DEPMIN*. *SBAMIN* is equal to *SBAPOP* times *HIGHM*, and *DEPMIN* is equal to *DEPPOP* times *HIGHM*. And *HIGHM* is an indicator variable equal to 1 if the percentage of minority population in the local market is greater than 25.55 percent; otherwise, *HIGHM* is equal to 0.0. The value 25.55 percent is equal to the mean (10.50) plus one standard deviation (15.05) from the mean for our sample.

$$EMPR_i = \alpha_0 + \alpha_1 PICAP_i + \alpha_2 HERF_i + \alpha_3 MSADUM_i + \alpha_4 DEPPOP_i$$
$$+ \alpha_5 SBAPOP_i + \alpha_6 HIGHM_i + \alpha_6 DEPMIN + \alpha_6 SBAMIN + \varepsilon_i. \qquad (2)$$

We use a measure of total deposits (*DEPPOP*) instead of a measure of total credit in the local market; we do this for two reasons. First, we cannot construct measures of bank lending at the local market level; however, market-level deposit data are available from the SUMD data. Total deposits should be highly correlated with lending. Using total local market deposits as an instrument for approximating cross-sectional differences in the level of total market lending is consistent with previous research from Petersen and Rajan (1995). Second, King and Levine (1993a) suggested that the local market deposit base is one of several reasonable measures of market liquidity and financial development.

The deposit market Herfindahl index (*HERF*) is included in equations (1) and (2) to control for the structure of the local market. Constructed at the market level using branch level deposit data from the SUMD database, *HERF* provides a measure of concentration, and presumably the competitiveness, of the local banking market. The definitions of the variables used in the empirical analysis are provided in Table 1.

The Empirical Results

Equations (1) and (2) are estimated using a simple OLS fixed effects method. Descriptive statistics for the variables used in the regression can be found in Table 2, and a correlation coefficients matrix in Table 3. Our regression estimation

TABLE 1
VARIABLE DEFINITIONS

Variable	Definition	Source
EMPR	Average employment percentage rate in the local market over the sample period	BLS
SBAPOP	Average per capita amount of new SBA guaranteed lending in the local market over the sample period	SBA, BLS
HERF	Average deposit market Herfindahl over the sample period	FDIC SUMD
PICAP	Average per capita income in the local market over our sample period	BEA
MSADUM	Indicator variable equal to one if local market is an MSA, zero otherwise	BEA
DEPPOP	Average annual per capita bank deposits in the local market over the sample period	FDIC SUMD
SBADEP	Interactive variable equal to SBAPOP times DEPPOP	—
HIGHM	Indicator variable equal to one if the minority population in the local market is greater than 25.55 percent of the total local market population; zero otherwise.	BLS
DEPMIN	Interactive variable equal to HIGHM times DEPPOP	—
SBAMIN	Interactive variable equal to HIGHM times SBAPOP	—

NOTE: SBA = Small Business Administration; FDIC SUMD = Federal Deposit Insurance Corporation Summary of Deposit Data; BEA = Bureau of Economic Analysis; BLS = Bureau of Labor Statistics; MSA = metropolitan statistical area.

results are presented in Table 4. Notice from Table 2 that our primary variables of interest display large dispersions. *EMPR*, our employment rate percentage, ranges from 98.67 percent to a low of 68.06 percent, with a mean of 93.67 percent.

Our per capita income variable (*PICAP*) has a mean of $15,562 with a high of $36,772 and a low of $6,637 and a standard deviation of $3,080. Our measure of financial market development, local market deposits per capita (*DEPPOP*), also displays a wide range. The high for *DEPPOP* is $106,313 deposits per capita, while the low is only $147 deposits per capita, and the mean is $8,314 per capita. Similar results appear in our measure of SBA guaranteed lending activity. Per capita SBA guaranteed lending (*SBAPOP*) ranges from a high of $416.39 per capita to a low of $0.00 per capita, with a mean of $28.33 per capita over our sample period.

In Table 3, we present a correlation matrix for our main variables. There are several correlation coefficients in Table 3 worth mentioning. For example, the local market employment rate (*EMPR*) is significantly positively correlated with

TABLE 2
DESCRIPTIVE STATISTICS ($N = 2,358$)

Variable	Mean	Minimum	Maximum	Standard Deviation
EMPR	93.67	68.06	98.67	3.00
HERF	0.53	0.03	1.00	0.28
PICAP	15.562	6.637	36.772	3.080
MSADUM	0.13	0	1.00	0.34
DEPPOP	8.314	0.147	106.313	6.114
SBAPOP	28.33	0.00	416.39	29.48
Minority	10.50	0.00	86.79	15.05
HIGHM	0.15	0.00	1.00	0.36

NOTE: EMPR is the average annual employment rate in percentage points over the sample period. HERF is the average Herfindahl ratio, calibrated to be between zero and one, in market i over the sample period. PICAP is average per capita income in local market i over our sample period. MSADUM is an indicator variable equal to one (zero otherwise) if market i is a metropolitan statistical area (MSA). DEPPOP is the average annual per capita bank deposits in market i. SBAPOP is the average annual amount of (new) Small Business Administration (SBA) guaranteed lending in market i over our sample period. SBAPOP is calibrated in dollars per capita, and DEPPOP is calibrated in thousands of dollars per capita. All dollar amounts are in 1990 dollars. Minority is the percentage of the local market population classified as racial minorities. HIGHM is an indicator variable equal to one if Minority is greater than 25.55 and zero otherwise.

TABLE 3
PEARSON CORRELATION COEFFICIENTS MATRIX ($N = 2,358$)

	EMPR	PICAP	HERF	MSADUM	DEPPOP	SBAPOP	HIGHM
EMPR	—						
PICAP	0.44(0.00)	—					
HERF	−0.18 (0.00)	−0.29 (0.00)	—				
MSADUM	0.08 (0.00)	0.43 (0.00)	−0.31 (0.00)	—			
DEPPOP	0.27 (0.00)	0.28 (0.00)	−0.23 (0.00)	0.04 (0.08)	—		
SBAPOP	0.18 (0.00)	0.20 (0.00)	−0.01 (0.67)	0.02 (0.42)	0.07 (0.00)	—	
HIGHM	−0.21 (0.00)	−0.09 (0.00)	0.06 (0.01)	0.14 (0.00)	−0.09 (0.00)	−0.12 (0.00)	—

NOTE: p-values are in parentheses. EMPR is the average annual employment rate in percentage points over the sample period. HERF is the average Herfindahl ratio, calibrated to be between zero and one, in market i over the sample period. PICAP is average per capita income in local market i over our sample period. MSADUM is an indicator variable equal to one (zero otherwise) if market i is a metropolitan statistical area (MSA). DEPPOP is the average annual per capita bank deposits in market i. SBAPOP is the average annual amount of (new) Small Business Administration (SBA) guaranteed lending in market i over our sample period. And SBADEP is an interaction variable equal to SBAPOP times DEPPOP. SBAPOP is calibrated in dollars in per capita, and DEPPOP is calibrated in thousands of dollars per capita. HIGHM is an indicator variable equal to one if the minority population in the local market is greater than 25.55 percent of the total local market population and zero otherwise.

TABLE 4
ORDINARY LEAST SQUARES (OLS) FIXED EFFECTS
REGRESSION ESTIMATION ($N = 2,358$)

Variable	Parameter Estimates and T-Statistics		
	Model 1	Model 2	Model 3
Intercept	87.02 (251.23)***	86.82 (243.42)***	87.14 (248.43)***
PICAP	0.41 (19.46)***	0.41 (19.45)***	0.39 (18.56)***
HERF	−0.69 (−3.26)***	−0.67 (−3.15)***	−0.43 (−2.05)**
MSADUM	−1.15 (−6.30)***	−1.14 (−6.29)***	−0.95 (−5.26)***
DEPPOP	0.07 (7.45)***	0.09 (6.83)***	0.10 (9.33)***
SBAPOP	0.008 (4.44)**	0.015 (4.46)***	0.006 (3.36)***
SBADEP		−0.001 (−2.34)**	—
HIGHM			−0.47 (−1.87)*
DEPMIN	—	—	−0.12 (−5.84)***
SBAMIN			0.012 (1.77)*
Adjusted R^2	.236	.238	.262
F-statistic	146.94***	123.59***	105.65***

NOTE: This table provides parameter estimates for equation (1): $EMPR_i = \alpha_0 + \alpha_1 PICAP_i + \alpha_2 HERF_i + \alpha_3 MSADUM_i + \alpha_4 DEPPOP_i + \alpha_5 SBAPOP_i + \alpha_6 SBADEP_i + \varepsilon_i$. EMPR is the average annual employment rate in percentage points over the sample period. PICAP is average per capita income in local market i over our sample period. HERF is the average Herfindahl ratio, calibrated to be between zero and one, in market i over the sample period. MSADUM is an indicator variable equal to one (zero otherwise) if market i is a metropolitan statistical area (MSA). DEPPOP is the average annual per capita bank deposits in market i. SBAPOP is the average annual amount of (new) Small Business Administration (SBA) guaranteed lending in market i over our sample period. And SBADEP is an interaction variable equal to SBAPOP times DEPPOP. SBAPOP is calibrated in dollars in per capita, and DEPPOP is calibrated in thousands of dollars per capita. This table also provides three variations of equation (1). In the first variation (model 1), the variable SBADEP is excluded. In the second variation (model 3), the variables SBAMIN and DEPMIN are substituted for SBADEP. SBAMIN and DEPMIN are equal to SBAPOP and DEPPOP times a dummy variable, respectively. That dummy variable (HIGHM) is equal to one, and zero otherwise, if the percentage of minority population in the local market is greater than 25.55. T-statistics are in parentheses.
*Significant at the 10 percent level. **Significant at the 5 percent level. ***Significant at the 1 percent level.

local market per capital income (PICAP), per capita deposits (DEPPOP), and SBA guaranteed lending per capita (SBAPOP). The correlation coefficients for the first two of these relationships are similarly rather large. EMPR is significantly negatively correlated with our high-minority population percentage variable (HIGHM) and HERF.

The correlation coefficients for our independent variables suggest that multicollinearity may be a concern for the relationships between local market per capita income (*PICAP*) and *MSADUM*, *HERF*, and *DEPPOP*. These and other concerns about multicollinearity are evaluated using a variance-inflation-factor (VIF) method.

In Table 4, we present the main results for our study. These results are estimated using an OLS fixed effects method. The fixed effects class variable is the state in which the local market is located. Focusing on individual states as our fixed effect allows us to control for variations in state specific factors associated with systematic influences on employment levels within the same state. Examples of these state-specific factors are levels of educational attainment and other human capital measures, technological endowment and advancement, and state-level public policies designed to influence employment rates.

From Table 4, our measure of financial development (*DEPPOP*) has a positive and significant coefficient, suggesting a positive and significant impact on *EMPR*. Recall that *DEPPOP* is per capita bank deposits in the local market. To some extent, this is a measure of cross-sectional local market liquidity levels. A similar measure of liquidity was used by King and Levine (1993a, 1993b) to proxy for the level of financial development across countries. The issue of endogeneity is a concern for this variable, for it could be argued that higher levels of employment cause higher levels of per capita bank deposits as forcefully as it can be argued that higher levels of per capita bank deposits cause higher levels of employment. However, as mentioned in our introduction, recent studies from Jayaratne and Strahan (1996); Rajan and Zingales (1998); and Guiso, Sapienza, and Zingales (2004) all reported significant evidence supporting the proposition that the causal relationship runs from more financial market development to better economic performance. Furthermore, this issue of endogeneity is not central to our analysis, as we are more concerned with the impact of our interaction variable *SBAMIN* on *EMPR* rather than the causal linkages between *EMPR* and *SBAPOP*, or between *EMPR* and *DEPPOP*.

Notice from Table 4 that *SBAPOP* has a positive and significant coefficient, suggesting a positive and significant impact on *EMPR*. But the impact appears to be economically small. For example, if one increased per capita SBA guaranteed lending in a local market by three standard deviations (approximately $100), the predicted result is an increase in the level of employment by 0.8 percentage points. Of course, the outcome of this example would change to about 1.5 percentage points if we use model 2 in Table 4.

The major variable of interest in model 2 of Table 4 is *SBADEP*. This is the interactive variable that represents the impact on *EMPR* of increasing *SBAPOP* at higher levels of financial market development (*DEPPOP*).

SBADEP has a negative and significant coefficient associated with it. This suggests that at higher levels of financial market development (*DEPPOP*), per capita SBA guaranteed lending has a lower impact on *EMPR* than it does at lower levels of financial market development. Given that high-minority areas are likely characterized by relatively lower levels of financial market development, it is possible that SBA guaranteed lending will have more of an impact on local market employment rates in high-minority markets.

This latter proposition is tested directly in model 3 of Table 4. The interaction variable (*SBAMIN*) in model 3 in Table 4 is equal to the dummy variable

(*HIGHM*) times local market per capita SBA guaranteed lending (*SBAPOP*). The dummy variable *HIGHM* is equal to one, zero otherwise, if the local market minority population is greater than 25.55 percent. Notice that the coefficient (–0.47) for *HIGHM* in Table 4 is negative, large, and statistically significant. This suggests that, other things being equal, high-minority local markets experience an employment rate that is on average 0.47 percentage points less than the employment rate for those markets that are not high-minority.

Our main variable of interest in model 3 is *SBAMIN*. The coefficient (0.012) for *SBAMIN* is positive and statistically significant at the 5 percent level using a one-tailed test. Also notice that for this specification the coefficient (0.006) for *SBAPOP* is only about one-half the size of the coefficient for *SBAMIN*. This suggests that *SBAPOP* has about three times the positive impact in high-minority markets as it does in low minority markets. Recall that the coefficient on *SBAMIN* is the marginal impact of *SBAPOP* in a high-minority market, the total impact is represented by the sum of the coefficients (0.018) for *SBAMIN* and *SBAPOP* in model 3.

Overall, the results from Table 4 suggest that per capita SBA guaranteed lending is significantly positively correlated with the local market employment rate. And the impact of SBA guaranteed lending on the level of employment is 200 percent greater in high-minority markets relative to low-minority markets. These results lead to the rejection of our null hypothesis, which was that the impact of SBA guaranteed lending on employment rates in high-minority markets is the same as it is in low-minority markets.

[P]er capita SBA guaranteed lending is significantly positively correlated with the local market employment rate.

Our results are consistent with the notion that less developed financial markets benefit relatively more from government interventions in small firm credit markets. This relatively higher benefit is consistent with a credit rationing argument like that of Stiglitz and Weiss (1981), where the intervention serves to ameliorate a market failure in the small firm credit market. More specifically, the results suggest that SBA guaranteed lending will have a larger positive impact on social welfare if it is targeted to certain high-minority areas.

Robustness checks

Several robustness checks were performed for equations (1) and (2). In particular, we estimated equations (1) and (2) separately for MSAs and non-MSA counties, using disaggregated guaranteed lending variables for the 7(a) and 504 lending programs. Additionally, we estimated the equations using a stacked regression (OLS) approach with our panel data.

These robustness checks yield results qualitatively consistent with those reported in Table 3. Because of the potential for multicollinearity in our regressors, we conducted a VIF analysis. Our VIF results suggest that multicollinearity was not a problem for the results reported in Table 4. We did not observe a significant problem when testing the standard errors in our regressions for possible heteroskedasticity.

We recognize that there may be some endogeneity concerns with certain variables in our models. For example, higher local market employment rate levels may influence local market per capita income and vice versa. To address this issue, we first removed the per capita income variable from our analysis. This did not materially change our results for our SBA guaranteed lending variable. Then we used per capita income before the beginning of our sample period (e.g., 1990) in the analysis. This latter analysis suggested that local markets with higher per capita income at the beginning of the sample period experienced higher levels of employment over the sample period. This provides some evidence that higher per capita income levels may result in higher levels of employment. Next, we use the average SBA lending per capita variable for the 1991 to 1995 period and the employment levels variable from the 1996 to 1999 period. All other variables (in model 1 of Table 4) were calculated as before. The results from the lagged SBA variable exercise were qualitatively the same as previous results. We used a stacked regression analysis and lagged the SBA lending variable by one and two periods. The results were again qualitatively the same.

Conclusions and Extensions to Our Analysis

SBA guaranteed lending programs are one of many government-sponsored market interventions aimed at promoting small business. The rationale for these guarantees is often based on the argument that credit market imperfections can result in small enterprises being credit rationed—particularly those in high-minority areas. If SBA loan guarantees indeed reduce credit rationing in high-minority markets for small business loans, then there should be a relationship between measures of SBA guaranteed lending activities and economic performance, and this relationship should be more evident in high-minority markets.

We find evidence consistent with this proposition in this study. In particular, we find a positive and significant impact on the average annual level of employment in a local market as we increase the level of SBA guaranteed lending in that local market, and the magnitude of this impact is relatively larger in high-minority markets. One interpretation of our results is that the impact is three times as large in high-minority markets.

However, all of our results should be interpreted with caution because of at least five issues. First, we are unable to control for small business lending at the local market level, and hence, we do not know whether SBA loan guarantees are contributing to economic performance by helping to complete the market or are simply substituting for small business lending in the market. Second, we are not able to test whether SBA loan guarantees materially increase the volume of small business lending in a market—a question that is related to who captures the subsidy associated with SBA loan guarantees.

Third, we do not have direct measures of whether SBA guaranteed lending is really reducing discrimination at the microeconomic level. Fourth, we do not have any measures of the actual demand for credit by potential and existing minority small business owners in the local market. And, fifth, we do not include measures of the costs of SBA guaranteed lending, which would include the performance of granted SBA loans.

All of these issues relate to a larger question: what is the optimal level of SBA guaranteed lending in U.S. small firm credit markets? Future research may seek to shed additional light on this larger question.

Notes

1. This is because each loan made would reflect a random draw from the pool of borrowers. If the bank made a large number of small loans to borrowers in the pool, then the bank's loan portfolio would have the same risk and return characteristics of the pool of borrowers.

2. The act that created the Small Business Administration (SBA) is Public Law 163.

References

Becker, G. S. 1971. *The economics of discrimination*. 2nd ed. Chicago: University of Chicago Press.

Berger, A. N. 1995. The profitstructure relationship in banking—tests of market-power and efficient-structure hypotheses. *Journal of Money, Credit, and Banking* 27:404-31.

Berger, A. N., and T. H. Hannon. 1989. The price-concentration relationship in banking. *Review of Economics and Statistics* 71:291-99.

———. 1995. Relationship lending and lines of credit in small firm finance. *Journal of Business* 68 (3): 351-81.

Blanchflower, D. G., P. B. Levine, and D. J. Zimmerman. 2003. Discrimination in the small business credit market. *Review of Economics and Statistics* 85 (4): 930-43.

Calem, P. S., and G. A. Carlino. 1991. The concentration/conduct relationship in bank deposit markets. *Review of Economics and Statistics* 73:268-76.

Cavalluzzo, K. S., L. C. Cavalluzzo, and J. D. Wolken. 2002. Competition, small business financing, and discrimination: Evidence from a new survey. *Journal of Business* 75 (4): 641-79.

Craig, Ben R., William E. Jackson III, and James B. Thomson. 2007. Small firm finance, credit rationing, and the impact of SBA guaranteed lending on local economic growth. *Journal of Small Business Management* 47 (1): 116-132.

Guiso, Luigi, Paola Sapienza, and Luigi Zingales. 2004. Does local financial development matter? *Quarterly Journal of Economics* 119:929-69.

Jackson, W. E., III. 1992a. Is the market well defined in bank merger and acquisition analysis? *Review of Economics and Statistics* 74:655-61.

———. 1992b. The price-concentration relationship in banking: A comment. *Review of Economics and Statistics* 74:373-76.

Jayaratne, Jith, and Philip Strahan. 1996. The finance-growth nexus: Evidence from bank branch deregulation. *Quarterly Journal of Economics* 111 (3): 639-70.

Kane, Edward J., and Burton G. Malkiel. 1965. Bank portfolio allocation, deposit variability, and the avail-ability doctrine. *Quarterly Journal of Economics* 79 (1): 113-34.

King, Robert G., and Ross Levine. 1993a. Finance and growth: Schumpeter might be right. *Quarterly Journal of Economics* 108 (3): 717-37.

———. 1993b. Finance, entrepreneurship, and growth: Theory and evidence. *Journal of Monetary Economics* 32 (3): 513-42.

Lang, W. W., and L.I. Nakamura. 1993. A model of redlining. *Journal of Urban Economics* 33:233-38.

Petersen, Mitchell, A., and Raghuram G. Rajan. 1994. The benefits of lending relationships: Evidence from small business data. *Journal of Finance* 49 (1): 3-37.

———. 1995. The effect of credit market competition on lending relationships. *Quarterly Journal of Economics* 110 (2): 407-43.

Rajan, Raghuram G., and Luigi Zingales. 1998. Financial dependence and growth. *American Economic Review* 88 (3): 559-86.

Robinson, Joan. 1952. *The generalization of the general theory: The rate of interest and other essays*. London: Macmillan.

Schumpeter, Joseph. 1911. *A theory of economic development*. Cambridge, MA: Harvard University Press.

Shaffer, Sherrill. 1994. Bank competition in concentrated markets. In *Business review*, 3-16. Philadelphia: Federal Reserve Bank of Philadelphia.

———. 2004. Patterns of competition in banking. *Journal of Economics and Business* 56:287-313.

Small Business Administration (SBA). 2005. Small and micro business lending for 2003-2004. Report no. 266, November. Washington, DC: U.S. Small Business Administration, Office of Advocacy.

Stiglitz, Joseph E., and Andrew Weiss. 1981. Credit rationing in markets with imperfect information. *American Economic Review* 71 (3): 393-410.

Traits and Performance of the Minority Venture-Capital Industry

This study analyzes the performance of investments made by venture-capital (VC) funds that specialize in financing minority business enterprises (MBEs). Existing studies document that MBEs have less access to financing—equity as well as debt—than similarly situated firms owned by nonminority whites. The apparent existence of a discriminatory financing environment creates an underserved market and, hence, attractive opportunities are available to firms capable of identifying and serving MBE financing needs. Analyzing cash-flow data on VC investments, we find that the minority-oriented funds earned yields on their realized equity investments that were slightly higher than the returns reported by mainstream VC funds. Considering differences in methodologies used to generate rate-of-return data for the MBE—as opposed to the nonminority-oriented funds—we conclude that the minority VC funds are earning yields on their realized investments that are at least equivalent to those of the broader VC industry.

Keywords: financing minority-owned businesses; venture capital

By
TIMOTHY BATES
and
WILLIAM BRADFORD

Overview

Minority business progress in recent decades is strongly rooted in the human-capital gains of business owners: the depth of expertise among minority entrepreneurs has grown substantially (Bates 2006). Market access has broadened and financial-capital availability has expanded (Bates 2001). Parity with nonminority entrepreneurs, however, has not been achieved. Capital-market access is an enduring barrier, thwarting the size and scope of minority

Timothy Bates is a distinguished professor of economics at Wayne State University. His current research focuses upon the minority-oriented venture-capital industry and the roles that small businesses might play in revitalizing low-income urban areas.

William Bradford is an endowed professor of business and economic development and professor of finance at the University of Washington Business School, Seattle. His research interests include minority business development issues, entrepreneurial finance, and venture capital.

DOI: 10.1177/0002716207303580

business enterprises (MBEs) (Cavalluzzo and Wolken 2005; Bates, Bradford, and Rubin 2006). Yet the very existence of discriminatory barriers limiting capital access creates an underserved market and, hence, attractive opportunities are available to firms capable of identifying and serving MBE financial-capital needs (Bradford and Bates forthcoming).

This study analyzes the nature and performance of the venture-capital (VC) funds that specialize in financing large-scale minority-owned businesses. We address three issues: (1) Where are the VC dollars that flow to MBEs coming from? (2) What kinds of MBEs get VC financing? (3) What is the investment performance of the MBE-focused VC funds?

Three relationships underlay our research. First, MBEs have less access to financial capital than nonminority firms with identical measured traits (other than owner race). Second, such unequal access creates opportunities for VC funds specializing in financing this underserved niche market. Third, VC funds that restrict their investments to minority firms are potentially harmed by forgoing opportunities to finance nonminority-owned ventures (Bradford and Bates forthcoming). The funds analyzed in our study, on balance, earned high returns relative to VC funds investing in mainstream markets. We conclude that the opportunities available in the underserved minority market offset possible negative impacts of forfeiting opportunities to invest in the nonminority business community.

Human-Capital Underpinnings of MBE Progress

The target market for VC investments is a small subset of the nation's minority business community. VC funds seeking to invest in MBEs commonly target firms whose owners have strong educational credentials and considerable managerial expertise. Firms receiving these investments typically have annual sales in the million-dollar-plus range as well as excellent growth prospects (Bates and Bradford 2003a, 2003b).

Among black-owned firms, for example, Census Bureau data indicate that only 10,727 of the 1.2 million firms covered by the Survey of Business Owners reported annual sales exceeding $1 million (U.S. Census Bureau 2006). Yet this subset—roughly 1 percent of black enterprises—employed 449,098 of the 756,679 workers on the payrolls of black-owned businesses in 2002 (see Table 1). These large firms generated 59.3 percent of all jobs found in the nation's black business community and were expanding at more than four times the rate of smaller firms. Helping to finance this high rate of growth and job creation is the task of the minority-oriented VC industry.

As the black business community has expanded in size and scope, highly educated and experienced entrepreneurs are increasingly present. A new African American entrepreneur has emerged, according to Boston and Ross (1997). "This new entrepreneur is young, well educated, operating increasingly in non-traditional

TABLE 1
SURVEY OF BUSINESS OWNERS DATA: BLACK-OWNED BUSINESSES WITH
PAID EMPLOYEES (NATIONWIDE)

Firms	Number of Employees in 2002
Annual sales under $1 million	307,581
Annual sales $1 million plus	449,098
All employer firms	756,679

SOURCE: U.S. Census Bureau.

industries . . ." (p. 339). Describing Atlanta's new black entrepreneurs, Boston and Ross observed that "they are heavily concentrated in providing business services . . . 80% of their employees are African American; 62% of their customers or clients are non African American" (340).

Gains in higher education underlay progress in entrepreneurship. Black students moving away from traditional career paths—teaching, most often—and preparing, instead, for careers in business and technical fields, are the underpinnings of the new African American entrepreneur. As career options have widened in recent decades, students shifted their fields of concentration dramatically to take advantage of opportunities in the business world (Bates 1997; Carter and Wilson 1992; Harvey 2003). Today, more than one hundred thousand African Americans hold MBA degrees.

Black students moving away from traditional career paths—teaching, most often—and preparing, instead, for careers in business and technical fields are the underpinnings of the new African American entrepreneur.

Compiling Data on Minority-Oriented VC Funds

In cooperation with the National Association of Investment Companies (NAIC), we have surveyed VC funds that focus their investments in minority-owned firms. Our 2001 survey described fund characteristics and performance

TABLE 2
PRESURVEY OF FIRMS THAT ARE ACTIVE MEMBERS OF THE NATIONAL
ASSOCIATION OF INVESTMENT COMPANIES (NAIC)

Presurvey universe: Forty-one firms holding active membership in the NAIC in early 2004.
Task: Identify the member firms operating funds that are actively investing venture capital in
minority business enterprises (MBEs).
Step 1: Identify member firms that do not actively invest in MBEs, or small businesses of
any sort: eight member firms.
Step 2: Contact thirty-three member firms to identify those focused upon investing venture
capital in MBEs: thirty-one firms responded, two refused. These latter two member firms
were dropped from further consideration.
Step 3: Apply three criteria to the thirty-one member firms responding to the presurvey
(some of these firms operate two or more funds):
(a) Are the majority of the fund's investments in MBEs?
(b) Are the majority of the fund's investments venture-capital (as opposed to straight debt)
oriented?
(c) Does the fund choose investments with a predominant focus upon generating profits?

through year-end 2000. Our 2004 to 2005 survey describes these VC funds
through year-end 2003.

Nearly all of the VC funds serving the minority business niche are NAIC
members, and we screened the NAIC membership initially to identify funds
meeting three conditions (see Table 2).

1. The fund's investments were equity-capital oriented (as opposed to debt).
2. Most investments were in minority-owned firms.
3. The fund was profit (as opposed to nonprofit) oriented.

Funds meeting these criteria were asked to complete a lengthy survey describing fund traits as well as characteristics of their investments. Response rates were
high, exceeding 60 percent for each of our surveys. Nonrespondents were most
often new VC funds lacking realized equity investments in MBEs. Of the thirty-
eight profit-oriented, minority-oriented VC funds that were surveyed in 2004 to
2005, twenty-four (63.1 percent) responded. Our 2001 survey, by way of contrast,
generated twenty-four responses from thirty-six funds, producing a response rate
of 66.7 percent.

Sources of Funds

The twenty-four responding VC funds raised most of their capital from five
sources. Public pension funds were dominant, providing more than $1 billion to
ten VC funds. The other four major sources—banks, funds of funds, corporate
pension funds, and corporations—collectively provided more than $800 million

TABLE 3
COMPARING FUNDING SOURCES FOR MINORITY-ORIENTED
VENTURE-CAPITAL FUNDS (VCs)

	Growing Sources			
	Number of Funds Tapping These Sources[a]		Median Dollar Amount of Capital Raised	
	2001 Survey	2004 Survey	2001 Survey	2004 Survey
Public pension funds	6	10	$55 million	$53 million
Fund of funds	7	12	$15 million	$16 million

a. The total number of funds responding to the 2001 and 2004 surveys was twenty-four for each survey.

in capital to the VC funds responding to our survey. Minor sources collectively providing more than $110 million for the minority-oriented VC funds were local, state, and federal government agencies; insurance companies; foundations; endowments; and individuals.

Comparing funding patterns for the minority-oriented VC funds through time indicates that public pension funds, and funds of funds, have aggressively increased their capital investments in this segment of the VC industry. Six of the twenty-four funds responding to our 2001 survey were financed by public pension funds; ten funds raised capital from this source, according to 2004 survey respondents (see Table 3). Similar increases typified funds of funds; while seven of the minority-oriented VCs indicated in the 2001 survey that they had raised capital from funds of funds, the corresponding figure in the 2004 survey was twelve funds. None of the other sources were expanding their scope of investments in the minority-oriented VC sector as aggressively as public pension funds and funds of funds.

The pattern of expanding institutional capital summarized in Table 3 reflects the fact that younger funds lacking track records have increasingly been successful in raising capital from public pension funds and funds of funds. These key sources of capital are not expanding their presence primarily by making larger investments in minority-oriented VC funds. Median investment amounts recorded in our 2001 and 2004 surveys were $55 million and $53 million for public pension fund sources; corresponding figures for the funds of funds were $15 million and $16 million (see Table 3). As successful minority VC firms set up new funds, they increasingly rely upon the public pension funds and funds of funds for capital. Now the strongest among the new industry entrants as well as the established, successful VC firms can tap these funding sources. Not only do the public pension funds and funds of funds provide more than 60 percent of the institutional capital invested in this sector (see Table 4); they also serve as expanding funding sources, driving continuing growth in the minority VC sector.

TABLE 4
TOTAL DOLLAR AMOUNT OF CAPITAL RAISED, BY SOURCE

1. Public pension funds	$1,010.3 million
2. Fund of funds	$212.2 million
3. Banks	$201.7 million
4. Insurance companies	$52.1 million
5. Corporate pension funds	$192.0 million
6. State, local government	$8.5 million
7. Federal government	$39.5 million
8. Corporations	$211.3 million
9. Foundations, endowments	$11.0 million
10. Individuals, families	$4.5 million
11. Other sources	$38.6 million
Total raised through year-end 2003: all sources	$1,981.4 million

*[F]ocus upon financing MBEs [minority
business enterprises], in fact, is often what
attracted the institutional investors in the first
place. . . . Self-proclaimed minority-oriented
VCs would risk alienating their funding sources
if they deviated from MBE investing.*

Our analysis of the individual investments made by the VC funds indicates that
nearly all are in minority-owned firms. Investments in black-owned firms are predominant; Hispanic businesses are a distant second; VC investments in Asian-
owned firms are least common. When making investment decisions, some
minority-focused funds have an explicit mandate from their institutional
investors to fund MBEs (Bates, Bradford, and Rubin 2006). Their strategic focus
upon financing MBEs, in fact, is often what attracted the institutional investors
in the first place. Banks providing capital to minority-oriented VC funds typically
qualify for Community Reinvestment Act (CRA) credit. State pension funds that
actively invest in minority-oriented VCs have high proportions of minority residents in their states. Minority-targeted investing is politically popular. Self-
proclaimed minority-oriented VCs would risk alienating their funding sources if
they deviated from MBE investing.

TABLE 5
TRENDS IN INVESTING IN MINORITY BUSINESS
ENTERPRISES (MBEs)—NUMBER OF FUNDS INVESTING
IN SELECTED INDUSTRY GROUPS

	2001 Survey	2004 Survey
Communications	20 funds	21 funds
Software and other IT	—[a]	15 funds
Manufacturing: electronics and computer-related fields	12 funds	6 funds
Manufacturing: other fields	15 funds	12 funds
Services: medical/health	9 funds	8 funds
Services: All other	16 funds	18 funds
Trade: wholesale and retail	13 funds	13 funds

a. Investments in software and other IT were sufficiently rare, therefore they did not justify a separate category. Note that the same number of funds—twenty-four—responded to each of the surveys.

Investing in Minority Business

An important trait differentiating the minority-oriented VC sector from mainstream VCs is its broad diversification regarding industries in which the funds invest. Mainstream VCs are heavily concentrated in several high-tech sectors while minority VCs are widely diversified across high- and low-tech fields (Bates and Bradford 2002). Table 5 summarizes the industry distribution of the companies receiving equity investments from minority VC funds through year-end 2003. A comparison of investment patterns reported in the 2001 and 2004 surveys reveals broadly similar patterns of investment diversity, but one important difference is starkly apparent. The software and IT fields have not traditionally attracted equity investments from minority VC funds, but this pattern, according to 2004 survey results, has changed: fifteen of the responding funds reported software and IT investments. This represents an aggressive move toward investment patterns more in line with mainstream VC industry practices. The move toward high-tech investing also became apparent at the top of the cycle—1998 through 2000—suggesting that some minority VCs might have been swept up in the euphoria of high-tech equity investing that peaked in 2000.

The next issue concerns the dollar magnitude of the investments made by minority-oriented VC funds. One fact is clear: equity capital invested in MBEs has grown enormously. Data from our 2004 survey verify that nearly all of the equity investments made by the surveyed VC funds were in MBEs. We were hoping that investments in nonminority firms would be common enough to permit comparison of returns generated from investing in MBEs, as opposed to nonminority firms. The latter, however, are too scarce to permit valid comparison.

Table 6 reports equity amounts invested in MBEs by the surveyed minority-oriented VCs: only those equity investments that had been realized by year-end 2003 are included. Table 6 should be read as follows: (1) $3.2 million was

TABLE 6
REALIZED EQUITY INVESTMENTS OF THE MINORITY
FUNDS: DOLLAR AMOUNTS INVESTED IN PORTFOLIO
COMPANIES (BY YEAR OF INVESTMENT)

Year Investment Was Made	Sum Invested by All Funds	Percentage Change from the Previous Year
1989	$1.5 million	NA
1990	$3.2 million	107
1991	$3.9 million	24
1992	$11.2 million	185
1993	$13.9 million	24
1994	$13.5 million	-3
1995	$7.7 million	-43
1996	$34.6 million	349
1997	$22.8 million	-34
1998	$27.7 million	21
1999	$55.9 million	102
2000	$25.6 million	-54
2001	$5.0 million	-80
2002	$1.5 million[a]	-70
2003	$0.2 million[a]	-87

NOTE: Data represent investments in 184 firms.
a. These dollar figures are low because only realized investments are being described in this table. Thus, $0.2 million was invested in 2003 in deals that were realized by year-end 2003.

invested in 1990 and realized by year-end 2003, (2) $55.9 million was invested in 1999 and realized by year-end 2003, (3) and so on. A comparison of amounts of equity invested in MBEs in 1990 ($3.2 million) and 1999 ($55.9 million), of course, highlights the enormous investment growth generated by the minority-oriented VC funds over the 1990s. Table 6's figures represent gross dollar inflows into equity investments.

Returns Generated from Realized Equity Investments

An initial look at the returns generated by the minority-oriented VC funds is provided in the Table 7 statistics. These numbers summarize returns solely for mature investments—those realized investments initially funded in 1998 or previous years. Many of the applicable 149 investments were first funded in the 1996 to 1998 period (boom years) and realized in the 2001 to 2003 period (bust years).

The average investment described in Table 7 was for $899.9 thousand; the corresponding average gross return was $1,891.8 thousand. Thus, mean net return

TABLE 7
INVESTMENT PERFORMANCE MEASURES FOR THE MINORITY-ORIENTED
VENTURE-CAPITAL FUNDS

A. Payback analysis	
Number of investments	149
Number with payback exceeding zero	89
Percentage with payback exceeding zero	59.7
B. Average investment performance ($ thousands)	
Mean investment outflow	$899.9
Mean investment gross return	$1,891.8
Mean investment net return	$991.9

NOTE: These dollar figures describe only those realized equity investments initially funded during or before 1998. When an investment payback equals zero, the amount invested exactly equals the amount returned (by definition).

on the 149 realized investments was $991.9 thousand. By way of comparison, mean investment reported in the 2001 survey data (as discussed in Bates and Bradford 2002) was $562.4 thousand and corresponding gross return was $1,623.9 thousand; the resulting mean net return was $1,061.5 thousand.

Lower average returns—in comparison to the 2001 survey figures—reflect the drop-off in equity investment returns realized after 2000. Of the 149 investments described in Table 7, note that 20.2 percent of them yielded absolutely nothing: they were complete losses. Among the realized investments initially funded in 1999, in comparison, nearly half yielded nothing (not reported in Table 7). These developments—sharp decline in returns—were not unique to the minority VC funds. These same patterns describe the mainstream VC industry's performance in the 2001 to 2003 period. Realized investments in the minority VC sector sometimes represent IPOs, but more common methods for VC funds to exit investments are buyouts by new owners or refinancings by existing owners.

The ability of the minority-oriented VC industry to expand its MBE investments depends critically upon its ability to attract capital from institutional investors. Offering attractive financial returns to such key capital sources as state pension funds, in turn, is a particularly effective strategy for ensuring the long-run viability and growth of the minority VC industry. We have attempted to calculate VC investment returns in ways that are of maximum interest to institutional investors. We have done this, first, by calculating the net returns that VC funds actually pay out to their limited partners (the institutional investors). In contrast, Table 7 reported returns that are not net of the fees and carried interest retained by general partners (the VC fund) and not paid out to the limited partners.

VC funds charge investors an annual fee—based on their total investment in the fund—to cover normal operating expenses. When investments in MBEs are realized, VC funds retain 20 percent of gains and pay out the remaining 80 percent to their limited partners. The bottom line for the institutional investor consists of the returns produced when all of the VC fund investments have been realized, net of annual fees and the 20 percent of gains retained by the general partners. We report estimated returns to institutional investors for all investments made by the minority-focused funds in the period from 1989 through 1995. We collected annual cash flow data for all such investments and tracked each investment through year-end 2003. All but 9 of the applicable 140 investments had been realized by then. For the 9 not exited, the cash flows consist of actual intermittent cash flows and the estimated market value of the investment at year-end 2003.[1] Utilizing the investments' cash flows, we compare the resulting internal rate of return (IRR) of each minority-focused fund to that of mainstream private equity funds that started investing in the same year as that of the minority-focused fund ("vintage funds").

The ability of the minority-oriented VC industry to expand its MBE investments depends critically upon its ability to attract capital from institutional investors.

In reporting the funds' IRRs, we adjusted the cash flows for the minority funds to reflect payment of 2 percent of the fund's assets for management fees, plus 20 percent of the net cash flow return on investment (carried interest) to the fund's managers. The fees and carried interest are standard for both the minority-focused funds and the mainstream industry. Eleven of the surveyed minority-oriented funds made VC investments during the applicable 1989 to 1995 period. The others began investing after year-end 1995 and were therefore excluded from our analysis of investment returns. Multiple investments by a fund in one firm were common; these were treated as one investment. As a group, the investment cash outflows of the minority VC funds totaled $104.7 million for the 140 investments that were undertaken. Cash inflows from these investments totaled $251.2 million. The VC funds thus netted $146.5 million from the realized investments that were initiated in the 1989 to 1995 period.

We report in Table 8 the performance of the minority-focused funds in two ways: (1) the overall average IRRs of the funds and (2) the public market equivalents (PMEs) based on the IRRs of private equity funds of the same vintage year as the minority funds (PME–Vintage PE). The PME–Vintage PE performance measure is found by dividing the present value of the minority fund's cash inflows (returns) by the present value of its cash outflows. The discount rate is the average

TABLE 8
PERFORMANCE THROUGH YEAR-END 2003 ON INVESTMENTS
MADE IN 1989 TO 1995: MINORITY-ORIENTED VENTURE CAPITAL FUNDS

Fund	a	b	c	d
IRR of the fund	46.6%	25.1%	3.2%	13.7%
PME-Vintage funds	2.93	1.17	0.46	1.01
	e	f	g	h
IRR of the fund	−28.3%	5.6%	25.9%	13.0%
PME-Vintage funds	0.16	0.74	1.14	0.99
	i	j	k	Totals
IRR of the fund	5.5%	46.8%	12.1%	17.7%
PME-Vintage funds	0.66	2.33	0.86	1.16

NOTE: PME = public market equivalents; IRR = internal rate of return. PME-Vintage is found by dividing the present value of the fund's cash returns by the present value of the fund's cash outflows. The discount rate is the average realized IRR of venture-capital funds in the Venture Economics database that began investing in the same year that the minority-focused fund began investing.

realized lifetime IRR of all private equity funds of the same vintage year in the Venture Economics database.[2] For example, if a minority fund made its first investment in 1990, the discount rate used for PME–Vintage PE is the average IRR (22 percent) of the forty-five private equity funds in the Venture Economics database that started investing in 1990. The PME–Vintage PE compares investing in the minority-focused fund to investing in the same vintage private equity fund: a PME greater (less) than one indicates that the minority-focused fund outperformed (underperformed) its vintage private equity funds.

The first row of Table 8 reports, by fund, the IRR of each fund's investments. A fund's IRR is found by calculating the IRR of the combined net cash flows of all of the fund's investments initiated in the 1989 to 1995 period. The second row reports the PME–Vintage PE for each fund. Fund names are withheld for purposes of confidentiality. The minority-focused funds earned an average IRR of 17.7 percent (see Table 8). To derive this figure, we treated all of the relevant cash flows of each fund as one big investment, for which we calculated one IRR. This produced eleven IRR values for eleven funds, the mean of which was 17.7 percent. However, the performance of individual minority-focused funds varied widely. Four funds earned IRRs less than 10 percent, and four funds earned IRRs exceeding 20 percent. The PME-Vintage compares the IRRs of the mainstream funds starting during the same year as the minority funds. Five of the eleven PMEs are equal to or greater than one. The total PME-Vintage for the minority-focused funds is 1.16, indicating that as a group, the minority-focused funds earned higher IRRs than the mainstream funds of the same vintage.

We also compared our findings to those of other studies examining the IRRs of private equity funds. Chen, Baierl, and Kaplan (2002) found a mean IRR of 13.4 percent for 148 VC funds in the Venture Economics data that had liquidated as of 1999. Ljungqvist and Richardson (2004) reported a mean IRR of 18.5 percent for 36 VC funds that started in 1989 to 1993 and had either been liquidated or were likely to have earned most of their returns. These older funds were less impacted by the post-2000 drop-off of realized investment returns than the minority-oriented funds. We view the mean IRRs of the minority-focused funds as broadly equivalent to these yields.

Concluding Remarks

We conclude that the returns on the minority-focused funds are certainly no lower—and perhaps higher—than those of mainstream funds. Furthermore, their market risk of investments is not higher than the risk of the mainstream funds (Bradford and Bates forthcoming). Thus, we accept the hypothesis that minority-focused funds are investing in an underserved market niche that offers attractive returns. Our conclusion is tempered by the reality of underlying databases that are not perfectly comparable. Our evidence, nonetheless, clearly suggests that, during the period observed, the investment performance of the minority-focused funds was at least equivalent to that of their vintage mainstream funds.

[T]he returns on the minority-focused funds are certainly no lower—and perhaps higher—than those of mainstream funds.

As we look to the future, should we expect mainstream VC funds to enter and exploit MBE investment opportunities? Such entry may be limited by three factors. First, fund general partners obtain the bulk of their investment opportunities through contacts and relationships that they have built over time. Minority entrepreneurs have traditionally been underrepresented in mainstream networks. Second, most minority funds are not high-tech oriented and do not fit the technical focus typifying mainstream VC funds. This increases information asymmetries surrounding investment opportunities in the minority business sector. Third, the existence of discrimination à la Becker (1971) can result in distaste for minority persons, spilling into distaste for investing in minority businesses. To the extent that general partners prefer not to work with ethnic minorities and are willing to forego economic profits in order to avoid transacting with minority owners, then fund entrance will be (self-) restricted. We conjecture that each of these factors plays a role in creating a profitable niche for minority-focused VC funds.

Notes

1. In each case, the estimated market value was made using industry guidelines. Any error in our measures caused by errors in measuring the market value of investments not exited should be negligible: the estimated market value of the investments not exited is only 1.8 percent of the investments' total cash flows, and less than that if they are adjusted for time value.

2. The internal rates of return (IRRs) of funds in a vintage year were calculated by Venture Economics. We are grateful to Elizabeth Schoar for providing us those data.

References

Bates, Timothy. 1997. *Race, self employment, and upward mobility*. Baltimore: Johns Hopkins University Press.

———. 2001. Minority business access to mainstream markets. *Journal of Urban Affairs* 23 (1): 41-56.

———. 2006. The urban development potential of black-owned businesses. *Journal of the American Planning Association* 72 (2): 227-38.

Bates, Timothy, and William Bradford. 2002. *Venture capital in minority business investment*. Report to the E.M. Kauffman Foundation, November. Kansas City, MO: E.M. Kauffman Foundation.

———. 2003a. Analysis of venture-capital funds that finance minority-owned businesses. *Review of Black Political Economy* 32 (1): 37-46.

———. 2003b. *Minorities and venture capital: A new wave in American business*. Kansas City, MO: E.M. Kauffman Foundation.

Bates, Timothy, William Bradford, and Julia Sass Rubin. 2006. The viability of the minority-oriented venture-capital industry under alternative financing arrangements. *Economic Development Quarterly* 20 (2): 178-91.

Becker, Gary. 1971. *The economics of discrimination*. 2nd ed. Chicago: University of Chicago Press.

Boston, Thomas, and Catherine Ross. 1997. Location preferences of successful African American-owned businesses in Atlanta. In *The inner city*, ed. Thomas Boston and Catherine Ross, 337-57. New Brunswick, NJ: Transaction Publishers.

Bradford, William, and Timothy Bates. Forthcoming. Venture capital investment in minority business. *Journal of Money, Credit, and Banking*.

Carter, D., and R. Wilson. 1992. *Minorities in higher education*. Washington, DC: American Council on Higher Education.

Cavalluzzo, Ken, and John Wolken. 2005. Small business loan turndowns, personal wealth, and discrimination. *Journal of Business* 78 (6): 2153-78.

Chen, Ping, Gary Baierl, and Paul Kaplan. 2002. Venture capital and its role in strategic asset allocation. *Journal of Portfolio Management* 28 (1): 83-89.

Harvey, W. 2003. *Minorities in higher education, 2001-2003*. Washington, DC: American Council on Higher Education.

Ljungqvist, Alexander, and Matthew Richardson. 2004. The cash flow, return and risk characteristics of private equity. Working Paper no. 9454, July, National Bureau of Economic Research, Cambridge, MA.

U.S. Census Bureau. 2006. *Survey of business owners*. www.census.gov/prod/ec02/sb0200csblkt.pdf.

Secrets of Gazelles: The Differences between High-Growth and Low-Growth Business Owned by African American Entrepreneurs

By
THOMAS D. BOSTON
and
LINJE R. BOSTON

The research findings are based on a national survey of 350 African American business owners whose companies had ten to one hundred employees. Each quarter of 2002 and 2003, owners were randomly selected and interviewed. Companies were classified into three groups according to their annual employment growth over five years: gazelles (20 percent or greater rate of growth), growth-oriented firms (1 to 19 percent), and no-growth firms (less than 1 percent or negative). In comparison to no-growth firms, gazelles were more likely to market to the government sector, less likely to compete on the basis of price, more likely to serve regional and national markets, and more likely to have fewer African Americans workers. CEOs of no-growth companies were more likely to have entered business because they lost a previous job. Surprisingly, no statistically significant differences appeared in thirty-nine other variables that defined owner attributes, firm characteristics, and business strategies of gazelles and no-growth firms.

Keywords: high-growth firms; black-owned firms; gazelles

Background

David Birch labeled fast-growing companies gazelles and defined them as firms that have achieved an annual rate of growth of at least 20 percent (cited in Gundry and Welsch 2001, 465). The National Commission on Entrepreneurship (NCOE) developed a similar measure, called the Growth Company Index (GCI). This index defined high-growth firms as those having achieved at least 15 percent annual employment growth for a period of five years (NCOE 2001, 6). GCI also defined high-growth ventures as firms that hired at least twenty employees within five years after their start-up date. By these criteria, NCOE found that less than one in twenty businesses will achieve high-growth status; they are located in all regions of the country; and they are most often found in manufacturing, business services,

DOI: 10.1177/0002716207303581

distribution and extractive industries, and retail industries. Contrary to popular opinion, NCOE did not find that fast-growing companies are primarily concentrated in high-tech industries (NCOE 2001, 1).

Using Birch's definition, we examined gazelles, owned and operated by African Americans that achieved a minimum annual rate of employment growth of 20 percent and had a minimum of ten employees and a maximum of one hundred employees. While most researchers focus on the growth in sales when discussing fast-growing companies, this study focused on employment growth because Dun and Bradstreet (D&B) data were used to generate the survey population. Using sales data generated by D&B to measure firm performance is not as accurate as using employment data because a significant percentage of registered firms do not report actual sales to D&B. As a result, the unreported sales information is estimated. For example, D&B had to estimate sales for 36 percent of the 3,843 firms that made up our survey population while it estimated employment for only 1 percent of these firms. Additionally, the accuracy of firms designated as African American–owned by D&B was validated during survey interviews. We found that 3.7 percent of firms in the survey population were incorrectly classified as African American–owned. These firms were excluded from subsequent analyses. Each survey instrument was designed by the authors and administered by a national survey company.

Purpose

This research seeks to extend our knowledge of the nation's fastest-growing African American–owned small ventures. Since gazelles have achieved extraordinary rates of growth, we compared them to two other groups. The first group consisted of low and moderately growing small businesses that we called growth-oriented firms. The second group consisted of firms whose annual employment growth was less than 1 percent or negative. We labeled this group no-growth firms. While 20 percent was the minimum employment growth a firm had to achieve to be classified as a gazelle, the average annual increase in employment (measured from 1998 to 2003) of the 208 gazelles in our survey was 40.9 percent.

Thomas D. Boston is a professor of economics at the Georgia Institute of Technology and CEO of EüQuant, a marketing research and consulting company. He is the former president of the National Economic Association and former editor of the Review of Black Political Economy. *He is the author or editor of six books and numerous scholarly articles, and he created the ING-Gazelle Index, a national quarterly survey of the nation's fastest-growing black-owned companies.*

Linje R. Boston is CFO and chief statistical analyst of EüQuant, a marketing research and consulting company. He holds a master's degree in statistics from the University of Michigan and is the former corecipient of Carnegie Mellon University's first-place prize in the Annual Economics and Statistics Competition. He is cocreator of the ING-Gazelle Index.

NOTE: This research is supported by a grant from the Ewing Marion Kauffman Foundation. We thank the Kauffman Foundation for its generous support, which has made possible a new national quarterly survey.

The average annual employment growth of the 320 growth-oriented businesses was 9.1 percent, and the average annual decline in employment for the 607 no-growth firms was –14 percent.

The survey results are derived from the Gazelle Index™, a national quarterly random survey of 350 African American business owners. The survey was designed by Boston (2002) and conducted for seven consecutive quarters starting in April 2002 and ending in the fourth quarter of 2003. During the first three weeks of each quarter, a national survey company randomly selected for interview 350 African Americans who owned enterprises having ten to one hundred employees. The probability of a firm being selected for inclusion in a quarterly survey was independent of its previous participation or nonparticipation status. On average, each respondent participated in two of the seven quarterly surveys. In each survey, four core questions were asked that were designed to gauge the owners' outlook and confidence regarding business and economic conditions.

1. In your opinion, are general economic conditions better today than six months ago?
2. In looking six months into the future, are you more optimistic or more pessimistic about the economy?
3. Is business activity in your company better today than six months ago?
4. As compared to six months ago, has employment in your company increased, decreased, or remained the same?

The responses to these four questions constituted the Gazelle Index. Each quarter these core questions were supplemented with different questions designed to capture information on the owners' background, attributes, perceptions, strategy, and operational plans. For example, owners were asked questions about their family's involvement in business, their education attainment, age, experience, method of acquiring the business, succession plans, risk tolerance, government contracting, business strategy, perceptions of factors that influenced their company's growth, investment spending plans, hours spent in the business, reasons for entering the business, intentions to go public, and racial composition of their market and employees. The survey was financially supported by ING Financial Services.[1] Under a grant from the Kauffman Foundation, a new survey will be issued during the first quarter of 2007.

Literature Review: The Differences between High-Growth and Low-Growth Firms

A major distinction is made in the literature between entrepreneurs and small business owners. Entrepreneurs are conceptualized as agents of innovation and firm growth. Schumpeter (1934) viewed innovative activity as a central function of entrepreneurs and one that separates them from more common managerial activities. The characteristics of entrepreneurs and the attributes of the businesses they operate have been researched extensively. But much less is known about how entrepreneurs whose enterprises achieve high rates of growth differ from those whose small businesses grow less dramatically, or not at all. Gundry and Welsch (2001) noted that researchers have distinguished small business owners from entrepreneurs by the willingness of the former to settle for status quo growth. Stewart et al. (1998) distinguished small business owners from entrepreneurs by the latter's ability to capitalize on innovative combinations of resources for the principal purpose of profit and growth. They also noted that entrepreneurs make greater use of strategic management practices. In contrast, small business owners operate their enterprises as simple extensions of their individual personality, and their primary purpose is to achieve personal goals and produce family income. So the two types of owners differ in regards to their strategies, personality, cognitive orientation, and preferences (p. 191).

A weakness of many studies of high-growth firms is that they seldom include low-growth or no-growth firms for comparison. Gundry and Welsch (2001, 454) analyzed both high-growth and slow-growth firms and found that growth aspirations are positively correlated with the entrepreneur's education, business organization, industry of operation, and past growth of revenue and employment. By contrast, they did not find a significant relationship between growth aspirations of entrepreneurs and their experience, gender, location, or the absolute size of employment.

Kim and Mauborgne (1998) found that high-growth entrepreneurs may be distinguished from low-growth entrepreneurs along several dimensions. These include greater strategic intentions (i.e., greater emphasis on vision, product and service quality, reputation, and market-driven focus), entrepreneurial intensity and growth (i.e., the degree of commitment to entrepreneurship), greater willingness to incur the opportunity costs of growing, more decentralized firm structure, higher levels of financial resources, and greater variety of funding sources. Their research indicated that high-growth-oriented entrepreneurs are more likely to pursue market expansion through product and service innovation and increased advertising expenditures. They are also more likely to pursue technological change (such as adding new equipment and computerizing existing operations), spend more time searching for financing, engage in operations planning (such as expanding the current facilities), and devote more resources to organizational development (such as off-site training of employees).

Kim and Mauborgne (1998, 26-27) noted that "the difference in approach was not a matter of managers choosing one analytical tool or planning model over another. The difference was in the company's fundamental, implicit assumption about strategy. The less successful companies took a conventional approach: their strategic thinking was dominated by the idea of staying ahead of the competition. In stark contrast, the high-growth companies paid little attention to matching or beating their rivals. Instead, they sought to make their competitors irrelevant through a strategic logic we call *value innovation*. The approach is aimed at making a quantum leap in value to dominate the market.

Woo, Cooper, and Dunkelburg (1991) examined the typologies within which entrepreneurs are classified and noted two predominant classifications: "craftsmen" and "opportunists." Craftsmen are thought to emerge from blue-collar backgrounds and have more limited education and managerial experience. Their primary motive for entering business is to earn a comfortable living. They avoid risk taking, are much less likely to seek investors or partners, and are more likely to experience lower rates of growth. In contrast, opportunists have more extensive education and work experience; they are future oriented, more inclined toward managerial challenges, grow their organizations by drawing upon external sources of funds, and pursue strategies that are diverse and innovative. The authors noted that opportunist entrepreneurs are more likely to be motivated by financial gain and by building successful organizations. As such, they tend to be associated with faster-growing businesses.

Opportunists have more extensive education and work experience; they are future oriented . . . and pursue strategies that are diverse and innovative.

Hamm (2002) has identified four hazardous tendencies that constitute the major reasons why entrepreneurs who are successful at starting new ventures are unsuccessful at scaling their enterprises. These included a blind loyalty to colleagues who were around at the founding of the enterprise; excessive attention to the task at hand rather than focusing on the larger view; tunnel vision that fails to overcome the single-mindedness that was important when the organization was founded; and a failure to interact with customers, investors, analysts, reporters, and others. By contrast, entrepreneurs who are successful at scaling do so by overcoming these limitations, seeking input from others, and being willing to shift their outlook (Hamm 2002).

Stewart et al. (1998) examined achievement motivation, risk-taking propensity, and preference for innovation as a means of distinguishing entrepreneurs from small business owners and corporate managers. They found that entrepreneurs, in contrast to small business owners, are highly motivated, have a greater propensity for risk taking, engage in innovative activities, exhibit a psychological profile that is consistent with the goal of growth and profitability, and plan systematically (p. 204). While noting that there is no consensus in the literature regarding the risk-taking propensity of entrepreneurs, they pointed out that it is generally thought that entrepreneurs have a greater tendency toward taking risk.

Research conducted on successful African American–owned small businesses has mainly sought to identify variables associated with business start-up, viability, or failure.[2] The influential variables are classified into individual-specific factors, environment-consequence factors, and group-specific factors (see Ahiarah 1993). On the other hand, Bates (2006) has developed a paradigm (titled the "Three M's"), which he uses to classify factors associated with firm viability. The three factors are money, markets, and management.

Description of Data and Survey Methodology

The Gazelle Index was initiated in the second quarter of 2002 and continued for seven successive quarters, ending in the fourth quarter of 2003. Working with D&B, African American–owned businesses were identified for inclusion in the survey population if they met the following criteria: (1) the business was registered with D&B as an African American–owned enterprise, (2) the business had a minimum of ten and a maximum of one hundred workers in 2002, and (3) total employment in 2002 was greater than 1997 total employment by 5 percent or more. There were 1,497 businesses that fit these criteria. We anticipated that this survey population might not yield the desired number of survey responses efficiently. Therefore, 1,503 additional African American–owned firms that fit the first and second criteria but not the third were randomly selected for inclusion in the survey population. These additional firms comprised the low-growth and no-growth sector of the survey population. We anticipated that during the seven-quarter survey period, some firms might grow beyond one hundred employees while others might decline to less than ten employees. Therefore, the survey population was renewed in the first quarter of 2003. In total, the survey population consisted of 3,990 different firms, 3,843 of which were subsequently verified as African American–owned. Of this number, 21 percent were gazelles, 28 percent were growth-oriented firms, and 51 percent were no-growth firms (see Figure 1). Each quarter, 350 owners of these businesses were randomly selected and surveyed by a national survey company. The sample size of 350 was used so that the results would have a margin of error of ±5 percent at the .05 level of statistical significance.

Table 1 provides the number of firms from each group that responded to the survey. By converting these numbers to percentages, we find that the response rates for firms classified as gazelles, growth oriented, and no-growth oriented were 25.0 percent, 28.8 percent, and 30.4 percent, respectively. The differences in group response rates were not statistically significant. On average, gazelles, growth-oriented firms, and no-growth firms employed twenty-nine, twenty-seven, and twenty-five workers, respectively, in 2003. Their respective average years of operation were twelve, fifteen, and twelve years. Again, the differences are not statistically significant.

Figure 2 provides a histogram of the annual employment growth of gazelles and growth-oriented firms. No-growth firms are excluded from the figure. A

FIGURE 1
GAZELLE INDEX SURVEY POPULATION DISTRIBUTION

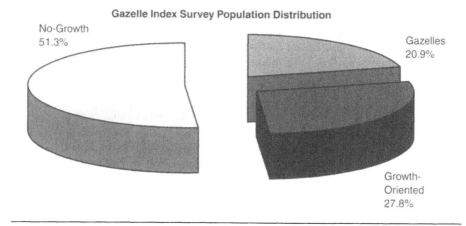

TABLE 1
SURVEY POPULATION AND SURVEY RESPONSE RATES

Group Category	Survey Population	Group Response Number	Group Response Rate
Gazelles	823	207	25.2%
Low growth	1,086	317	29.2%
No growth	1,934	607	31.4%
Total	3,843	1,131	29.4%

slight discontinuity occurs in the histogram for the distribution of companies experiencing less than a 20 percent employment growth (annually). This discontinuity is convenient in that it corresponds neatly to the definition of gazelles in the literature. Therefore, we split gazelles from growth-oriented companies at 20 percent annual employment growth. No-growth companies were defined as those having less than 1 percent annual employment growth.

The geographic location of the respondents to the survey was not statistically different from the distribution of all African American businesses as indicated by the 1997 Survey of Minority-Owned Business Enterprise (SMOBE), conducted every five years by the U.S. Census Bureau. According to SMOBE, the geographic distribution of African American–owned businesses in 1997 was as follows: 52.8 percent in the South, 12.9 percent in the Northeast, 16.8 percent in the Midwest, and 10.0 percent in the West. In comparison, respondents to the gazelle survey were distributed geographically as follows: 52.3 percent in the South, 11.7

FIGURE 2
FREQUENCY DISTRIBUTION FOR ANNUAL EMPLOYMENT
GROWTH (RESULTS FOR GAZELLES AND GROWTH-ORIENTED FIRMS ONLY)

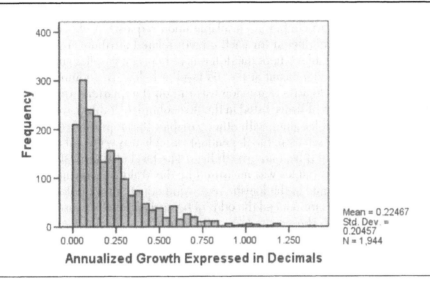

TABLE 2
REGIONAL DISTRIBUTION OF SURVEY RESPONDENTS BY
GROWTH CLASSIFICATION

	South		Northeast		Midwest		West	
	Number	Row %	Number	Row %	Number	Row %	Number	Row %
Gazelles	125	60.4	19	9.2	42	20.3	21	10.1
Growth-oriented businesses	173	54.6	41	12.9	62	19.6	41	12.9
No-growth businesses	293	48.3	72	11.9	141	23.2	101	16.6
Total	591	52.3	132	11.7	245	21.7	163	14.4

percent in the Northeast, 21.7 percent in the Midwest, and 14.4 percent in the West. Gazelles are more likely to be found in the South (60.4 percent of gazelles and 48 percent of no-growth companies) and much less likely to be found in the West (10 percent of gazelles and 17 percent of no-growth companies) (see Table 2). Overall, 78 percent of businesses surveyed were owned by men. This included 75 percent of gazelle owners, 76 percent of the owners of growth-oriented businesses, and 80 percent of the owners of no-growth businesses.

Summary of Major Results

Responses to survey questions were cross-tabulated with firms classified as either gazelles or no-growth (survey results for the growth-oriented firms are not reported in this article but are available upon request). A chi-square test of independence was conducted for each growth-related attribute. In Table 3, an asterisk indicates variables where the differences between gazelles and no-growth firms are statistically significant at the .05 level or below. In addition to the chi-square test, a binary logistic regression was run on the quarterly results of each survey. The attributes of firms, listed in the first column of Table 3, were included as independent variables along with other variables that represented the characteristics of firms. In each case, the dependent variable was set to 1 if the response was by a gazelle and 0 if by a no-growth firm. The level of statistical significance of the independent variables was measured by the Wald statistic, and the exponents of the coefficients in the logistic regression equations indicated the extent to which the variables influenced the odds of being a gazelle (because of the large number of equations, the results of logistic regressions are not reported in this article but are available upon request). In every case, they supported the results of the chi-square test.

Some of the survey questions were as follows. Did someone in your immediate family own a business prior to you starting this business? What was the highest level of education you attained? What is your age? How many years of work experience did you have before starting this business? How would you characterize yourself regarding risk taking? How did the following factors affect the growth of your business: marketing expenditures, expenditures on product and service innovation, expenditures on e-commerce, participation in minority business procurement programs, and discriminatory business practices? How did you acquire this business and what are your succession plans for the business? What percentage of total revenue is generated from African American customers and clients? How has the percentage of total revenue from government contracting changed over time? What percentage do African American employees comprise of your total workforce? Did you attend a historically black college or university? On average, how many hours do you spend in the business each week? Respondents were also asked to indicate how they adjusted their business strategy during periods of economic slowdown. That is, did they increase or decrease the prices of goods and services, the quality of their products, the size of the workforce, expenditures on wages and benefits, expenditures on technology, expenditures on research and development, other capital expenditures, marketing expenditures, and government-oriented marketing? Finally, they were asked to indicate the specific reason(s) why they entered business, the amount of satisfaction they derive as a business owner, and whether they would take their company public if the opportunity presented itself.

Figure 3 provides a typical illustration of how the group responses differed but not by a wide enough margin to be attributed to anything but chance. The Gazelle Index score is derived from responses to the four core questions described earlier. For each question, the percentage of neutral responses (i.e.,

TABLE 3
RESEARCH FINDINGS BASED ON GAZELLE INDEX™ SURVEYS, 2002 THROUGH 2003

Attributes of Gazelles (Relative to No-Growth Firms)	Theoretical Expectation: Gazelles vs. No-Growth Companies [a]	Empirical Finding [b]	Results Confirm or Reject Expectations [c]	Statistical Sign	Gazelle Survey Response	No-Growth Survey Response	Explanation of Response
Traits and self-perceptions							
High risk-taking behavior	>>	∨	Ø		22%	29%	Percentage of high risk takers
Index of confidence and optimism	>>	∧	+		.56	.49	Average from Gazelle Index
Has forward-looking optimism	∧	∧	+		.70	.64	Average from Gazelle Index
Legacy of business in family	>>	∧	+		46%	39%	Percentage stating yes
More satisfied as entrepreneur	∨	~	+		93%	86%	More satisfied now
Believes business acumen is inborn	∧	∧	+		27%	18%	Percentage that believes it is inborn
Motives for entering business							
Sought profit or personal wealth	>>	~	Ø		73%	76%	A significant motive
Opportunity presented itself	>>	~	Ø		71%	71%	A significant motive
Sought control over destiny	∨	∨	+		80%	87%	A significant motive
Sought power and social status	∨	∨	+		13%	26%	A significant motive
Dissatisfied with previous job	<<	∨	+		41%	54%	A significant motive
Lost previous job	<<	∨	+		13%	39%	A significant motive
To overcome racial barriers	∨	∨	+	°	65%	71%	A significant motive
Desire to use experience and education	∧	∨	Ø		74%	82%	A significant motive
To serve my community	∨	∨	+		64%	76%	A significant motive
Influenced by family member	∨	∨	+		40%	58%	A significant motive
Owner Attributes							
Years of schooling	∧	∧	+		38%	31%	Percentage with graduate studies
Attended a historically black college or university	∨	∧	Ø		40%	29%	Percentage stating yes
Years of business-related experience	∧	∧	+		60%	50%	Percentage with > 15 years
Male business owners	?	∧			80%	75%	Percentage of group owners male
Age	∨	~	+		59%	62%	Percentage in 45 to 64 age group
Business founder	∧	∧	+		83%	75%	Percentage founding their business
Succession plans within family	∨	∧	Ø		63%	56%	Family member to succeed
Hours worked per week in business	∧	~	Ø		56	54	Hours per week in business

(continued)

TABLE 3 (CONTINUED)

Attributes of Gazelles (Relative to No-Growth Firms)	Theoretical Expectation: Gazelles vs. No-Growth Companies[a]	Empirical Finding[b]	Results Confirm or Reject Expectations[c]	Statistical Sign	Gazelle Survey Response	No-Growth Survey Response	Explanation of Response
Business management and characteristics							
Positive current hiring plans	>>	>>	†	○	.53	.43	Average from Gazelle Index
Positive future hiring plans	>>	>>	†		58%	44%	Hiring three months ahead
Rapid growth	>>	>>	†	○	40%	Negative	Yearly employment growth
Future investment plans	>>	∧	†		42%	35%	Invest three months ahead
Located in South	?	~			60%	48%	Percentage located in South
Three largest industries	>>	~	Ø		25%; 16%; 11%	16%; 19%; 8%	Percentage in engineering; businesss services; comp
Percentage of workforce that is black	<	<	†	○	56%	67%	Percentage of workforce black
Age of business	<	< ?	Ø		12	12	Years in operation
Employment size of business	>>	~	Ø		29	25	Mean number of employees
Growth strategy							
Willingness to go public	>>	∧	†		70%	61%	Yes
Innovation expenditures important	>>	∧	†		44%	34%	Significant to past growth
Marketing expenditures important	>>	∧	Ø		35%	46%	Significant to past growth
E-commerce significant	∧	~ ?	Ø		27%	28%	Significant to past growth
Discriminatory significant	<	~ ?	Ø		38%	41%	Significant to past growth
Significant spending on research and development	>>	∧	†		29%	21%	Significant to past growth
Significant technology experience	>>	∨	Ø		35%	40%	Significant to past growth
Competitive strategy							
Reduced price during slowdown	<<	<<	†	○	13%	26%	Action during slow economy
Improved quality during slowdown	<<	∨	†		25%	30%	Action during slow economy
Increased wages and benefits	>>	∧	†		42%	32%	Action during slow economy
Increased size of workforce	>>	∧	†		32%	24%	Action during slow economy
Marketing strategy							
Marketing to government	<<	>>	Ø	○	59%	35%	Increase over past 5 years
Regional, national, international marketing	>>	>>	†	○	14%; 24%; 1%	12%; 18%; 0%	Percentage with regional, national, international marketing
Percentage revenue from blacks	<<	~	Ø		23%	27%	Percentage of total revenue from group
Importance of minority business programs	<<	∧	Ø		43%	38%	Significant to past growth

a. > or < indicates responses were expected to be more positive or more negative; >> or << indicates responses were expected to be strongly positive or negative; and a question mark (?) reflects cases where the expected direction of the outcome is unknown.

b. > and < and >> and << indicate actual direction of survey results; ~ indicates that the group responses were very similar.

c. Ø and † indicate survey results contradicted or supported the expectations.

118

FIGURE 3
GAZELLE INDEX BY GROUP CLASSIFICATION

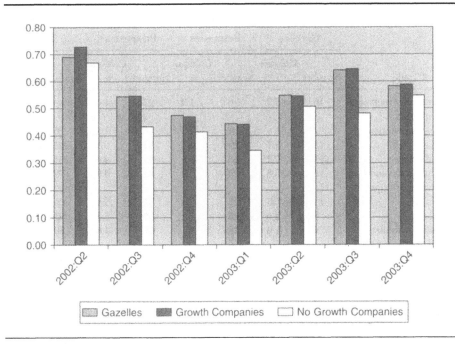

those stating that conditions are about the same) were omitted. The percentage of positive responses was divided by the sum of the percentage of positive and negative responses. The average value for the four questions constituted the Gazelle Index. A chi-square test of statistical independence was conducted for each quarterly index score.

The null hypothesis is that percentage responses for the three groups are not significantly different. Simply put, the null hypothesis is that the groups have a similar outlook on the economy. An observed chi-square statistic of .05 or less indicates that the group's outlooks differ, leading to a rejection of the null hypothesis. Using data from the seven quarterly surveys, the null hypothesis was tested twenty-eight times (i.e., four questions on each survey by seven quarterly surveys) and rejected only three times. The rejections were first quarter 2003 (question 4 observed chi-square = .034) and third quarter 2003 (question 1 observed chi-square = .013 and question 3 observed chi-square = .008). Each rejection of the null hypothesis was caused by a more pessimistic response of owners of no-growth companies. Overall, the small number of times the null hypothesis was rejected (three out of twenty-seven) led us to conclude that the difference in outlook on the economy by gazelles, growth-oriented firms, and no-growth firms was not statistically significant, even though the outlook of the no-growth company owners was usually more pessimistic than was the outlook of owners of gazelles

TABLE 4
INDUSTRY DISTRIBUTION OF SURVEY RESPONDENTS BY GROWTH CLASS

Type of Trade	Gazelles		Growth-Oriented Businesses		No-Growth Businesses		Total	
	Number	Column %	Number	Column %	Number	Column %	Number	Column %
General construction contractors	16	7.7	6	1.9	27	4.4	49	4.3
Heavy construction	2	1	4	1.3	20	3.3	26	2.3
Special trades	18	8.7	29	9.1	55	9.1	102	9
Manufacturing	15	7.2	28	8.8	58	9.6	101	8.9
Transportation and communications	12	5.8	26	8.2	41	6.8	79	7
Wholesale	11	5.3	27	8.5	31	5.1	69	6.1
Retail	5	2.4	26	8.2	32	5.3	63	5.6
Finance, insurance, real estate	4	1.9	18	5.7	28	4.6	50	4.4
Personal, and other businesses services	33	15.9	48	15.1	115	18.9	196	17.3
Building maintenance	17	8.2	10	3.2	56	9.2	83	7.3
Computer and data processing	22	10.6	35	11	48	7.9	105	9.3
Engineering, architectural, consulting	52	25.1	60	18.9	96	15.8	208	18.4
Total	207	100	317	100	607	100	1,131	100

and growth-oriented companies. Based on the literature review, we expected gazelle owners to be significantly more optimistic than owners of no-growth firms.

Gazelles were more likely than nongazelles to operate businesses in general construction (7.7 percent) and engineering, architectural, and consulting services (25.1 percent; see Table 4). Gazelles were less likely than nongazelles to operate businesses in retail (2.4 percent) and finance, insurance, and real estate (1.9 percent). The five-year average annual employment growth for gazelles (see Table 5) was 41 percent. Industries in which gazelles achieved above-average growth rates were computer and data processing (48.9 percent); personal and other business services (47.8 percent); engineering, architecture, and consulting services (41.3 percent); and transportation and communications (40.9 percent).[3] Industries where gazelles achieved below-average employment growth were finance, insurance, and real estate (30.8 percent); special trades contracting (31.9 percent); retail (33.2 percent); general construction (34.5 percent); manufacturing (36.5 percent); building maintenance (37.7 percent); and wholesale (38.2 percent). The results show that gazelles are most heavily concentrated in engineering, architectural, and consulting services, but they are experiencing the fastest rate of growth in information technology industries.

TABLE 5
ANNUAL EMPLOYMENT GROWTH BY INDUSTRY DISTRIBUTION
OF RESPONDENTS

Type of Trade	Percentage Growth of Employment Growth Class	
	Gazelles Mean %	Growth-Oriented Business Mean %
General construction contractors	34.5	10
Heavy construction	73.9	5.2
Special trades	31.9	8.5
Manufacturing	36.5	8.1
Transportation and communications	40.9	8.8
Wholesale	38.2	9.2
Retail	33.2	8
Finance, insurance, real estate	30.8	7.8
Personal, and other businesses services	47.8	9.8
Building maintenance	37.7	9.3
Computer and data processing	48.9	10.9
Engineering, architectural, consulting	41.3	9.2
Total	40.9	9.1

Results of the logistic regression indicated that firms that increased their contracting to the government sector over the past five years, as opposed to those that decrease their contracting to the government sector, had 4.6 times greater odds of being a gazelle as compared to a no-growth company. Firms whose government contracting remained the same over the past five years (as opposed to decreasing) had 2.6 times greater odds of being a gazelle as compared to a no-growth company. See Table 6 for the tabular responses to this question.

Second, lowering product and service prices during a period of economic slowdown as opposed to keeping prices unchanged decreased the odds of being a gazelle by 65 percent (see Table 7). Gazelle owners were much less likely to have entered business because they lost their previous job—13.3 percent for gazelle owners and 39.8 percent for owners of no-growth firms (see Table 8). The difference is statistically significant and coincides with our theoretical and intuitive expectations. That is, we expected that gazelle owners were more likely to have been attracted into entrepreneurship, while owners of no-growth firms were more likely to have been pushed into it. Finally, the mean percentage of African Americans employed in gazelles, growth-oriented companies, and no-growth companies were 56 percent, 60 percent, and 63 percent, respectively. With this in mind, we found a marginally significant difference (p-value of the Wald statistic of .058) associated with the percentage of African Americans in the company's workforce. Logistic regression results indicated that an increase of

TABLE 6
CHANGE OVER THE PAST FIVE YEARS IN THE PERCENTAGE OF COMPANY
REVENUE GENERATED IN THE GOVERNMENT SECTOR

	Percentage Has Increased		Percent Has Not Changed		Percentage Has Decreased	
	Number	Row %	Number	Row %	Number	Row %
Gazelles	33	58.9	16	28.6	7	12.5
Growth-oriented businesses	41	47.1	26	29.9	20	23
No-growth businesses	55	35	48	30.6	54	34.4
Total	129	43	90	30	81	27

TABLE 7
PRICING STRATEGY DURING THE SLOW ECONOMY

	Increased		Decreased		No Change	
	Number	Row %	Number	Row %	Number	Row %
Gazelles	8	17	6	12.8	33	70.2
Growth-oriented businesses	22	23.9	24	26.1	46	50
No-growth businesses	47	22.2	56	26.4	109	51.4
Total	77	21.9	86	24.5	188	53.6

TABLE 8
HOW THE LOSS OF A PREVIOUS JOB INFLUENCED MY DECISION TO
BECOME A BUSINESS OWNER

	Significant Influence		Minor Influence		No Influence	
	Number	Row %	Number	Row %	Number	Row %
Gazelles	2	13.3	5	33.3	8	53.3
Growth-oriented businesses	12	27.9	1	2.3	30	69.8
No-growth businesses	39	39.8	14	14.3	45	45.9
Total	53	34	20	12.8	83	53.2

1 percent in the share of African Americans in the company's workforce lowered the odds of being a gazelle by 1 percent. We also found that 14 percent of gazelles marketed their goods and services regionally and 24 percent marketed nationally. In comparison, 12 percent of no-growth firms marketed regionally and 18 percent marketed nationally. The difference in marketing was statistically significant.[4]

The most important finding is that the large number of variables reflecting personal attributes of owners, characteristics of businesses, and business strategies cannot explain the intraracial differences in high-growth and no-growth companies. This is important because researchers have historically explained firm growth by focusing on these factors. Even the mean hours spent per week running an enterprise were not significantly different—fifty-four, fifty-six, and fifty-five hours for owners of gazelles, growth-oriented companies, and no-growth companies, respectively.

This means that the real explanation behind the achievement of high-growth status lies in something that we have not yet measured. We believe part of the puzzle has been explained by Kim and Mauborgne (1998). They noted, "In a five-year study of high-growth companies and their less successful competitors, we found that the answer lies in the way each group approached strategy. . . . The less successful companies took the conventional approach: their strategic thinking was dominated by the idea of staying ahead of the competition. In stark contrast, high-growth companies paid little attention to matching or beating their rivals. Instead, they sought to make their competitors irrelevant through a strategic logic we call *value innovation*" (pp. 26-27).

Detailed Summary of Survey Results

The forty-eight survey questions in Table 3 are grouped into one of seven categories. The categories are as follows: traits and self-perceptions, motives for entering business, owner attributes, business management and characteristics, growth strategy, competitive strategy, and marketing strategy. These classifications allow us to generate expectations (based upon experience and the relevant literature) about how a variable would influence high-growth status. The theoretical expectations are documented in the column labeled "Theoretical Expectation, Gazelles versus No-Growth Companies." In each case, we compared the responses of gazelle owners to the responses by owners of no-growth companies. In cases where we expect the response of gazelle owners to be more positive or more negative than the response of owners of no-growth companies, these expectations are represented by the symbols > or <, respectively. In cases where we expect the response to be strongly positive or strongly negative, the corresponding symbols will be >> and <<, respectively. A question mark (?) reflects cases where the expected direction of the outcome is unknown.

The next column gives a symbol that shows the actual direction of the survey results such as >, which indicates that a larger percentage of gazelles responded positively to the question than was the case for owners of no-growth companies. In contrast, a < symbol indicates that a smaller percentage of gazelles in comparison to owners of no-growth companies responded positively to the question, and ~ indicates that the group responses were very similar. That column is followed by one containing a symbol indicating whether the actual survey results contradicted (Ø) or supported (†) the expectations. Finally, an asterisk (°) in the next column indicates that the results are statistically significant at the .05 level. The next two columns give the actual percentage response for gazelle owners and no-growth owners respectively, while the final column provides a short explanation of the response.

Traits and self-perceptions

The first category, traits and self-perceptions, contains six survey questions. Statistical tests on all of the questions did not lead to a rejection of the null hypothesis. The first question asked owners to identify their risk-taking behavior; we expected to find that gazelle owners would be much higher risk takers than no-growth owners. The results were surprising in that a higher proportion of no-growth owners considered themselves high risk takers (no-growth = 28.9 percent, gazelles = 22 percent), while a higher proportion of the gazelle owners considered themselves moderate risk takers (no-growth = 64.3 percent, gazelles = 73.8 percent). The differences were not statistically significant, however.

> A [high] proportion of no-growth
> [business] owners considered themselves
> high risk takers . . . while a [high] proportion
> of the gazelle owners considered themselves
> moderate risk takers.

The second question represents the Gazelle Index measurement for the optimism and confidence of the owners. The index value .56 is the average value for gazelle owners over the seven successive surveys, while .49 represents the average index value for owners of no-growth firms. Using one-way analysis of variance, we concluded that there is no statistically significant difference between gazelles and no-growth firms in their general optimism, confidence, and outlook on the economy. The p-value for the resulting F-statistic is $\approx.178$, which suggests we cannot reject the null hypothesis that the two index values come from one distribution. This result contradicts our theoretical expectations, as we assumed high-growth firms would possess greater optimism and business confidence than their no-growth counterparts. In summary, gazelle owners do hold slightly more positive views about the economy; however, the difference is not large enough to attribute it to anything more than chance.

One widely held notion in the entrepreneurship literature suggests there is a strong positive relationship between being an entrepreneur and having a family member, or family members, who are themselves entrepreneurs. We anticipated that having a family member who owned a business would significantly improve the chances that one would operate a high-growth firm. Although a higher proportion of gazelle owners have family members who own businesses (gazelle = 46 percent, no-growth = 39 percent), this difference is not statistically significant. The results also indicated that while a greater proportion of gazelle owners are more satisfied with their current positions as an entrepreneur than are owners of no-growth firms, the difference is not statistically significant.

We asked respondents to describe the main mechanism through which they acquired the skills that made them successful. They could respond in one of two ways: the skills "were mainly inborn," or they were "mainly learned through experience and education." While a slightly greater proportion of gazelle owners reported that their skills were inborn (27.4 percent) compared to the percentage of no-growth owners (17.7 percent), the differences were not statistically significant.

Motives for entering business

The next category of questions is related to owners' motivations for entering into business. These questions had three possible outcomes: the factor under consideration had a significant influence, a minor influence, or no influence on their decision to enter into business. None of these questions proved to be statistically significant.

The first question asked owners how their desire to build personal wealth played in their decision to enter business. In comparison to no-growth owners, we expected a greater proportion of gazelle owners to rate this as a significant motive for entering business. In fact, a greater proportion of no-growth owners rated this as a significant motive. The next question asked whether the presence of a business opportunity influenced their decision. Again, there was no difference between the responses of gazelle owners and no-growth owners to this question.

The desire to control one's destiny was the most significant motivating factor in the decision to enter into business. It seemed reasonable to assume that because gazelle owners exhibit strong growth-oriented tendencies, they would be less likely to be driven by this desire. This is because there is a strong relationship between growth and capital infusion, and firms that are interested in growing rapidly often seek outside investors (Woo, Cooper, and Dunkelburg 1991; Kim and Mauborgne 1998). This may result in less independence of decision making. If this is correct, gazelle owners will not have as much control over their destiny as their business grows. The results presented in Table 3 are consistent with this view because fewer gazelle owners (gazelle = 80 percent vs. no-growth = 87 percent) rate control over their destiny as a significant motive for entering into business. Again, this difference is not statistically significant.

We expected the pursuit of power and social status to be much less important to gazelle owners, and the results confirmed this as 13 percent of gazelle owners and 26 percent of no-growth owners indicated this was a primary motive for entering business. A larger percentage of gazelle owners rated this as a minor influence than did no-growth owners (gazelle = 56 percent vs. no-growth = 34.8 percent). Again, the chi-square test for independence fails to reject the null hypothesis.

Respondents were asked if their dissatisfaction with a previous job led them to enter into business. We expected fewer of the gazelle owners to indicate that this was a significant motivating factor. This assumption was consistent with our survey results in that gazelle owners entered business because they were attracted to opportunities, not pushed by adverse circumstances.

The desire to control one's destiny was the most significant motivating factor in the decision to enter into business.

Respondents were asked to indicate the importance that the loss of a previous job had on their decision to enter business. We expected that a much lower percentage of gazelle owners would rate this as a significant factor. The data support this expectation because only 13 percent of gazelle owners rated this as an important factor while 39 percent of no-growth owners rated this as a significant factor. In this case, the chi-square test of independence rejected the null hypothesis. This indicated that gazelle owners were much less likely to have entered business because of a job loss.

Other questions asked if owners entered business because they wanted to overcome racial barriers, they wanted to serve their communities, or they were inspired by someone outside of their family. None of the differences in responses to these questions were statistically significant. However, the small differences that were noted are consistent with our intuitive expectations. In other words, 65 percent of gazelle owners and 71 percent of no-growth owners rated overcoming racial barriers as a significant motivation for entering business; 64 percent of gazelle owners and 76 percent of no-growth owners rated a desire to serve their community as a significant motivation for entering business.

Respondents were asked how the desire to use their experience and education influenced their decision to enter business; 74 percent of gazelle owners considered this to be a significant factor, while 82 percent of no-growth owners considered this to be a significant motivating factor. While this difference was not statistically significant, there was a statistically significant difference in the racial composition of the workforce of gazelles versus that of no-growth companies. We have discussed this difference earlier.

Owner attributes

None of the group differences in responses to questions in this category were statistically significant, including the difference in education for gazelle owners and owners of no-growth firms, the fact that 40 percent of gazelle owners attended a historically black college or university while 29 percent of no-growth owners did so,[5] years of work-related experience, age of the business, or employment size of the business. One question asks respondents, on average, how many hours per week they spend working in their firm? Our expectation was that high-growth owners would spend more time on average than owners of no-growth firms. The data revealed that there was only a two-hour difference in the reported average number of hours spent weekly in the enterprise. Finally, 83 percent of gazelle owners compared to 75 percent of no-growth owners founded their business.

Business management and characteristics

Of the nine questions in this category, the responses to four are statistically significant. However, three of the significant results are trivial in that they are the outcome of how we defined the group classifications. By definition, we expected gazelles to have a higher rate of growth than no-growth companies. But the results also showed that a smaller percentage of the workforce of gazelles is African American. Specifically, 56 percent of gazelle's workforce and 67 percent of the workforce of no-growth firms are African American employees. This difference is statistically significant.

Growth strategy

The first question under this category asked whether individual owners are willing to take their company public if the opportunity arises. As expected, more gazelle owners than no-growth owners indicated a willingness to do so. However, the difference is not statistically significant. The results of this section also revealed that gazelle owners devoted more resources to expenditures on innovation and on research and development. However, they devoted fewer resources on marketing and advertising, e-commerce, and technology than did no-growth companies, but the differences are not statistically significant. Respondents were asked to evaluate the impact of discriminatory business practices on the ability of their firms to grow. An equal percentage of both groups of owners feel the same about the impact of discrimination on the ability of their firm to grow.

Competitive strategy

Respondents were asked about their pricing strategy: whether they increased, decreased, or did not change their prices during the economic slowdown that occurred in 2001 and 2002. It is important to note that a significantly smaller percentage of gazelle owners, in comparison to owners of no-growth firms, reacted to the economic slowdown by reducing their prices. Approximately 13 percent of gazelle owners reduced their prices, while 26 percent of no-growth owners reduced their prices. In contrast, a greater percentage of no-growth owners responded to the economic slowdown by increasing the price of their products/services. The chi-square test for independence reveals a statistically significant interaction between a company's growth classification and the way it changes prices in response to an economic slowdown. The response to this question suggests that gazelles are less likely to engage in competitive pricing strategies.

Marketing strategy

The final category related to marketing behavior. The results indicated that 59 percent of gazelle owners increased their marketing to the government over the past five years in comparison to only 35 percent of owners of no-growth companies. This difference is statistically significant and contradicts the expectation that faster-growing African American–owned firms have reduced their dependence on government contracting. We discussed this point earlier. Gazelles were also more likely to engage in regional and national marketing in comparison to no-growth firms. This difference is also statistically significant and has been discussed previously. Finally, the results show that gazelles received a smaller percentage of the total revenue from African Americans (23 percent for gazelles versus 27 percent for no-growth firms). Gazelle owners also indicated that participating in minority business procurement programs can significantly affect their firm growth.

Fifty-nine percent of gazelle owners increased their marketing to the government over the past five years in comparison to only 35 percent of no-growth companies.

Conclusion

Our findings suggest that the large differences in rates of growth among African American–owned firms cannot be explained simply by evaluating differences in owner attributes, firm attributes, characteristics of markets, and environmental constraints. We must broaden our research to consider the role of strategy and innovation more carefully in future research. On the surface, it is surprising that firms experiencing rates of growth of 40 percent annually have characteristics that are very similar to firms experiencing declining rates of growth. But when we think of how some of today's most rapidly growing companies have dominated their market space by relying on new forms of value innovation, our results are perhaps more understandable. The small number of variables that we found to be statistically significant forced us to conclude that the real explanation of high growth remains a "black box." But we have eliminated many variables that are typically assumed to be correlated with high-growth status and hopefully have provided a more promising direction for future research.

Notes

1. Quarterly results are posted on the Gazelle Index Web site: www.gazelleindex.com.

2. For further information, see studies by Ahiarah (1993); Audretsch (1991); Bates (1985, 1989, 1990, 1997); Cooper (1993); Cavalluzzo, Cavalluzzo, and Wolken (2002); Christopher (1998); and Fairlie (1999).

3. While gazelles grew fastest in heavy construction (73.9 percent), there were only two such firms in this category.

4. One percent of gazelles marketed internationally while none of the no-growth firms did.

5. This difference was insignificant after controlling for age.

References

Ahiarah, Sol. 1993. Black Americans' business ownership factors: A theoretical perspective. *Review of Black Political Economy* 22 (Fall): 15-37.

Audretsch, D. B. 1991. New-firm survival and the technological regime. *Review of Economics and Statistics* 73 (3): 441-50.

Bates, T. 1985. Entrepreneur human capital endowments and minority business viability. *Journal of Human Resources* 20 (4): 540-54.

———. 1989. Small business viability in the urban ghetto. *Journal of Regional Science* 29 (4): 625-43.

———. 1990. Entrepreneur human capital inputs and small business longevity. *Review of Economics and Statistics* 72 (4): 551-59.

———. 1997. Financing small business creation: The case of Chinese and Korean immigrant entrepreneurs. *Journal of Business Venturing* 12:109-24.

Bates, T., W. Bradford. 2006. Tracking the development of, and the returns generated by the minority-oriented venture capital industry. Paper presented at the Bootcamp Research Conference, Chapel Hill, North Carolina, June 16-20, 2006.

Boston, T. 2002. http://www.inggazelleindex.com/.

Cavalluzzo, K. S., L. S. Cavalluzzo, and J. Wolken. 2002. Competition, small business financing and discrimination: Evidence from a new survey. *Journal of Business* 75 (4): 641-80.

Christopher, J. E. 1998. Minority business formation and survival: Evidence on business performance and viability. *Review of Black Political Economy* 26 (1): 37-73.

Cooper, A. C. 1993. Challenges in predicting new firm performance. *Journal of Business Venturing* 8:241-53.

Fairlie, R. W. 1999. The absence of the African-American owned business: An analysis of the dynamics of self-employment. *Journal of Labor Economics* 17 (1): 80-108.

Gundry, L. K., and H. P. Welsch. 2001. The ambitious entrepreneur: High growth strategies of women-owned enterprises. *Journal of Business Venturing* 16:453-70.

Hamm, J. 2002. Why entrepreneurs don't scale. *The Entrepreneur* 4 (6): 2-7.

Kim, W. C., and R. Mauborgne. 1998. Value innovation: The strategic logic of high growth. In *Harvard Business Review on Strategies for Growth* (pp. 25-53). Boston: Harvard Business School Press.

National Commission on Entrepreneurship. 2001. *High-growth companies: Mapping America's entrepreneurial landscape*. Washington, DC: National Commission on Entrepreneurship.

Schumpeter, J. 1934. *The theory of economic development*. Cambridge, MA, Harvard University Press.

Stewart, W. H., Jr., Warren E. Watson, Joann Carland, and James Carland. 1998. A Proclivity for entrepreneurship: A comparison of entrepreneurs, small business owners, and corporate managers. *Journal of Business Venturing* 14:189-214.

Woo, Carolyn Y., Arnold C. Cooper, and William C. Dunkelberg. 1991. The development and interpretation of entrepreneurial typologies. *Journal of Business Venturing* 6 (2): 93-114.

Exploring Stratification and Entrepreneurship: African American Women Entrepreneurs Redefine Success in Growth Ventures

By
JEFFREY ROBINSON,
LAQUITA BLOCKSON,
and
SAMMIE ROBINSON

The relationship between social stratification and entrepreneurship is one that is underexplored in the literature of management and organizations. In the authors' view, social stratification (social structure, institutions, and culture) influences the context, process, experience, and outcomes of entrepreneurship. In this article, the authors discuss these relationships in the context of African American women engaged in high-growth entrepreneurship. The authors support their premise by presenting the limitations of prevailing approaches that exist within the current minority and women entrepreneurship literatures. Using the concept of entrepreneurial success as an example, the authors demonstrate how a social stratification and entrepreneurship framework may be useful for scholars who seek to understand the process of entrepreneurship.

Keywords: African Americans; women; entrepreneurship; social stratification

Accarding to the National Women's Business Council (2004), in 2004, 365,110 majority-owned, privately held firms were owned by African American women in the United States, more than 6 percent of all women-owned firms. These African American women entrepreneurs employ nearly two hundred thousand people and create more than $14 billion in revenues. In one study of the survival rates of firms owned by women and minorities, African American women–owned firms fared better than those owned by African American men (Robb 2002). In Fairlie's (2004) analysis of the trends of African American entrepreneurs, African American women entrepreneurs appear to be increasing in numbers faster than African American men for the first time in the past one hundred years. Taken in combination, these trends point to the increasing presence of women in African American entrepreneurship, have implications for the U.S. economy, and provide a road map for economic

DOI: 10.1177/0002716207303586

development in the African American community through productive entrepreneurship (Baumol 1990).

Surprisingly, very little academic literature has been written about African American women in entrepreneurship. We believe the gap exists because of the lack of an orienting framework in an area we call social stratification and entrepreneurship. We define social stratification as the end result of institutional processes that partition society into advantaged and disadvantaged socially constructed groups. This article focuses on African American women in entrepreneurship as a starting point for exploring the influences of social stratification on entrepreneurship and vice versa.

We begin this article by providing a brief overview of our framework for exploring social stratification and entrepreneurship. We then turn our attention to the topic of African American women entrepreneurship as an area of study that would benefit from our framework. We present an overview of the existing literature in the area of minority and women entrepreneurship. We demonstrate through this review what is missing from the discourse and the limitations of the prevailing approaches. We conclude by demonstrating how the social stratification and entrepreneurship framework is useful for scholars seeking to understand the process of entrepreneurship using the concept of entrepreneurial success as an example of new research directions.

Social Stratification and Entrepreneurship

As early as Max Weber and W.E.B. Dubois (1995), sociologists have long held to the notion of stratification in society. Following a long conversation in sociology

Jeffrey Robinson is an assistant professor of management and entrepreneurship at the Leonard N. Stern School of Business of New York University. He currently spends much of his time writing and researching about the role of entrepreneurs and entrepreneurship in society, communities, and in developing the competitive advantage of regions and nations. He is committed to research and informed policy making in the areas of community economic development, social venturing, and social and institutional barriers to markets. He believes that long-lasting change for inner-city communities is stimulated when religious institutions, community leaders, and businesspeople work together toward the common goal of community revitalization.

Laquita Blockson is an assistant professor of ethics and entrepreneurship at the College of Charleston's School of Business and Economics. She earned her doctorate in business ethics and public policy from the University of Pittsburgh. Her primary research focuses on ethics in entrepreneurship/venturing and the role entrepreneurs/businesses play in addressing social justice issues. She also studies how multisector collaborations (business-nonprofit-government) address urban economic development problems.

Sammie Robinson is an assistant professor in the College of Business at Prairie View A&M University. She holds a Ph.D. in business from the University of Kansas. Her primary research focuses on women in business, including both entrepreneurs and career professionals. Other research interests include management issues facing small and family-owned businesses. She has conducted research on comparing the experiences of majority and minority entrepreneurs and risk management issues facing women entrepreneurs.

(Davis and Moore 1945; Hatt 1950; Tumin 1953; Buckley 1958; Spilerman 2000), we define social stratification as the end result of institutional processes that partition society into advantaged and disadvantaged socially constructed groups. In the United States, it is well documented that the basis of social stratification can include groupings by gender, race/ethnicity, wealth, and class (Massey and Denton 1993; Spilerman 2000). The result is some groups are advantaged because of their group membership. These advantages and disadvantages can be reinforced by the accumulation of power and resources by the advantaged group over time.

Social stratification and entrepreneurship interact in at least three ways. Entrepreneurship can be a means of social mobility. Entrepreneurs can create ventures that create wealth and allow the entrepreneurs and their families to move from lower-status to higher-status positions. Second, entrepreneurship can play a role in addressing the challenges of a fractious, stratified society. Typically, this takes on the form of programs supporting entrepreneurship (self-employment) as an alternative to traditional labor markets. A second approach to meeting the challenge is entrepreneurship that uses market processes to directly solve social problems (as in social entrepreneurship). This type of entrepreneurship requires some nuanced understanding of social stratification processes (see Robinson [2006] for a more detailed explanation).

The third type of interactions between social stratification and entrepreneurship is the focus of this article. Social stratification profoundly influences the process of entrepreneurship for those actors who hold lower-status positions in society. We explain this further in the next section.

The process of entrepreneurship

Before we continue with our argument for more research at the intersection of social stratification and entrepreneurship, we should be clear about what we mean by entrepreneurship. Of the many definitions of the term *entrepreneurship*, the opportunities-oriented definition proposed by Shane and Venkatraman (2000) is the most useful for our purposes. Therefore, entrepreneurship is the process of identifying, evaluating, and pursuing opportunities. Variation among entrepreneurs is related to how entrepreneurs go about the process of entrepreneurship. This variation relates to the type and level of capital they can apply toward developing the new venture, the type of opportunity and innovation exploited by the entrepreneur, and the type and substance of the networks employed to achieve their entrepreneurial goals. Researchers have examined the variation of inputs and outcomes related to entrepreneurs and entrepreneurship. This is an essential step and easily transferable to the classroom. We consider this a first step toward understanding entrepreneurship.

As scholars, we are advocating that our colleagues go further by studying entrepreneurship in relation to its impact and influence on society and vice versa. Our

FIGURE 1
STRATIFICATION AND ENTREPRENEURSHIP

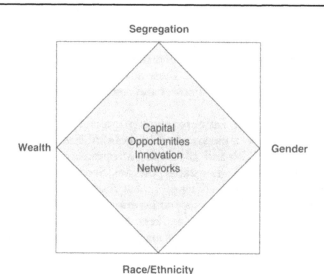

framework proposes that studying entrepreneurs with a social stratification lens will lead to different conclusions about the process and possibilities of entrepreneurship.

Stratification processes and entrepreneurship

We are advocating the study of entrepreneurship with the lens of social stratification because stratification is a multidimensional construct and allows for more nuanced considerations of the intersection of entrepreneurship and society.

Our view of the relationship between social stratification and entrepreneurship is captured in Figure 1. At its core, the idea of entrepreneurship is a process that entrepreneurial actors will go through to create and grow ventures. Through mainly popular accounts, we have agreed upon a set of norms and assumptions about what it takes to be successful as an entrepreneur. The academic literature provides some insight into the process but seldom into the context of the entrepreneurship. Entrepreneurship does not take place in a vacuum; it takes place in various social settings, and these settings can make a difference in how the process of entrepreneurship unfolds. Rarely have the assumptions regarding entrepreneurship been challenged.

We find this problematic for a field in its adolescence (Low 2001). In the academic literature, the processes and activities of entrepreneurs were developed with primarily white and generally male subjects, and this has led to a set of assumptions about how entrepreneurship should proceed for *all* entrepreneurs. We generally agree that the core processes of identifying, evaluating, and pursuing opportunities are a broad enough umbrella for all to fit beneath. However, the arrangement of capital, opportunities, innovation, and networks are influenced by a modern society that has social structures in place that advantage some and disadvantage others. In our view, social stratification based on race, class, wealth, gender, and segregation processes circumscribes entrepreneurship.

For some entrepreneurs, the effects of social stratification are not noticeable because they are advantaged by the institutional structures that govern the norms and processes of entrepreneurship. For those entrepreneurs who hold disadvantaged positions in the social structure, social stratification can have profound effects on how they identify, shape, and pursue entrepreneurship.

For those entrepreneurs who hold disadvantaged positions in the social structure, social stratification can have profound effects on how they identify, shape, and pursue entrepreneurship.

For example, we often evaluate the survival of a new venture based upon the amount of financial capital raised by the entrepreneurial team. For most entrepreneurs, the initial investment for a new venture comes from the founders and their family. Researchers have pointed to this type of statistical evidence to explain the higher failure rates of African American– and woman-owned firms.

If we challenge the underlying assumptions for a moment, we must first ask the question, Where does the initial investment come from for a new venture? If the initial investment comes from the founders and their family, then we are no longer examining the financial means; we are measuring wealth. Personal and family wealth is much more than cash on hand. Wealth is inextricably tied to social stratification (Spilerman 2000) and to that end interrelated to race, gender, and class. To show statistical evidence of the link between start-up capital and venture success leaves out aspects of the story that may be important for policy making or future research.

Those familiar with the literature on ethnic or female entrepreneurship may wonder if our framework is any different than previous research in these areas. Scholars who have researched protected markets (Light 1972; Aldrich et al.

1985) and networks and entrepreneurship (Aldrich 1989; Aldrich and Waldinger 1990; Uzzi 1997, 1999) have come the closest to the approach we are advocating in this article. We believe our approach, however, is an improvement on previous research because it allows for the influence of multiple dimensions on entrepreneurship simultaneously. Using the social stratification lens, we can account for multiple influences from society on the process of entrepreneurship. One dimensional accounts lack explanatory power and can lead to dangerous assumptions and ineffective public policy.

In the next section, we demonstrate the limitations of the previous approaches to researching women in entrepreneurship and ethnic entrepreneurship by considering previous work on African American women.

Limitations of Current Entrepreneurship Research on African American Women

Early research on women in entrepreneurship, such as Hisrich and Brush (1984), incorporated very descriptive studies of women entrepreneurs with surveys. More recently, programs of research (e.g., The Diana Project) have taken a broader look at the patterns of women entrepreneurs in hi-tech industries and venture capital. Brush (1992); Brush et al. (2004); Baker, Aldrich, and Liou (1997); and others have noted that many opportunities exist for research on women's entrepreneurship. We take up this challenge in this article by presenting aspects of women's entrepreneurship that have not been fully researched or understood: African American women in entrepreneurship.

Recently, large-scale research projects by consortia of researchers have moved the dialogue further along in this area. Brush and her colleagues in The Diana Project (Brush et al. 2004) have provided a more nuanced view of high-growth and technology entrepreneurship by women, but minority women were not present in significant numbers in their study. The Panel Study of Entrepreneurial Dynamics (PSED; Reynolds 2000; Reynolds et al. 2004) offers an oversample of both women and minority respondents. The PSED sample of nascent entrepreneurs does not have large enough numbers of minority female respondents for an adequate study.

Our intention here is not to completely review the literature of women's entrepreneurship or research on African American entrepreneurship. Several authors (Aldrich and Waldinger 1990; Brush 1992; Bates 1997; Brush and Bird 2002; Brush et al. 2004) have provided notable reviews of the literature. We have explored this literature to understand its relevance to studies about African American women in entrepreneurship. In this section, we examine studies from both streams of literature.

Lack of research

To fully appreciate the dearth of research in this area, we first considered Brush's (1992) review of the women in entrepreneurship literature. She noted

TABLE 1
CATEGORIZATION OF RECENT DISSERTATIONS BY TOPIC (1981-2004) ON
AFRICAN AMERICAN WOMEN IN ENTREPRENEURSHIP

Topic	Number of Dissertations
Nascent entrepreneurs/self-employment	5
Start-up	1
Characteristics of the business	3
Financing ventures	1
Characteristics of business owners	4
History	2
Social networks	1
Total	17

that only two of the fifty-seven articles on women and entrepreneurship she analyzed from 1977 to 1991 focused on minority women. When we shift to the literature on African American entrepreneurship, little has specifically been written
about African American women. Reviews by Aldrich and Waldinger (1990) and
books by Bates (1997), Light and Rosenstein (1995), and Butler (1991) said little
about African American women and their experiences as business owners. The
most that is said in this research is in the form of comparisons with African
American men or with women in other ethnic groups.

We wanted to also understand the potential for papers in the pipeline
generated out of dissertation research. To do so, we conducted a keyword search
of the Proquest Dissertation and Theses Database. Between 1981 and 2004,
972 dissertations were written on entrepreneurship, 304 dissertations on self-
employment.[1] Upon further analysis, we found 108 total dissertations using keywords *women* and *entrepreneurs* and 104 total dissertations using keywords
women and *self employment*. Using various combinations of keywords (*women*,
female, *African American*, *black*, *entrepreneurship*, and *self employment*), we
found only 17 dissertations related to African American women entrepreneurs
and self-employment. Table 1 categorizes these 17 dissertations by topic.

For this article, we chose to examine the state of the literature since 1991.
We found a marked increase in number but not necessarily in the breadth or
depth of the research. We have organized the notable ones according to their levels
of analysis.

Individual and firm level

The majority of the studies that explore African American women in entrepreneurship consider issues at the individual level. This is consistent with Brush's
(1992) presentation of the distribution of research papers.

Two studies have explored the individual characteristics of African American entrepreneurs and included separate tables for women and men. Fairlie and Meyer (1996) presented data on ethnic and racial differences in entrepreneurship. In one section of this paper, the entrepreneurship (self-employment) rates of each ethnic or racial group are presented. Each group is further divided by gender. Their findings indicate that African American women have a 2 percent rate of entrepreneurship, while African American men have a 4.4 percent rate based upon the 1990 census. Fairlie and Meyer made contribution to the areas of ethnic entrepreneurship by testing three competing explanations (sojourners theory, cultural theory, and disadvantage theory) concerning African American entrepreneurship using their data. Unfortunately, these explanations do not explain the significant differences within group and between genders.

The second study picks up where Fairlie and Meyer (1996) left off. Robb (2002) went directly to the research question at the intersection of race/ethnicity, gender, and entrepreneurship. This study provides some insight into the predictors of firm survival across women and minority groups. Robb concluded that the survival rate of African American women–owned businesses is slightly higher than those owned by African American men and that a number of other factors also correlated with survival (i.e., location, form of organization, number of employees).

Our first critique of these studies is that they lack nuance. While these data enable us to understand broad patterns in the characteristics of African American women in entrepreneurship (i.e., education level, wealth, age, family composition, etc.), they do not provide the more nuanced data that explain more than grand comparisons. We recognize the significance of highlighting the disparities in the human capital and personal wealth data between men and women and African Americans and other groups. Nevertheless, we are concerned that further studies in this stream will only incrementally enrich our understanding of the challenges faced by African American women in founding and sustaining viable firms.

Two other studies were able to address this issue. Inman's (1999) study of black and white women entrepreneurs found a link between motivations and resources at the individual level. Inman's qualitative and survey approach to this study of start-up ventures uncovered nuances that large quantitative studies often overlook. Black women and white women entrepreneurs often have different lived experiences that lead to completely different approaches and motivations when starting up new ventures. These findings were similar in content and breadth to the findings of Bell and Nkomo (2001) in corporate settings.

Smith-Hunter and Boyd (2004) made a contribution by testing competing theoretical explanations for differences between white and minority (mostly African American) women. In a sample of sixty (thirty white and thirty minority) women entrepreneurs in the personal services industry, they found some of the differences in individual characteristics that previous studies have highlighted. But they also found that the motivations of the minority women in their study do not differ greatly from their white counterparts. This is contrary to the prevailing disadvantage theories and culture-based explanations of these differences. Smith-Hunter's (2004) dissertation work in the same area created a space for research to be conducted that challenges the prevailing theories about African American women entrepreneurs.

Black women and white women entrepreneurs often have different lived experiences that lead to completely different approaches and motivations when starting up new ventures.

This leads us to our second critique. We agree with sociologists Basu and Werbner (2001; Werbner 1999) that simple comparisons without theory may do more harm than good because they can lead unsophisticated readers to believing that each racial/ethnic group's history, values, motivations, and goals are the same. This approach assumes that the "objective" measures of human capital explain the differences between groups and can lead to positive ascriptions of "entrepreneurial tendencies" to certain groups. While this approach is easily accepted here in the United States, it is not only approach to take. Two international studies of women entrepreneurs, Mitra (2002) and Lerner, Brush, and Hisrich (1997) reflect alternate approaches to theory building research. These studies explore the nature of women's entrepreneurship in India and Israel (respectively) without comparing them to other groups. This approach assumes that these women entrepreneurs have practical value and theoretical significance without the need for comparison.

It should be noted that both Smith-Hunter and Boyd (2004) and Inman (1999) were able to avoid this critique in their qualitative work by writing their findings not as simple comparisons but as indications that the differences between these women could be traced back to significant differences in the cultural and personal history of the subjects. Neither study devalued one group or the other. One of their many conclusions is that traditional economic rational choice theoretical approaches did little to explain these differences. Furthermore, functionalist paradigms will not uncover the richness at the individual level in accord with calls for alternative perspectives in entrepreneurship research (Jennings, Perren, and Carter 2005).

Market/environment/population level

The macro-level of analysis of African American women entrepreneurs is by far the least studied area of all. This is consistent with Brush's (1992) assessment of women's entrepreneurship research and the discourse analysis of Baker, Aldrich, and Liou (1997).

A follow-up to the previously mentioned Fairlie and Meyer (1996) paper reveals that the entrepreneurship rate for African Americans has been flat for most of the past one hundred years. Only within the past twenty years has there been a marked increase in the number of African American–owned firms (Fairlie 2004). Some reports indicate that the increase has been generated by African American women (National Women's Business Council 2004).

Most notably, two scholars, Bates (1997) and Butler (1991) have written extensively about African American entrepreneurship. In *Race, Self-Employment and Upward Mobility*, Bates took a look at the statistical evidence related to self-employment and black entrepreneurship. He made several comparisons across ethnic groups to make the point that sociological approaches to explaining the differences do not hold up under statistical scrutiny. He concluded that successful entrepreneurship is independent of race or ethnicity. In *Entrepreneurship and Self-Help among Black Americans*, Butler took a more historical comparative approach to understanding African American entrepreneurship. His central thesis is an arrested development of entrepreneurship in the African American community because of establishment of Jim Crow and other discriminatory laws. These laws prevented blacks from selling their goods and services to whites and others, and therefore, the economic development of the African American community was greatly minimized. Neither Butler or Bates fully addressed African American women in entrepreneurship in their books or subsequent articles. Both provided statistical evidence of the trends, types, and history of African American entrepreneurship, but neither considered the additional challenges of African American women in entrepreneurship. To their credit, each of these books provided enormous depth in the area of African American entrepreneurship and subsequent work (including our own) builds upon their insights.

Recent studies have followed the work of Butler and Bates and tackled specific entrepreneurship issues in the African American community. A paper by Rhodes and Butler (2004) presented a conceptual model of "black American small business performance" based largely on the family background of and the community resources of the black community around the entrepreneur. Whereas we see the merits of this approach to study firm performance, we cannot ignore the notion that African American men and African American women may experience entrepreneurship differently and that these variations may also have an impact on performance.

Rasheed (2004) demonstrated in his study the moderating effects of ethnicity and gender on the relationship between capital access barriers and market penetration. Both ethnicity and gender (along with education) were found to influence the market penetration of the firms in the study. These results are certainly interesting from a policy perspective because of the interaction between ethnicity and capital, gender and capital, and education and capital. But how is the relationship between capital access barriers and market penetration (sales) influenced when the entrepreneur is both a member of a minority group and a woman? Are the effects combined or are they independent? Rasheed did not answer this question.

Other studies have been challenged to address these difficult questions. And herein lies another conundrum of functionalist work: for academic precision, we would like the variables to be independent of one another. We argue here that as scholars truly interested in the subject of African American women entrepreneurs, we will have to rigorously investigate the nature of being both African American and female as it relates to entrepreneurship. The multidimensional nature of social identity has implications for how entrepreneurs pursue entrepreneurship.

We found only one study that attempted to tackle this issue. Levent, Masurel, and Nijkamp (2003) described the entrepreneurship experiences of ethnic (Turkish) females in the Netherlands. Their study wrestles with the idea that ethnic women entrepreneurs' experiences, attitudes, and choices vary. They were particularly interested in the idea of characterizing the entrepreneurship as primarily female entrepreneurship or ethnic entrepreneurship. Based on their field surveys, they concluded from their study of their personal and business characteristics and motivation that the ethnic female entrepreneurs are "special female entrepreneurs" and not "special ethnic entrepreneurs." In other words, these Turkish women used the strategies that have been described as female entrepreneurship strategies (interacting and servicing women of all ethnic groups) more often than they used strategies described as "ethnic" entrepreneurship strategies (interacting and servicing ethnic protected markets).

We find this paper interesting because of the very idea of dual identity of ethnic minority women. Levent, Masurel, and Nijkamp (2003, 1158) admitted that their findings may not be generalizable beyond the Netherlands: "Different ethnic groups and different cultures may show different characteristics in terms of their driving forces, motivation, performance, and success conditions." This idea can help us construct a broader framework for studying the intersection of entrepreneurship and society.

A Framework for Understanding Social Stratification and Entrepreneurship

From the literature review of the previous section, it is clear to us that the field gains much when researchers explore social stratification and entrepreneurship together. When we consider how social stratification influences entrepreneurship, the approach we are advocating has two advantages. First, we are able to account for the multidimensional nature of social identity. Since the basis of social stratification can be multidimensional, we can use additive language (e.g., African American *and* female) instead of one-dimensional language to discuss the process of entrepreneurship. Second, this approach allows us to move beyond the functionalist paradigm to understand how entrepreneurship unfolds differently for these subjects. This second point requires a paradigm shift in the way entrepreneurship research is conducted, reported, and evaluated.

Shifting paradigms for research on
African American women in entrepreneurship

Using a social stratification lens requires a paradigm shift for entrepreneurship researchers. Burrell and Morgan (1979) in their seminal work proposed that organizational research was trapped in a functionalist paradigm and that this limited the explanatory power and the potential impact of the research. We embrace the perspective of similar recent critiques of the entrepreneurship literature:

> Assumptions that researchers make, both about philosophy of science and the theory of society, represent two independent dimensions which, taken together, delineate four distinct paradigms: "Functionalist," "Interpretive," "Radical Humanist," and "Radical Structuralist" (Burrell and Morgan, 2003). These paradigms reflect basic metatheoretical assumptions that underpin the shared philosophy, perspective, mode of theorizing, and approach of researchers who operate within them. . . . (Jennings, Perren, and Carter 2005, 145-46)

Using the two-by-two table of the types of research described by Burrell and Morgan (1979) and reviewed in Jennings, Perren, and Carter (2005), we present in Figure 2 how the four approaches lead to different questions.

We begin with the highly functionalist research question that compares rates of entrepreneurship between African American women and women in other racial/ethnic groups. This is the status quo. When we consider the same set of comparisons from one of the three other sociological perspectives, the questions and the approach are quite different. Jennings, Perren, and Carter (2005) defined the three other quadrants as follows:

> Interpretivists, like Functionalists, are interested in how society maintains order and regulates the status quo, but view reality as subjective and are interested in the world through the eyes of individuals. Radical Humanists share Interpretivists' subjective view of the world, but see the purpose of research as understanding how radical change can occur within society. As the name suggests, Radical Structuralists are interested in understanding radical change of what they view as objective and hard structures within society. (pp. 146-147)

The point here is that completely different theoretical approaches to the topic will yield different types of explanations of a phenomenon. We believe that a purely functionalist research agenda will yield more the same types of research and will explain little about the phenomenon of African American women in entrepreneurship.

Robb (2002, 395) admits that "additional factors may play a role in the differences according to race and gender in business survival. Whether these differences are due to discrimination or other obstacles remains a topic for further research." A functionalist paradigm will not be able to address the nuances found in the lived experiences of those being discriminated against. Statistical evidence may not fully characterize what remains an entrenched problem in society.

An example of using the interpretivist approach in entrepreneurship research is Feagin and Imani (1994). They used this approach to explore the various

FIGURE 2
EXAMPLES OF RESEARCH QUESTIONS FROM FOUR RESEARCH PARADIGMS

Radical Humanist How did the increases in number of African American women entrepreneurs take place in U.S. society over the last 20 years?	**Radical Structuralist** What kinds of changes would have to take place in U.S. society to change the status quo of African American women entrepreneurs?	
Subjective		*Objective*
Interpretive How do African American women view entrepreneurship in U.S. society (in their own words)?	**Functionalist** Comparisons of rates of entrepreneurship between African American women and women in other racial/ethnic groups	

aspects of discrimination against African American construction contractors. Their scholarship yielded a multidimensional construct for discrimination useful in future studies of entrepreneurship where discrimination is a barrier to entry and growth.

Using the social stratification lens in entrepreneurship research leads to research conducted from a nonfunctionalist paradigm. We believe this is a healthy progression for the field of entrepreneurship.

Social stratification influences on entrepreneurship

Throughout this article, we have argued that the study of entrepreneurship will be enhanced if scholars research the effects of stratification on the entrepreneurial process. It is a useful lens that can help researchers consider alternative paradigms for research and close significant gaps in the literature.

Of course, the issue here is not whether stratification exists in American society but how gender and race present barriers and opportunities for these women. The challenge we have for our colleagues is to move beyond one-dimensional accounts of entrepreneurship. We propose an increased emphasis on the influence of stratification on the entrepreneurship process because it affects every step of the process. Stratification may influence who pursues entrepreneurship and who does not. It influences the types of opportunities that are seen and evaluated. It also shapes how a venture opportunity will be pursued.

Specifically, this means acknowledging the inequality in the United States and other nations and considering how that inequality interacts with the identification and the shaping of entrepreneurial opportunities (see Figure 3) by constraining some activities and providing opportunities for others. It also means recognizing how the variation of entrepreneurial success and failure is based upon a more

FIGURE 3
HOW SOCIAL STRATIFICATION INFLUENCES ENTREPRENEURSHIP

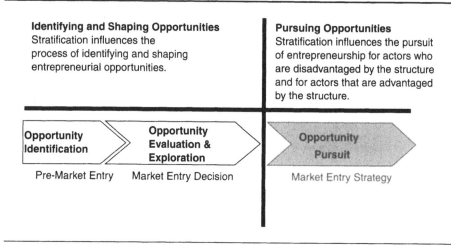

nuanced set of social and institutional factors than we have previously understood. Therefore, the pursuit of entrepreneurship is tied directly to the historical, social, and institutional processes of social stratification. Since this cannot be easily achieved using a functionalist paradigm, we advocate the study of African American women entrepreneurs and other complex identities with distinctly interpretivist approaches.

A Study of African American Women in Growth Firms

Between February 2005 and May 2006, we conducted qualitative, in-depth interviews with sixty-two African American women entrepreneurs (AAWEs) in seven U.S. metropolitan areas, where the women tell "their entrepreneurial story." We interviewed women who were founders/leaders of growth/growing firms, with a minimum of three years' ownership and management. In this light, we focused our study on AAWEs who lead ventures that provide services and/or products that fulfill wants and needs in an innovative and/or unique manner. Some of these ventures include engineering consulting firms, corporate/professional event planning, specialty product manufacturing, specialty construction companies, information technology firms, and large-scale hospitality services, among others.

Our criterion of a minimum three years' ownership and management implies some assumptions about business viability; however, the criterion itself does not necessarily assume business success. This is different from some scholars' assumptions about entrepreneurial success, where an entrepreneur was viewed as successful if she or he met specific criteria. In other words, our criterion does not—in and of itself—*define* success.

Another criterion the AAWEs must meet for our study is that the ventures are owned completely (100 percent) by either one African American woman or two African American women. Persons of another race and/or gender could not be a financial and/or managing partner. This enabled us to focus clearly on African American women's experiences, without the need to explore explicitly the differences between male- and female-led entrepreneurial ventures or the differences between majority- and minority-led entrepreneurial ventures. For the purpose of this particular study, we explore the experiences of African American women, in their own right, from their own perspective.

Preliminary observations

In this article, we present preliminary observation based upon our "first cut" of our interview data. We believe these observations are an example of using different approaches to shed light on the question of what defines success for entrepreneurs. We have organized our observations into four categories: the double minority challenge, the trade-off between passion and growth, the importance of family history and family support, and personal calling and community orientations. Two of these categories represent perspectives on success at the individual level; the remaining two represent the group/family and societal levels.

Individual level: The double minority challenge

The current entrepreneurship literature provides conflicting evidence regarding whether gender plays a significant role in determining economic entrepreneurial success. Fasci and Valdez (1998), Reynolds (1993), Loscocco et al. (1991), and Loscocco and Robinson (1989) all indicated that female-owned businesses are less profitable than male-owned businesses. On the other hand, Watson (2002), Chaganti and Parasuraman (1996), and Kallenberg and Leicht (1991) noted that few financial performance differences exist when comparing female- and male-owned businesses.

Previous studies have shown that race/ethnicity plays a role in entrepreneurial identity, which may contribute to entrepreneurial success. Levent, Masurel, and Nijkamp (2003), in their study of Turkish women entrepreneurs in Amsterdam, investigated whether the women (given their location in the Netherlands and within a strong extended family) saw themselves as ethnic entrepreneurs or as female entrepreneurs. In our preliminary observations, many of the AAWEs expressed some tension in being both a woman and an African American. Most of the AAWEs also noted that their social identity as a "woman first" or an "African American" first varied depending on context. Among other African Americans, the AAWEs often viewed themselves primarily as women, while they viewed themselves as African Americans when among other racial/ethnic groups (regardless of gender present). The AAWEs mentioned that their identity was not an issue when they participated in activities with other African American women. Therefore, success became a function of overcoming racism and sexism in the marketplace.

The current entrepreneurship literature provides conflicting evidence regarding whether gender plays a significant role in determining economic entrepreneurial success.

Eleanor Evans,[2] who founded and operates a construction company in Chicago, notes,

> People always thought that because we were black and female we had a double advantage. When in fact it was a double disadvantage. You know, we were never allowed to participate for the twenty-five percent [government contracting set-asides for minority/women-owned businesses]. That was for the white women who were prized contractors. And we had to fight for that little five percent [of the set-asides]. One of the blurbs that Winnie [another African American woman entrepreneur] sent me was called, "How do you know you're gonna make it?" Once I could bond . . . once I began to see that they stopped looking at me as a female contractor and started looking at me as a minority contractor . . . now that I am in the twenty-five percent arena. You know, but now I've got to fight the brothers. And I didn't want to fight them. I wanted to line myself with them, but they weren't having that. You know, it's gotta be a fight. You know, why I gotta fight you? I have a son! You know, I wanna show him [that] black man [and] black woman [can] work together.

As the previous quote indicates, most of the AAWEs also raised questions about being taken seriously or taken for granted. This was particularly the case for AAWEs who chose to compete for government contracts. Those who chose to compete for government contracts and set-asides discussed the challenges they faced to ensure they were not being used by majority firms solely for their minority/women status. Nevertheless, these same women proclaimed that they did not want to forsake any opportunities (i.e., government contracts and set-asides) that they believed were fairly available to them. Interestingly, those who chose not to compete for government contracts did so because they did not want their venture to be perceived as inferior, needy, or labeled as a minority- or woman-owned enterprise.

Based on our observations, the AAWEs believed they were successful in their ventures. Our understanding is that this is because they learned how to be tenacious and to persevere when race and/or gender became an operational issue/challenge.

Individual level: The trade-off between passion and growth

Many subjects expressed a desire to pursue a passion *and* growth. Several AAWEs mentioned that the ability to stabilize and grow their ventures was an important criterion for success; however, some provided a caveat when saying so. Some women mentioned that the ability to sustain and grow their ventures was an important external indicator (i.e., a measure used by outsiders for legitimacy and/or validation purposes); nevertheless, financial stability and financial growth was not these women's predominant definition for success.

The overwhelming majority of AAWEs defined success holistically rather than in pure economic or financial terms. They mentioned two or more of the following reasons that they believed they (and their businesses) are successful: (1) they are able to provide wealth for their family, (2) they are able to spend more time with their family, (3) they are able to give back to their community, (4) they are able to meet a specific customer need, and (5) they are able to fulfill a personal or spiritual calling.

When the AAWEs were asked, "What does the future hold for you and your venture?" approximately half of the women mentioned they intend to grow the business into a larger concern. The other half of the AAWEs mentioned that, now that their venture has attained and surpassed the survival, stability, and initial growth stages, they are not as concerned about growing their venture any further. In this light, some women defined success as an ability to maintain her venture's current level of performance (i.e., "going concern"), while other women defined success as an ability to enhance the venture's level of performance (i.e., "growing concern"). Interestingly, these women did express that their definition of success does not imply that they did not/do not face challenges in any/all of the above areas. In fact, most attribute their *personal* success to their ability to overcome some/all of these challenges.

Valerie Young, founder and owner of an information technology firm in Washington, D.C., notes,

> My goal each year is whatever the dollar value that was done or the biggest contract, dollar-wise, that we had, my goal would always be to try to double it. Okay, but also, the ultimate goal is, because the big companies aren't going to let you get to their status, they will buy you out first before you get there. Now, let's be honest here. So, I don't have a problem: buy me out, signing off; and, I'm fine with that. So, if I get to a status where you gonna buy me off at what I know I'm worth, you're not buying me cheap. So, I have two options: either I position ourselves where one of the big prime companies wants to buy us out . . . that's no problem; I'd be willing to sell. Or, I turn the running of the company to an individual that I feel could take it further."

AAWEs mentioned that they choose to resolve the tension between passion and growth in different ways. For instance, some women purposely are maintaining specific geographical market boundaries. Some women are placing their energies on fulfilling niche markets and customer bases. Furthermore, the majority of the AAWEs mentioned that a primary objective is to ensure that their venture does not compromise its founding values.

Group/family level: The significance of family history and family support

Family history and support factored significantly in the lives of AAWEs. A large number of AAWEs had entrepreneurial influences—both traditional and nontraditional—from family members (e.g., Shelton 2006). Some AAWEs were raised in families where the parent(s) or extended family members own/owned a business. Some others were inspired or encouraged by family members who might not have owned a business but have/had an entrepreneurial spirit or a sense of economic self-determination (e.g., bootstrapping; creating own sources of income). Some AAWEs defined success as being able to continue a family tradition of entrepreneurship and/or to continue a tradition of economic self-determination. Eleanor Evans, speaking of her parents' work ethic, notes that "my mother . . . started [a business] in the house for extra money. My dad was doing little extra side jobs for extra money. You know, he taught us how to value every single penny. Like I said, we were hustling. I hustled my way through high school; hustled my way through college."

The average age of the AAWEs interviewed was forty-nine; more than half of the AAWEs (across all ages) were mothers. A number of the AAWEs aged forty or older worked in corporate environments before launching their ventures and shared the challenges they faced when attempting to fulfill simultaneously their familial and professional obligations. In response to the oft-times conflicting obligations, a large number of the AAWEs parlayed their professional experiences and resources in a manner that enabled them to conduct business on their terms while continuing to meet their family's needs. Many of those AAWEs who did not yet have children expressed that one of the reasons they created their venture was so that they could structure their business in a manner that would be family-friendly (for themselves and their employees). Thus, many AAWEs defined success as being able to create a venture that does not force them to compromise their familial commitments. Marcia Quarles, founder and owner of a consumer products company in New York City, notes,

> Yes, juggling family and stuff has been difficult. It's weird, it's difficult and then it's easier because I make my own schedule. So, if I want to go to something and it's going on in their school, I don't have to ask anyone for their permission. But it's hard when they [her children] feel that I work all the time 'cause I work at home. Or I can't talk to them 'cause I'm on the phone, and they want to tell me something exciting. But in the beginning, when they were babies . . . I had a woman who helped me . . . it was great to be able to have them [her children] here. And not have to send them off someplace, you know, because I nursed both of them. So, I couldn't have done that with a nine-to-five job. So as hectic as it was, it wasn't as difficult but it was, it was definitely the way to go . . . but it was always a juggling act. You work at home; so, your work is here. So, it

becomes very hard to turn it off because it's right here, you know [laughs]. You walk past your desk and it's like, "Oh, let me check my e-mails." Then an hour later [laughs], you know you're still sitting there. But I don't think I would like it any other way.

Societal level: Calling and community orientations

Besser (1999) noted that greater social responsibility on the part of business operators will be positively related to business success as measured by the operator's evaluation of success. Besser asserted that business success precedes increased social responsibility. We asked, Is it also possible that a high level of social or civic responsibility precedes business success? In fact, some—particularly many of our interviewees—would argue that a high level of social and civic responsibility is a success criterion in and of itself.

Boston and Ross (1997) noted that the most successful African American businesses locate themselves in low-income inner-city areas, employ African American workers, and recruit a significant portion of their workforce from the inner city. In our study, most of the AAWEs expressed a responsibility toward their local and racial community; many AAWEs defined success for themselves as being able to provide employment and economic support for their chosen communities. A few AAWEs mentioned that they purposely hire and train a significant number of high school dropouts, former felons, and public assistance recipients, with the charge that, as one firm owner in Atlanta mentioned, "If I don't hire them, who will? I want to provide those most at-risk with an opportunity to improve their lives and the lives of their families."

In our study, most of the AAWEs [African American women entrepreneurs] expressed a responsibility toward their local and racial community; many AAWEs defined success for themselves as being able to provide employment and economic support for their chosen communities.

Theresa Thomas speaks of her ownership of an event marketing/public relations company in Chicago:

It's really important to find a way to stay grounded. . . . Our [fellow African-American] business people need to somehow understand that and be willing to share and give back . . . when you go down [with setbacks], there's nobody down there with you. But then, it inspires you to continue because I know that God . . . hasn't put me here to be down. . . . I know my mission is true; and I believe it is an appointed one by Him. I believe that He recognizes that our people are in need of so much; and, there are a lot of people giving on lots of levels. But, I don't see people really giving on this level that I'm talking about. There are people that are out here that are doing a lot of good in the nonprofit sector, you know, lots of social services organizations out there that help the people. Nobody's talking business; so, I stay on the business tip. I don't get off of that because, when I do whatever, someone says, "Well, who are you giving a contribution to?" I'm giving a contribution to a business . . . because we've got to stay as a business. Basically, my role is to help other businesses; that's what my business is . . . a lot of what I did with [my company] came out of a spirit of hope than purely looking at bottom line numbers and making the decision that this should go forward because, even though it's not making the "right" numbers and the margins weren't there, all the things that you're supposed to look at in business, you know. I put all those aside because I saw people, there were a lot of faces out there.

Some women explicitly defined success as being able to serve as a positive role model within their chosen communities. While serving as a role model may not have been a priority for most AAWEs, these women realize that their success enables them to influence and mentor others to perform well in their educational and professional endeavors.

As the previous quote notes, one interesting observation we made during our interviews is the strong influence of faith and spirituality in the lives of AAWEs. The overwhelmingly majority of the AAWEs interviewed perceived a spiritual calling when establishing their business. Many AAWEs defined success as being able to fulfill a spiritual calling or to serve God through their venture. As one of our AAWEs put it, meeting "God's criteria, above all others," was her barometer for measuring success.

Discussion

Based on these preliminary observations, it appears that AAWEs define success more broadly than do management and entrepreneurship scholars. We believe these women's stories provide some evidence that supports creating an augmented definition for success—one that reflects populations that are currently absent, underrepresented, or misrepresented in current entrepreneurship statistics. It is known among entrepreneurship scholars that no single agreed-upon definition exists for business success or failure. Rogoff, Lee, and Suh (2004) noted that the empirical work in entrepreneurial success and failure is limited because conducting studies on entrepreneurial success is difficult and requires significant time to conduct meaningful longitudinal studies. Given this development, exploring definitions of success beyond the management and entrepreneurship literatures provides additional insight.

While the history of American/Western business values has conditioned us to believe that economic indicators of success are predominant, entrepreneurial success is defined much more broadly in other cultures and environments. Pnina Werbner (1999), in her study of ethnic entrepreneurship, provided great insight on what determines entrepreneurial success. Werbner described it best when she noted that success may be defined as "the competitive achievement of prestige or honor, and of the symbolic goods signaling these, within a specific regime of value" (p. 556). Her main point is that we must expand our definition of success. Using purely economic measures for success does not provide a complete assessment. Things that are valuable (or deemed significant) to entrepreneurs when defining success for their ventures (and/or themselves) often cannot be translated cleanly into economistic terms. Noneconomic measures of success may be viewed as being as valuable as—if not more valuable than—economic measures of success. Depending on the context (which may include personal history, cultural environment, work environment, social networks, and personal values), success may be defined in a myriad of ways.

Our preliminary observations would validate Werbner's (1999) argument. For our subjects, entrepreneurial success is contextual. Using solely economic indicators to determine entrepreneurial success may mask whether entrepreneurs are, indeed, successful. It appears evident from our initial observations that the context of African American women is important for this discussion and has implications for the field of entrepreneurship.

Implications

Why should we study AAWEs? What do we learn from studying these entrepreneurs, and what are the implications of this research? In this article, we have established that scarce research has explored the intersection of race, gender, and entrepreneurship. For some the very idea that we know little about entrepreneurship is enough to pursue these new directions. But the case for studying African American women (or other unique intersections) in entrepreneurship is not complete without exploring the possible implications of conducting such research.

It is our position that *context* matters in entrepreneurship. The process of entrepreneurship may have many similarities across contexts, but the process is influenced by society's norms, values, rules, regulations, and public policies. A social stratification lens speaks to each of these aspects. In the United States, African American women have been marginalized as a result of racism and sexism. We should not perpetuate this marginalization in our research.

Second, studying African American women in entrepreneurship with an eye on social stratification perspectives provides an opportunity to use different research *approaches* in entrepreneurship research. As a field, we must stop privileging the traditional functionalist approach in our journals and classrooms. By using a different method, one that values the voice of the entrepreneur, we can answer different questions than before and see nuance in the old questions we have asked. We demonstrated the usefulness of this approach in this article by exploring the dimensions of success that emerge from rich group dialogue with high-growth AAWEs.

Third, the recognition of the importance of context and relevance of research approach will lead to more informed *policy making*. For example, if a policy maker were to ask what could be done to triple the number of African American women entrepreneurs with million-dollar firms, the current literature would do little to inform him or her. A review of the few papers that address the topic might only yield the answer, "provide more seed capital." Through our preliminary study, we know that this is just scratching the surface of the challenge. Solid entrepreneurship policy cannot be developed in a vacuum; the framework we have outlined here begins to put these issues into perspective. (Gilbert, Audretsch, and McDougall 2004).

We have highlighted the limitations of prevailing approaches to the study of entrepreneurship. Doing so raises the question, Does this research destabilize the entrepreneurship narrative? Our response is, Perhaps, though justifiably so. We have argued that research that privileges one group, by normalizing their experience such that another group's appears lacking in comparison, lacks nuance, results in competing theoretical explanations, and generates ascriptions that have been challenged by our work and by other researchers whose work is noted herein.

Our goal in writing this article was to present the usefulness of analysis that explicitly addresses the complexities of race, gender, class, wealth, and entrepreneurship. As a result, the implication is that further research in this area should be conducted from an interpretivist perspective, adopting a lens that considers several important factors. First, entrepreneurship is defined and characterized as a process. Our interest is in how such a process unfolds for a particular group that is underrepresented and, we would argue, mischaracterized in the current literature. Second, current research fails to see the nuances that are present when entrepreneurship is viewed as a social construction, which is grounded in the lived experiences of the women involved, and reflected in, among other features, their differing definitions of success. Third, research should take into account both the complexity in the field and the multidimensional nature of the phenomena.

Taken together, these factors produce investigations whose outcomes have practical value and enhance the theoretical significance of their results. Our hope is that we have encouraged other researchers to follow our lead and develop research questions that go beyond the traditional functionalist paradigm. By taking these radical departures from the prevailing narrative, we move the field forward.

Notes

1. For the purposes of this article, we use *self-employment* and *entrepreneurship* interchangeably.
2. This article uses pseudonyms to protect the identity of the subjects.

References

Aldrich, H. E. 1989. Networking among women entrepreneurs. In *Women-owned businesses*, ed. O. Hagan, C. Rivchun, and D. L. Sexton, 102-32. New York: Praeger.

Aldrich, H. E., J. Cater, T. Jones, D. McEvoy, and P. Velleman. 1985. Ethnic residential concentration and the protected market hypothesis. *Social Forces* 64 (4): 996-1009.

Aldrich, H. E., and R. Waldinger. 1990. Ethnicity and entrepreneurship. *Annual Review of Sociology* 16:111-35.

Baker, T., H. E. Aldrich, and N. Liou 1997. Invisible entrepreneurs: The neglect of women business owners by mass media and scholarly journals in the USA. *Entrepreneurship and Regional Development* 9:221-38.

Basu, D., and P. Werbner. 2001. Bootstrap capitalism and the culture industries: A critique of invidious comparisons in the study of ethnic entrepreneurship. *Ethnic and Racial Studies* 24 (2): 236-62.

Bates, T. 1997. *Race, self-employment and upward mobility: An illusive American dream*. Baltimore: Johns Hopkins University Press.

Baumol, W. J. 1990. Entrepreneurship: Productive, unproductive, and destructive. *Journal of Political Economy* 98 (5): 893-919.

Bell, E., and S. Nkomo. 2001. *Our separate ways: Black and white women and the struggle for professional identity*. Cambridge, MA: Harvard Business School Press.

Besser, T. L. 1999. Community involvement and the perception of success among small business operators in small towns. *Journal of Small Business Management* 37 (4): 16-30.

Boston, T. D., and C. Ross, eds. 1997. *The inner city: Urban poverty and economic development*. New Brunswick, NJ: Transaction Publishers.

Brush, C. G. 1992. Research on women business owners: Past trends, a new perspective and future directions. *Entrepreneurship Theory and Practice* 16: 5-30.

Brush, C. G., and B. Bird. 2002. A gendered perspective on organizational creation. *Entrepreneurship Theory and Practice* 22 (3): 41-65.

Brush, C. G., N. Carter, E. Gatewood, P. Greene, and M. Hart. 2004. *Clearing the hurdles: Women building high growth businesses*. Upper Saddle River, NJ: Financial Times–Prentice Hall.

Buckley, W. 1958. Social stratification and the functional theory of social differentiation. *American Sociological Review* 23 (4): 369-75.

Burrell, G., and G. Morgan. 1979. *Sociological paradigms and organizational analysis*. London: Heinemann.

Butler, J. S. 1991. *Entrepreneurship and self-help among black Americans: A reconsideration of race and economics*. Albany: State University of New York Press.

Chaganti, R., and S. Parasuraman. 1996. A study of the impacts of gender on business performance and management patterns in small business. *Entrepreneurship Theory and Practice* 21 (2): 73-95.

Davis, K., and W. E. Moore. 1945. Some principles of stratification. *American Sociological Review* 10:242-49.

Dubois, W. E. B. 1995. *The Philadelphia Negro*. Philadelphia: University of Pennsylvania Press.

Fairlie, R. W. 2004. Recent trends in ethnic and racial business ownership. *Small Business Economics* 23:203-18.

Fairlie, R. W., and B. D. Meyer. 1996. Ethnic and racial self-employment differences and possible explanations. *Journal of Human Resources* 31 (4): 757-93.

Fasci, M. A., and J. Valdez. 1998. A performance contrast of male- and female-owned small accounting practices. *Journal of Small Business Management* 36 (3): 1-7.

Feagin, J. R., and N. Imani. 1994. Racial barriers to African American entrepreneurship: An exploratory study. *Social Problems* 41 (4): 562-84.

Gilbert, B. A., D. B. Audretsch, and P. P. McDougall. 2004. The emergence of entrepreneurship policy. *Small Business Economics* 22 (3-4): 313-23.

Hatt, P. K. 1950. Stratification in the mass society. *American Sociological Review* 15 (2): 216-22.

Hisrich, R. and C. Brush. 1984. The woman entrepreneur: Management skills and business problems. *Journal of Small Business Management*, 22 (1): 31-37.

Inman, K. 1999. *Women's resources in business start-up: A study of black and white women entrepreneurs*. New York: Garland Publishing.

Jennings, P. L., L. Perren, and S. Carter. 2005. Guest editor's introduction: alternative perspectives on entrepreneurship research. *Entrepreneurship Theory and Practice* 29 (2): 145-52.

Kallenberg, A. L., and K. T. Leicht. 1991. Gender and organizational performance: Determinants of small business survival and success. *Academy of Management Journal* 34 (1): 136-61.

Lerner, M., C. Brush, and R. Hisrich. 1997. Israeli women entrepreneurs: An examination of factors affecting performance. *Journal of Business Venturing* 12:315-39.

Levent, T. B., E. Masurel, and P. Nijkamp. 2003. Diversity in entrepreneurship: Ethnic and female roles in urban economic life. *International Journal of Social Economics* 30 (11): 1131-61.

Light, I. 1972. *Ethnic enterprises in America: Business and welfare among Chinese, Japanese and blacks.* Los Angeles: University of California Press.

Light, I., and C. Rosenstein. 1995. *Race, ethnicity, and entrepreneurship in urban America.* New York: Aldine de Gruyter.

Loscocco, K. A., and J. Robinson. 1989. *Barriers to small business success among women.* Albany: State University of New York Press.

Loscocco, K. A., J. Robinson, R. H. Hall, and J. K. Allen. 1991. Gender and small business success: An inquiry into women's relative disadvantage. *Social Forces* 70 (1): 65-85.

Low, M. B. 2001. The adolescence of entrepreneurship research: Specification of purpose. *Entrepreneurship Theory and Practice* 25 (4): 17.

Massey, D. S., and N. A. Denton. 1993. *American apartheid: Segregation and the making of the underclass.* Cambridge, MA: Harvard University Press.

Mitra, R. 2002. The growth pattern of women-run enterprises: An empirical study in India. *Journal of Developmental Entrepreneurship* 7 (2): 217-37.

National Women's Business Council (NWBC). 2004. *Fact sheet: African American women and entrepreneurship.* Washington DC: NWBC.

Rasheed, H. S. 2004. Capital access barriers to government procurement performance: Moderating efforts for ethnicity and education. *Journal of Developmental Entrepreneurship* 9 (2): 109-26.

Reynolds, P. D. 1993. High performance entrepreneurship: What makes it different? In *Frontiers in entrepreneurship research*, ed. N. C. Churchill and V. L. Lewis. Babson Park, MA: Babson College.

————. 2000. National panel study of U.S. business start-ups: Background and methodology. In *Advances in entrepreneurship, firm emergence, and growth*, ed. J. Katz, 153-227. Stamford, CT: JAI.

Reynolds, P. D., K. G. Shaver, N. Carter, and W. Gartner. 2004. *Panel studies of entrepreneurial dynamics codebook by questionnaires used.* Ann Arbor: Survey Research Center, University of Michigan.

Rhodes, C., and J. S. Butler. 2004. Understanding self-perceptions of business performance: An examination of black American entrepreneurs. *Journal of Developmental Entrepreneurship* 9 (1): 55-71.

Robb, A. 2002. Entrepreneurial performance by women and minorities: The case of new firms. *Journal of Developmental Entrepreneurship* 7 (4): 383-97.

Robinson, J. A. 2006. Navigating social and institutional barriers to markets: How social entrepreneurs identify and evaluate opportunities. In *Social entrepreneurship*, ed. J. Mair, J. A. Robinson, and K. Hockerts. London: Palgrave.

Rogoff, E. G., M. S. Lee, and D. C. Suh. 2004. Attributions by entrepreneurs and experts of the factors that cause and impede small business success. *Journal of Small Business Management* 42 (4): 364.

Shane, S., and S. Venkatraman. 2000. The promise of entrepreneurship as a field of research. *Academy of Management Review* 25 (1): 217.

Shelton, L. 2006. Women entrepreneurs, work-family conflict and venture performance: New insights into the work family interface. *Journal of Small Business Management* 44 (2): 285-97.

Smith-Hunter, A. E., and R. L. Boyd. 2004. Applying theories of entrepreneurship to a comparative analysis of white and minority women business owners. *Women in Management Review* 19 (1): 18-28.

Spilerman, S. 2000. Wealth and stratification processes. *Annual Review of Sociology* 26:497-524.

Tumin, M. M. 1953. Some principles of stratification: A critical analysis. *American Sociological Review* 18 (4): 387-94.

Uzzi, B. 1997. Social structure and competition in interfirm networks: The paradox of embeddedness. *Administrative Science Quarterly* 42:35-67.

————. 1999. Embeddedness in the making of financial capital: How social relations and networks benefit firms seeking financing. *American Sociological Review* 64:481-505.

Watson, J. 2002. Comparing the performance of male- and female-owned businesses: Relating outputs to inputs. *Entrepreneurship Theory and Practice* 26 (3): 91-100.

Werbner, P. 1999. What colour "success"? Distorting value in studies of ethnic entrepreneurship. In *The sociological review 1999*, 548-79. Oxford, UK: Blackwell.

Building Ventures through Civic Capitalism

CANDIDA BRUSH,
DANIEL MONTI,
ANDREA RYAN,
and
AMY M. GANNON

An exploratory study of urban entrepreneurs participating in a technical assistance program finds that they focus on the bottom line and often have an explicit wish to improve their community. This integrated combination of economic and social values, a kind of civicminded capitalism, guides their positioning for growth and yields a business that can best be called a "civic enterprise." A descriptive analysis of qualitative and quantitative research yields propositions for future research on these hybrid business ventures.

Keywords: civic enterprising; minority entrepreneurs; hybrid ventures; civic capitalism

The importance of entrepreneurs working in urban settings is undeniable. Entrepreneurship and business development are vehicles for accelerating the revitalization of urban areas (Porter 1995; Robinson 2004; Monti 1999). This is especially important for American inner cities, which have higher poverty rates, lower median household incomes, and higher unemployment rates than places that are not cities.[1] But while there are nearly 12.7 million jobs in America's cities—representing about 8 percent of the country's private sector employment base— the average annual salary for these jobs— $38,000—is lower than that of jobs found in the areas surrounding cities.[2]

Many depressed urban neighborhoods have mostly minority populations whose rate of population growth vastly outstrips their ability to develop their own businesses. This makes the urban economic situation even worse. Even though minority business development is growing at a rate of 10 percent annually, it is lower than the national average for all businesses. And while the rate of job creation for minority businesses rose by 23 percent between 1987 and 1992, a substantial part of that growth was in the nonprofit sector (Y. Lowrey 2005). More recently, growth has slowed. While the percentage of minorities in the total U.S. population

DOI: 10.1177/0002716207303590

increased from 21 percent in 1982 to 23 percent in 2002, their share of businesses did not keep pace. At 6.8 percent in 1982, it rose to only 15.1 percent in 1997 (Y. Lowrey 2005).

It is interesting to note that recent research from the Panel Study of Entrepreneurial Dynamics (PSED) shows that the prevalence of entrepreneurial behavior among black men and women is 50 percent greater than for whites. For Hispanic men, it is 20 percent greater (Reynolds et al. 2004). Yet despite clear increases in minority business *start-ups*, over the long term, these enterprises have lower survival rates than nonminority establishments (J. Lowrey and Associates 2005). The core of the problem, it seems, lies not in entrepreneurial motivation, but in something else that happens once the doors of their new business open.

Not surprisingly, larger firms seem to have more staying power. Minority-owned firms with more than $500,000 annual revenues (171,000 businesses) accounted for 76 percent of revenue generated by minority-owned firms and 70 percent of all employment for these firms (J. Lowrey and Associates 2005). Yet when compared with all U.S. firms, the difference is clear. Minorities own only 5 percent of all U.S. firms with more than five employees, and more than 80 percent

Candida Brush is a professor of entrepreneurship, chair of the Entrepreneurship Division, director of the Doctoral Program at Babson College, and holds the Paul T. Babson Chair in Entrepreneurship. She has authored four books, two edited volumes, and more than eighty publications. A recent book, Clearing the Hurdles, provides strategies and approaches for growth-oriented women entrepreneurs. Her research investigates women's growth businesses and resource acquisition strategies in emerging ventures. She is a founding member of the Diana Project International, which is the 2007 recipient of the FSF-NUTEK International Research Award for Outstanding Contribution to Entrepreneurship Research.

Daniel Monti is a professor and associate chairman in the Sociology Department of Boston University. He has written six books and is the recipient of a Woodrow Wilson Fellowship. His most recent book, The American City: A Social and Cultural History, is a detailed description of American civic culture. He has served as a consultant to government agencies and for-profit and nonprofit organizations. He was a member of the Missouri State Advisory Board to the United States Commission on Civil Rights. He is founder of InnerCity Entrepreneurs, a technical assistance program for existing businesses that want to grow.

Andrea Ryan completed her PhD in sociology at Boston University in 2007. Her dissertation on Lawrence, Massachusetts, is titled "Economic and Civic Roles of Small Businesses and Hispanics in the Revitalization of a Majority-Minority City." She is currently engaged in a number of projects related to the relationship between businesses and communities. Her professional background includes program management, consulting, and research with municipal agencies, schools, nonprofits, and businesses.

Amy M. Gannon is a fourth-year doctoral student in the Organizational Behavior Department at Boston University's School of Management. She is a research assistant for the Human Resources Policy Institute. Her research interests include minority and social entrepreneurship, careers, identity, and adult learning and development. She has ten years of experience managing projects in corporate, nonprofit, and government settings.

NOTE: The authors are most grateful to the Kauffman Foundation for generous support of this research. An earlier version of this article was presented at the Babson College Entrepreneurship Research Conference, Bloomington, Indiana, in 2006.

of their larger firms operate in only four sectors: services, retail, wholesale trade, and construction.

Minorities own only 5 percent of all U.S. firms with more than five employees, and more than 80 percent of their larger firms operate in only four sectors: services, retail, wholesale trade, and construction.

Research to date exploring ways that smaller urban and minority businesses grow is very limited. Studies of new ventures suggest a variety of factors including entrepreneurial experience and motivations, resources, and strategy influence growth (Carter et al. 1994; Kirchhoff 1994; Cooper, Gimeno-Gascon, and Woo 1994; Davidsson and Wiklund 2000; Covin and Slevin 1997). But most of these studies sample by region, industry, size, or age, and nearly all investigate firms founded and run by populations of white men (Covin and Slevin 1997). The studies that do consider differences by race and ethnicity find that human capital, access to money, and industry structures may produce systematic differences (Bates 1993; Fairlie 1999; Greene and Butler 1996). This also reflects what the PSED suggested: motivation is not the limiting factor. Access to resources seems to be the more salient characteristic.

Research from sociology shows us that some minorities—particularly immigrants and ethnics in tight-knit ethnic communities—are able to create their own access to resources and cohesive industry structure based on ethnic solidarity and a commitment to their ethnic community. While the role of small businesses is largely overlooked in much of the sociology literature, many studies have examined the way business people in these ethnic enclaves are tied to their neighborhoods and seek to provide contributions to the community (Light and Bonacich 1988; Butler 1991; Light and Gold 2000). They survive and even prosper to the extent that they are socially embedded in their community. That is, they have good ties to their customers and other neighborhood organizations and local people trust them, two crucial elements in achieving effective social capital. Unfortunately, sociological research usually does not examine how minority businesses (i.e., ethnic and minority businesses generally) grow or expand their markets throughout larger geographic areas or with disparate groups or individuals (Jones and Conway 2000; Portes and Sensenbrenner 1993; Chaganti and Greene 2002).

In sum, there is an unfortunate gap in our knowledge of how smaller urban and minority businesses position for growth. This calls for a more organizational approach to studying minority businesses. In particular, how does the way they *manage* their enterprises, access *money* to establish themselves and grow, and define and expand their *markets* (i.e., the "three Ms") influence their ability to establish a sustainable and successful business enterprise?

Given this gap in the literature, the importance of urban revitalization efforts, and the demonstrated weaker performance levels of minority businesses, we developed an exploratory study to examine how urban and particularly minority-owned businesses position for growth. We draw from a panel study of twenty-nine white and minority entrepreneurs who wanted to make their ventures grow. They participated in a technical assistance program called InnerCity Entrepreneurs.

In this article, we begin by reviewing the role of the three Ms and how they influence growth. We then provide a brief description of the local context. Finally, we present the methods and findings of our study and point out how we might build on what we have learned in future studies.

Background

Key factors influencing business growth and success are money, market access, and management capability (Bates 2004; Timmons and Spinelli 2007). When these three Ms are in place—management is well prepared, the firm is better capitalized, and it competes effectively in the market—the business is better positioned for growth. On the other hand, when management is less well prepared and experienced, growth capital is minimal, and market access is limited or restricted, then growth cannot be achieved (Sexton and Kasarda 1997; Robb and Fairlie 2007; Bates 2004).

The relative lack of access of minority businessmen and women to the three Ms has been crucial to their lack of success and the slow growth of their ventures. First, the first M, management, is weaker for minority businesses on the whole. Experience is an important factor. Research has shown that prior business experience and education increase the survival and profitability of minority businesses (Robb and Fairlie 2007). Those with less experience than their white counterparts make less profit and hire fewer persons.

Of course, money (i.e., access to capital, credit, and equity) is also important. Several studies illustrate the different ways that money and access to resources affect minority versus nonminority businesses. For example, a study of minority business owners who applied for credit provides two key insights. First, Hispanics paid more for credit than did their white counterparts. Second, African Americans were more likely to be denied credit even in less competitive markets (Cavalluzzo, Cavalluzzo, and Wolken 2002). Furthermore, while both minority and nonminority business owners tended to shy away from applying for credit—even when they needed it—for fear of denial, minorities were more likely to avoid applying in the first place.

On the other hand, these discouraging facts do not tell us the whole story, particularly for those minority-owned businesses that start out a bit "stronger." A study of venture capital investment in minority businesses showed that venture capital returns on these investments were equal or better compared to investments in nonminority businesses (Bradford and Bates 2004).

Markets—their type, size, and location—are important to all businesses but may be even more so for minority businesses that are located in predominantly minority communities and/or inner cities. The relationships that a business can maintain in the local community are very important. Studies of immigrant and ethnic communities, in particular, show that minority businesses that are better embedded in the local community, serve a large share of area residents, and help their community as a whole do better than they might have otherwise (Monti 1999; Appold and Kasarda 2004). This is good news for the entrepreneurs, the businesses, and the community.

But it is also important to extend the market beyond the local community. It may be that the ability to do so enables a business to grow beyond what could otherwise be expected. Government procurement programs have been helpful in this regard. By giving preferential treatment to minority businesses, they help these firms expand their share of the market (Boston 2004). Certainly, many minority business owners have leveraged their own personal and professional resources to grow their businesses as well. But given their relative lack of success, we must ask both what helps to foster their growth and what barriers sit in the way.

As the research above suggests, entrepreneurial perceptions and motivations, the business organization, and the role of community all play a role in the success of a business. We reasoned that an elaboration of the three Ms might yield more insight about growth positioning in particular. To address these points, we developed a research framework using the following dimensions: the individual's motives and goals; the venture-strategy, structure, and growth objectives; and community participation and membership (see Figure 1).

Method

The subjects of this study participated in a technical assistance program, InnerCity Entrepreneurs (ICE), which was launched in Boston, Massachusetts. The training program is built on three core components: (1) classroom training (and specialized supplemental seminars), (2) access to a private sector network of experts in various fields, and (3) peer-to-peer coaching. The initial program lasts nine months. Graduates can then join the ICE Alumni Network, which allows them continued participation and access to program benefits.

As part of their commitment to ICE, the entrepreneurs agree to participate in the research study for a period of five years. For this study, we employed multiple data collection methods, including surveys, qualitative interviews, "archival research" that included reviewing selected classroom materials and completed assignments, and publicly available information about the organizations (i.e., Web site information, newspaper articles).

FIGURE 1
CONCEPTUAL FRAMEWORK

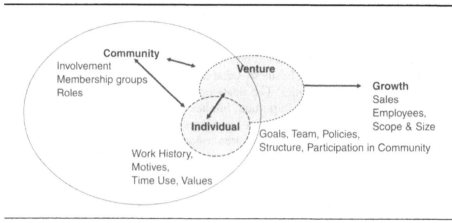

Consistent with our research questions, we collected data across three levels of analysis: the individual entrepreneur (i.e., demographics, motivations, values), the firm (i.e., business structure and operations), and the relationship between business and the community (i.e., voluntary and organizational memberships, donations, and participation in community events). We considered what drives the individual to become an entrepreneur and how the venture survives and succeeds. We also included measures of the entrepreneur's work history, motives, and values; group membership and roles; and demographic data on the businesses, employees, customers, and geographic "communities" or localities (Monti 1999; Brush and Chaganti 1998).

Our sample comprised twenty-nine entrepreneurs who participated in the first two cohorts of the ICE program (2004 and 2005). Responses from the 160-question survey were put into a statistical database for analysis. The statistical data were analyzed in straightforward ways (i.e., using cross-tabs rather than complex statistical measures) to determine levels of association among these different variables. Interview data were compiled into transcripts and were analyzed using qualitative data analysis techniques.

Results

Who are the ICE entrepreneurs?

The sample of entrepreneurs was 55 percent minority and 45 percent white, 65 percent male and 35 percent female. The twenty-nine entrepreneurs included seven black men, five black women, nine white men, five white women, and three

Hispanic men. Almost two-thirds of them are forty-five years old or younger. Nearly 80 percent of them have at least four years of college to their credit. Most of the entrepreneurs (62 percent) started their ventures from scratch, and 25 percent of them have owned two or more ventures. Sixty percent of entrepreneurs indicated that they had always wanted to be business owners (see Table 1).

Personal values and goals were related to the decision to start an enterprise. Nearly 80 percent of the entrepreneurs indicated that values were an important factor in starting their business. Most of the entrepreneurs (86 percent) felt that they had more opportunity to live by their values when running their own business than by working for someone else. Virtually all of the entrepreneurs indicated that, as business owners, they felt an obligation to give something back to the community (93 percent).

Seventy percent of our entrepreneurs stated that they or their partners carry out most of the management responsibilities. Nearly half of the ventures have a division of labor in which different people assume responsibility for certain tasks. Between 50 and 60 percent of the ventures have individuals responsible for sales, finance, and daily operations. Human resources and product development are least likely to be someone's primary responsibility.

This sample of entrepreneurs has a collaborative management style. Nearly 80 percent state that they share sensitive information with employees, and 96 percent say they have a flat administrative hierarchy. The entrepreneurs combine research and instinct when making business decisions. The majority indicate that their business decisions are guided by their values (97 percent).

What is the nature of their ventures?

The overwhelming majority of the ventures are small, with 70 percent having fewer than ten employees. Of the businesses, 44 percent had annual sales of more than $500,000, while more than 25 percent posted revenues of more than $1 million. These businesses were on average four years old (see Table 2).

Most of the entrepreneurs indicated they received most of their advice from family and friends when launching their ventures, but over time they began to use professional advice more often. While only 32 percent reported using professional advice at founding, at the point of growth this rose to 86 percent. These ventures were also governed more informally. Nearly half (48 percent) of the businesses have boards of directors, but they do not meet regularly. Most have informal advisers (65 percent) and mentors (41 percent).

More than 80 percent indicated that their organizational structure reflects their values and that their decisions are guided by their values. Those who reported that their organizational structure reflected their values felt their values were *not* similar to typical U.S. business values. They were also significantly more likely to set what we might call "nontraditional" business goals. They were more likely to say their goals were to provide jobs or create a quality work environment than to make a profit or create personal wealth.

TABLE 1
THE ENTREPRENEURS: DESCRIPTIVE STATISTICS ($N = 29$)

Variable	Number	Percentage
Sex		
Male	19	65.5
Female	10	34.5
Race/ethnicity		
White	13	44.8
Black	12	41.4
Hispanic	3	10.3
Missing	1	3.4
Age		
25-35 years old	5	17.2
36-45 years old	14	48.3
46-55 years old	6	20.7
56-65 years old	4	13.8
Years in business		
0-2 years	2	6.9
3-5 years	6	20.7
6-7 years	3	10.3
8-10 years	4	13.8
11-14 years	6	20.7
18-20 years	2	6.9
21-22 years	1	3.4
23-26 years	3	10.3
27 or more years	2	6.9
Education		
High school	1	3.4
Some college	4	13.8
2-year college	1	3.4
4-year college	15	51.7
Graduate school +	8	27.6
Entrepreneurial experience		
Started business himself/herself	18	62.1
First business owned	3	10.3
Number of other ventures		
started (mean = 2.38)		
1	6	20.7
2	9	31.0
3	7	24.1
5	2	6.9
6	1	3.4
8	1	3.4
Someone has primary responsibility for:		
Marketing and sales	16	55.2
Finance and accounting	17	58.6
Strategic leadership	13	44.8

TABLE 2
THE BUSINESSES: DESCRIPTIVE STATISTICS ($N = 29$)

Variable	Number	Percentage
Employees: part time		
0	6	20.7
1-3	10	34.5
4-6	2	6.9
7-10	3	10.3
11-20	4	13.8
41-50	1	3.4
51 or more	1	3.4
1-5 (old survey)	2	6.9
Employees: full time		
1-3	10	34.5
4-6	7	24.1
7-10	3	10.3
11-20	3	10.3
21-30	1	3.4
41-50	1	3.4
51 or more	1	3.4
21-50 (old survey)	1	3.4
1-5 (old survey)	2	6.9
Sales previous year ($)		
< 100K	2	6.9
101-250K	4	13.8
251-400K	5	17.2
401-550K	2	6.9
551-700K	1	3.4
701-850K	2	6.9
850-999K	2	6.9
1 million to 1.25 million	3	10.3
> 1.25 million	5	17.2
750 to 1 million (old survey)	1	3.4
250-500K (old survey)	1	3.4
Profits previous year ($)		
< 250K	1	3.4
1-25K	11	37.9
26-50K	4	13.8
76-100K	2	6.9
101-200K	2	6.9
201-300K	1	3.4
301-400K	1	3.4
Missing	6	21
Percentage local customers		
< 10	8	27.6
11-20	1	3.4
21-30	4	13.8

(continued)

TABLE 2 (CONTINUED)

Variable	Number	Percentage
41-50	1	3.4
51-60	1	3.4
61-70	2	6.9
71-80	1	3.4
81-100	7	24.1
Missing	4	13.7
Current boards		
Board of directors	14	48.3
Advisory board	4	13.8

Approximately 46 percent of the entrepreneurs specified that they market their products to members of their racial and/or ethnic group. Twenty-five percent of the ventures have mostly local customers, while 29 percent have mostly nonlocal customers. The remaining half of the sample has a mixed customer base of both local and nonlocal.

[InnerCity entrepreneurs] were more likely to say their goals were to provide jobs or create a quality work environment than to make a profit or create personal wealth.

The study tracks thirty-three different ways in which ventures "give something back" to their community. The venture that does the least amount of "giving back" still makes five different kinds of contributions to the larger community. The most active contributor gives back in twenty-five different ways. The remaining entrepreneurs in the sample spread themselves out pretty uniformly between these two extremes.

The more popular ways of "giving back" to the community include providing jobs to local people; offering in-kind contributions, free services, and donations; making referrals for people looking for assistance; letting their business be used for meetings and as a site for public announcements; and participating in neighborhood initiatives and celebrations. Somewhere between 28 and 50 percent of the ventures in our sample give back in these ways. This collection of entrepreneurs

TABLE 3
POSITION FOR GROWTH: DESCRIPTIVE STATISTICS ($N = 29$)

Variable	Number	Percentage
Sources of advice		
Professionals	25	86.2
Mentor	12	41.2
Family and friends	12	24.1
Access		
Access to technological skills	19	65.5
Access to markets	19	65.5
Access to capital	11	37.9
Customer base		
Primarily coethnics	9	31.0

also thinks that these kinds of activities garner their business more recognition from local people and the media.

How do the urban entrepreneurs organize for growth?

Approximately 70 percent of the ventures indicate they have access to the technological skills and markets they need, but only 41 percent felt they have access to adequate capital. At one time or another, entrepreneurs have used a combination of the following strategies to find a manager: friends (38 percent), advertisements (28 percent), other business owners (7 percent), consultants (14 percent), conferences (3 percent), and neighborhood groups (7 percent). Interestingly, 41 percent of our entrepreneurs indicated that the people they chose as managers had "found them" (see Table 3).

While these entrepreneurs say that they have clear business goals, when asked what those business goals were there seemed to be less focus. Most of the entrepreneurs agreed with a number of types of goals, including increasing sales, making more money, making the business attractive to buyers, providing jobs, and giving back to the community (see Table 4).

While the ventures are considering a number of options for growth, including acquisition of or merger with other businesses, the overwhelming majority (93 percent) intend to keep and expand their current business. Like most entrepreneurs, this sample of urban entrepreneurs believes their ventures are different, perhaps even unique. They have a better business model (39 percent) or they have better technology and better products (39 percent) than their competitors. What may very well be unique to this sample, however, is that nearly 20 percent believe that having a broader social mission or "social consciousness" is what distinguishes them from the competition.

TABLE 4
BUSINESS GOALS: DESCRIPTIVE STATISTICS (N = 29)

Variable	Number	Percentage
Main goals		
Keep and expand business	27	93.1
Keep and acquire different businesses	15	51.7
Keep and acquire similar business	12	41.4
Merge with similar business	11	37.9
Sell and start new and different business	10	34.5
Make business stable	29	100.0
Increase sales	28	96.6
Quality work environment	26	89.7
Make more money	26	89.7
Give back to community	24	82.8
Provide jobs	23	79.3
Become industry leader	22	75.9
Make business attractive to buyers	22	75.9

Significant differences by race/ethnicity

There were some significant differences between the minority entrepreneurs and their white counterparts. First, the minority business owners (black and Hispanic) were more likely to be running their first venture (60 percent). Only 23 percent of the white entrepreneurs were running their first venture. Second, minority entrepreneurs spend significantly more time on community activities in general and are more likely to indicate that they are deeply involved with their ethnic communities. Also, they were more likely to market their products to members of their racial and/or ethnic group. Interestingly, entrepreneurs who say that their ethnic group values business ownership were more likely to say they always wanted to be business owners. Finally, minority entrepreneurs (100 percent) indicated they believed they were more likely to meet their professional goals through business ownership than through employment for someone else, compared to 69 percent of white entrepreneurs (see Table 5).

Discussion

Because the premise of our study was to understand urban entrepreneurs and the growth of their ventures, the analyses focused on the broad context of entrepreneurship: the motivations of the entrepreneurs, the organizing practices of the ventures (e.g., strategy, structure, goals), and their engagement with their communities. Yet even given these complexities, most of the research to date tends to split ventures into one of two main categories—economic or social.

TABLE 5
CORRELATION MATRIX (N = 29)

Variable	1	2	3	4	5	6	7	8	9	10	11	12	13	14
1. Hours spent working (daily)	1													
2. Hours spent on community activities (daily)	-.131	1												
3. First business	.207	.222	1											
4. Values like U.S. values	-.02	.472*	.202	1										
5. Values are valued in business	.065	.332	.108	.594**	1									
6. Involved in ethnic community	.370*	.472**	.198	.239	.3	1								
7. Can be myself and succeed	-.123	.17	-.111	.222	.258	.154	1							
8. Clearly defined personal goals	.162	.239	.155	.471*	.255	.16	-.229	1						
9. Hadn't planned to own business	0	-.055	.314	.073	-.087	-.3	-.104	.177	1					
10. Want to merge with similar business	-.044	.409*	.035	.439*	.115	.328	.519**	.19	.03	1				
11. Goal is to increase sales	-.022	.295	-.092	.435*	.193	.27	.315	.163	-.329	.411*	1			
12. Someone's primary job is strategy	.042	-.008	.048	.036	-.027	.245	.295	-.521**	-.123	.21	.143	1		
13. Race	.268	.413*	.464*	.360	.341	.593**	.136	.088	-.175	.288	.356	.357	1	
14. Gender	.111	-.279	.127	.043	-.063	-.117	-.436*	.355	-.13	-.357	-.171	-.197	-.09	1

*$p \leq .05$. **$p \leq .01$.

"Traditional" economic ventures are guided by a profit motivation, follow business strategy and practices, and focus on obtaining resources to achieve competitive superiority (Lumpkin and Dess 1996).

This view emerges from historical perspectives that define entrepreneurship by the recognition and exploitation of previously unexploited profit opportunities that involved new combinations of ideas, production methods, or markets (Kirzner 1973; Schumpeter 1935). A long history of theory suggests the entrepreneur is the economic change agent who is alert to opportunities and exploits them in the market arena (Hebert and Link 1982). The traditional entrepreneur is guided by profit motivation whereby products/services are launched in the market setting. We know, however, that industry economics, market factors, and competitive dynamics directly influence a new or small firm's ability to grow (Porter 1985). Here we find a bit of a mismatch. While business strategy and practices focus on achieving competitive superiority, the entrepreneur is preoccupied with obtaining needed resources to achieve this growth (Lumpkin and Dess 1996).

Entrepreneurs do not operate only in the business arena. Innovative thinkers and entrepreneurial actors are getting increasingly involved in, and getting increasing attention for, their attempts to bring about a "social good." While social ventures are usually thought of as nonprofits, many for-profit ventures are led by socially motivated entrepreneurs whose core mission is to bring about social change or innovation (Dees 1998). A wide variety of terms characterize the intersection of entrepreneurship and social issues including social-purpose businesses, sustainable ventures, ecopreneurship, environmental entrepreneurship, and others (Gerlach 2003).

While our sample did reflect ventures at both ends of the spectrum, our preliminary findings showed that many of our ventures were in fact quite mixed. They did not fall neatly into one or the other of the categories outlined in previous research where primacy of economic goals would trade off social goals or visa versa. Instead of having either a bottom-line focus or a "do-gooding" focus, they *blend* business and community improvement goals in a variety of creative ways (Monti 1999). The good they do is sometimes by design and sometimes not. Doing good can be a natural by-product or elaboration of their business dealings and/or an explicit part of their business plan. We labeled these entrepreneurs *civic capitalists* and their ventures *civic enterprises* (Brush et al. 2006).

The ways in which the civic capitalists combine and integrate their economic and social missions varies. For some, their social engagement is at an individual level, while for others, it is organizational. This preliminary research suggests that the various kinds of civic capitalists depend on the complex and interacting patterns of individual motivations, business type, and community needs or expectations (see Figure 2). We discuss each of these below, drawing from both our qualitative and quantitative data.

Influence of individual motivations

Entrepreneurs have different motivations for starting their businesses that are influenced by cultural values and prior work experiences (Busenitz and Lau 1996;

FIGURE 2
CIVIC ENTERPRISE

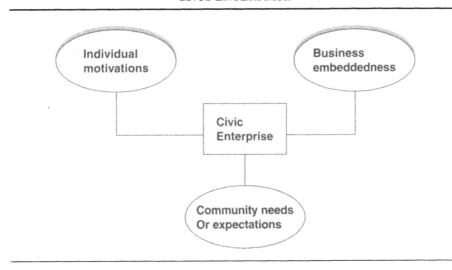

Bird 1989). The act of venture creation does not happen in a vacuum but, rather, is a continuation of their professional and personal experiences. For some, the motivation to start a business was based on a desire to integrate their personal and professional lives. They may want to live and work in the same neighborhood. Or they may want to live and work by a set of values that appeals to people in their area.

For some, however, the decision to start their own business came as a result of a "value mismatch." Some individuals felt that their roles as employees in other organizations challenged their personal values and created frustration or tension. As one entrepreneur, Judith (black, female), describes how she came to consider business ownership after an engineering career,

> There were some decisions that were made that I really did not agree with and found that I was still responsible for implementing them; whether I agree with them or not; whether they fit within my values. . . . I spent many years thinking I needed to change myself to fit better within these companies. One day I just decided that I don't have to fit into some mold I don't like. . . . I should be able to have the kind of job where I like myself, where I am happy with myself. . . . I started to think about having my own business where I worked on things that I cared about and I treated the employees the way I thought people should be treated. All the things that I felt I didn't like about my career in various companies . . . I thought if I could create my own business where I get to treat people the way I want to treat them. And have the culture I want to have.

Another entrepreneur, Daniel (white, male), described his experiences working with a construction company and how his values were challenged. While he initially loved working for the organization, as it grew things seemed to change. As he describes it, "We had gone from like this real family feeling to this big company where the owners were somehow now of a different class than the folks

[who] were working for him." The company clients had changed from more middle-class families to millionaires, to whom Daniel suggests he could not relate to a personal level. The business became all about "selling things to the customers and the customers are the extremely wealthy and so, what you are trying to get them to do is spend more money on their homes and they already have homes that are complete luxuries." In his description, Daniel used words such as greed and waste and indicated that he felt uncomfortable with the power dynamics that were developing. He says the client relations were "evolving in a way that I didn't really want to be a part of."

For other entrepreneurs, there was the perception that they would not be able to achieve their professional goals by working for someone else. Similar to previous research on minority entrepreneurs, business ownership provided a means for overcoming perceived barriers to advancement—barriers that could be based on social identities such as race, gender, dimensions of social class (e.g., education level), and/or beliefs about the nature of corporate settings (Butler and Kozmetsky 2004).

Deborah (black, female) describes her experiences working for a large, local retail chain. She entered a management training program, which she finished early, but says that she "was punished for every idea she had. It was misery." She describes how they assigned her to the worst department, and when she started to make progress improving it, they took her resources away. Deborah indicates the structures of the organization prevented people from benefiting from their hard work. "I just didn't see the benefits of trying to do better and better." She says that she was accused of "showing off" and not being a "team player." Deborah indicated that she felt her identity as an African American woman affected her professional opportunities and ability to reach her goals.

These different entrepreneurial motivations influence how the business owner approaches venture creation. The professional and personal experiences of the individual has influence over the type of business an entrepreneur chooses to open, how she or he chooses to organize it, and how she or he defines success, including rate and type of growth. Judith, for example, chose to purchase a horticulture business, quite different from her engineering background. She intentionally avoiding starting or buying a business that would require venture capital funding despite being quite familiar with the process. She wanted a business that she could control and in which she could define the organizational culture—a culture that supported certain social values. Daniel left construction to start a small grocery/café in his local neighborhood. He described the decision to start the business as "an opportunity to be in an economic relationship with my *peers*." Daniel views the relationship with his diverse community as critical to his business model, and it is the "idea" about which he is most excited. His social values are intertwined with his economic goals.

The embeddedness of small business

Besides the motivations of individual entrepreneurs, the various ways in which many urban entrepreneurs express their hybrid missions of having an economic and social impact may be affected by how they are embedded in the community—whether they serve their immediate neighborhood or a larger part of the city and metropolitan area. By definition, they are embedded if they are located in an ongoing system of social relations relevant to their ability to obtain resources, produce products/services, and sustain interactions (Uzzi 1997; Granovetter 1985; Jack and Anderson 2002). Our preliminary data suggest that entrepreneurs whose customers come primarily from the immediate area provide a number of direct services to their community and assistance to their customers. It also seems that businesses whose customer base is more local than not feel more closely tied to their community. This sort of locational or "place-based" connection may prove particularly important as we further explore the roles of entrepreneurs who are starting and running businesses in their own inner-city communities.

Our preliminary data suggest that entrepreneurs whose customers come primarily from the immediate area provide a number of direct services to their community and assistance to their customers.

To start to flesh out these distinctions and determine their usefulness, we provide a preliminary taxonomy based on this place-based notion of embeddedness. What follows are three categories of embeddedness, ranging from high to low. Preliminary definitions and an example of each one are provided.

1. High embeddedness—Fresh Foods, Inc.

These businesses have a significant number of local customers. They are typically retail or service businesses. Fresh Foods, Inc., is located in an inner-city neighborhood that has seen its share of business disinvestment and disinterest. The entrepreneur saw a need and opportunity to "do well by doing good" by, for, and with this community. Built around a strong social mission, this civic enterprise venture illustrates how emphasizing equity, fairness, and "social justice" are not incompatible with running an effective and profitable business.

Fresh Foods was founded in 1994 as a take-out lunch operation that used local talent to deliver fresh, home-style ethnic foods. Soon after start-up, the entrepreneurs were asked to provide ethnic meals to the growing population of homebound seniors in the local ethnic community. They now have a well-respected and thriving business that produces more than four thousand meals a day for homebound elders and school children. The company has experienced steady growth, with revenues exceeding $2 million, and it currently employs approximately 50 people.

Fresh Foods operates on the principle that people should not be forced to leave their communities to find decent jobs and quality goods and services. Its commitment to hiring and developing local talent is seen as one important way to help build the economic capacity of the community. As the CEO describes, "We want everyone to think like an owner" so that they can eventually manage Fresh Foods or start their own ventures. His ultimate goal is to build financial capital, human capital (i.e., education levels), and social capital (i.e., reciprocal sharing of resources between individuals and/or groups) within the community so that the business and surrounding neighborhood can be locally sustained.[3]

2. Medium embeddedness—Creation Catering

These entrepreneurs tend to serve a mix of local and nonlocal customers. Creation Catering is an off-premise catering and event-planning business that specializes in gourmet Caribbean, southern, and vegetarian cuisines. Owned by a Haitian man and his wife, the business collects revenues of approximately $300,000 a year. Its primary business comes from weddings, but it also has corporate, nonprofit, and private clients. Many of these clients are Caribbean American or African American. Creation Catering also works closely with other businesses such as florists, photographers, and entertainment companies to provide one-stop shopping for their customers.

Creation Catering is an immigrant-owned business in an underserved, inner-city neighborhood. However, its founder and CEO takes care to serve a "higher-end" clientele than he might find living next door. This is a significant point of tension for him. He wants his business to do well, not only to benefit himself and his family, but also to serve as a role model for other minority and immigrant business owners. He believes that by demonstrating that minority-owned businesses can provide high-end, quality services, he can dispel myths and stereotypes about what minority entrepreneurs can do. In this way, his mission is clearly mixed. He is a businessman, yet he also considers himself a leader in his community and a role model for other immigrant and black-owned businesses.

The changes he hopes to make also reflect his community-oriented thinking. For example, he is currently working on transitioning from his off-site catering work to running an on-site business. He believes it will help him create a gathering place for the black community, something he says is sorely missing. He sees this change as an opportunity to stabilize the business, raise his profile in the community, and even build a legacy establishment that provides connection and history in the black community.

3. Low embeddedness—Latino News Source

Ventures classified with low embeddedness tend to serve nonlocal customers. These were often technology-based ventures where face-to-face interactions were not essential for sales or business transactions. Latino News Source, a news media business started by three Venezuelan immigrants, provides a good example of the traditional economic model. These entrepreneurs used their personal and professional expertise in public relations and journalism to fill a gap in the growing Hispanic media market. Their approach was more "standard" than not. They began by drawing up a business plan and securing venture capital funds to get things going. Their goal is to become recognized as the "go-to" place for major companies who want to access the Hispanic and Latin American markets.

Although they are mostly involved in newspaper publications and radio at present, they hope to branch into TV in the future. They even named their business with this future in mind, giving it a three-letter abbreviation similar to other major news media outlets (e.g., NBC, CNN). This team of entrepreneurs wants to do well—very well. They want to position the business as a leader in the marketplace and secure a better living for themselves.

Latino News Source has no explicit social or community mission. It is not located in a Hispanic neighborhood but in a predominantly upper-class and largely white Boston community. Its founders' core focus is on running a profitable business, not connecting with local folks. Even so, while they clearly have an economic mission, it could be argued that they are still promoting a larger social good, even if only by "default." That is, they are creating a media opportunity that will serve and represent the largely underserved Hispanic population in the United States. Furthermore, these minority entrepreneurs illustrate that white men are not the only ones who develop "traditional economic ventures."

Based on this exploratory analysis and discussion, we reasoned that social capital theory provides a reasonable umbrella for thinking about the ways these urban ventures approach growth. We apply the theory broadly here to discuss the relationship between businesses and their communities (i.e., their levels of embeddedness) as well as to focus on the business-customer relationship specifically.

We consider two types of social capital when we look at how ventures approach and achieve growth—bonding and bridging (Putnam 2000). At the community level, strong intracommunity ties are "bonds," while weaker extra-community networks are "bridges" (Simmel 1971; Woolcock and Narayan 1999). Bonding takes place between "like" individuals and groups. Bonding strategies are cooperative activities that take place *within* their existing community. Bridging takes place between more disparate individuals and groups. Bridging is often weaker, but broader and is characterized by cooperative activities *between* groups.

Influence of community dynamics

The entrepreneurs who participated in the ICE program are influenced not only by their values and motivations but also by the communities in which they operate. Inner-city communities vary, and the unique nature of the community affects the venture's organizing efforts. As Reggie from Creation Catering describes, certain judgments are made about his business because it is located in a distressed, urban neighborhood populated by immigrants. In talking about his business, he describes the challenges he has in overcoming general stereotypes of minority-owned businesses as the low-cost option with "the worst service, the worst quality." He also finds that his immigrant community brings cultural notions to how business should be conducted.

The role he takes as an entrepreneur and the way he organizes his venture for growth in large part is determined by the needs of his community. To be successful (or perhaps even to begin to define success), Reggie must respond to the specific economic and social issues in his community, which are often intertwined. Similarly, Building Supply and Repair Co-Op (BSRC) located near the heart of Boston's predominantly black neighborhood takes care to provide an inventory of building supplies for the local community and, at the same time, provides environmentally conscious products. Fertilizers are organic and wood moldings are remanufactured and recycled from scrap wood.

In both cases, these businesses developed growth strategies using policies and programs that would develop local talent to fill supervisory and management roles. Strategic choices about product/market expansion were taken with careful consideration of ways to source talent and expend resources.

Conclusions and Implications

Based on the qualitative and quantitative results in this exploratory study, we conclude that to understand the processes of growing ventures in urban neighborhoods, we must understand the interactions of people and place and how these interactions affect the economic and social missions of these ventures. We propose that the dual mission of these *civic capitalists* influences many decisions the entrepreneurs make and can sometimes create special challenges. For example, the owner and CEO of Fresh Foods admits that developing local talent, as opposed to hiring experienced talent from outside the community, has slowed the business's growth. Yet his mission is clear, and he believes strongly that he is doing the "right thing." So while he certainly wants to grow, he must constantly negotiate a balance between his complementary economic and social missions.

Ethnicity and culture also play a role creating both advantages and disadvantages. For example, the owner of Creation Catering is a Haitian immigrant who strives to serve other minorities in the city while wanting to bridge out of his local community into a broader, wealthier market. To do this, he tries to run his business in more formal ways than many of his coethnics are used to. This means he is trying to serve a largely ethnic community, and at the same time he is attempting to do it from a more "mainstream" business model. It does not always work well. This discrepancy, and the difficulties one can face when trying to bridge social and economic differences, creates a dilemma for the entrepreneur. *How do minority entrepreneurs bridge the gap between their ethnic community and the demands of the mainstream economy so that their ventures can grow?*

On the other hand, it might be argued that business owners who are interested only in sustaining a modest income need not worry so much about these distinctions. But if they wish to grow, particularly in communities with relatively weaker institutional infrastructures and more unstable economic situations, they encounter a variety of challenges. For *civic capitalists*, a poor balance of social and economic missions can put the business at risk. Balancing them well can make the business thrive. Yet there is still a risk. As a business grows, the entrepreneur becomes less involved in every decision, perhaps making it more difficult to manage both missions well. Given these challenges, *How does a venture ensure that the dual social and economic missions are held by the organization itself and not simply part of the owner's approach?*

While this study of entrepreneurs from communities in and around Boston is limited due to our small sample ($n = 29$) and the fact that we did not consider a control group, it is but the first step of a panel study. Future research will follow the two cohorts reported on herein for three to four more years. In addition, we plan to add additional cohorts and a comparison sample. Some might argue this sample had a survival bias. This is true inasmuch as we were interested how urban ventures position for growth and expand. Their ability to survive and their motivation to succeed puts these businesses in a better position to positively impact the economic and social environment of urban communities—to create jobs, serve the community, and become entrepreneurial leaders.

Notes

1. Inner cities are defined as core urban areas that have higher unemployment and poverty rates and lower median income than surrounding metropolitan statistical areas (MSAs). Using Census data, the Initiative for a Competitive Inner City (ICIC) estimates that inner cities have a 20 percent poverty rate or higher based on the following criteria: a poverty rate of 1.5 or more times that of their MSA, a median household income of 0.5 or less than their MSA, and an unemployment rate of 1.5 or more times that of their MSA. See http://www.icic.org/vsm/bin/smRenderFS.php.

2. See http://www.riverwestcurrents.org/2004/December/002309html.

3. Increasingly emphasized in a variety of sociological literatures as well as in public discourse, *social capital* is loosely defined here as the resources that flow between people as a result of relationships based on mutual trust and reciprocity (Bourdieu 1983; Coleman 1990; Portes 1998; Putnam 2000). Trust and information channels foster links between people that promote stronger bonds and reinforce norms and values within the group or community (Coleman 1990).

References

Appold, S. J., and J. Kasarda. 2004. Building community through entrepreneurship: Lessons from the US and Vietnam. In *Immigrant and minority entrepreneurship*, ed. J. S. Butler and G. Kozmetsky, 61-84. Westport, CT: Praeger.

Bates, T. 1993. *Major studies of minority business*. Washington, DC: Joint Center for Political and Economic Studies.

———. 2004. Building blocks of viable businesses. Presentation at the Kauffman-UNC Bootcamp on Minority and Women Entrepreneurs, Chapel Hill, NC.

Bird, B. 1989. *Entrepreneurial behavior*. Glenview, IL: Scott, Foresman.

Boston, T. 2004. Research on business dynamics. Presentation at the Kauffman-UNC Bootcamp on Minority and Women Entrepreneurs, Chapel Hill, NC.

Bourdieu, P. 1983. Forms of capital. In *Handbook of theory and research for the sociology of education*, ed. J. Richardson, 241-58. New York: Greenwood.

Bradford, W., and T. Bates. 2004. Venture capital investment in minority business. Working paper presented at the Kauffman-UNC Bootcamp on Minority and Women Entrepreneurs, Chapel Hill, NC.

Brush, C. G., and R. Chaganti. 1998. Businesses without glamour. An analysis of resources on performance by size and age in small service and retail firms. *Journal of Business Venturing* 14 (1): 233-57.

Brush, C. G., D. Monti, A. Gannon, and A. Ryan. 2006. Inner city entrepreneurs: Building ventures and expanding community ties. Conference Presentation at the annual Babson College Entrepreneurship Research Conference, Indianapolis, IN.

Busenitz, L., and C. Lau. 1996. A cross cultural-cognitive model of new venture creation. *Entrepreneurship Theory and Practice* 20 (4): 25-39.

Butler, C. S. 1991. *Entrepreneurship and self-help among black Americans*. Albany: State University of New York Press.

Butler, J., and G. Kozmetsky, G., eds. 2004. *Immigrant and minority entrepreneurship: The continuous rebirth of American communities*. Westport, CT: Praeger.

Carter, N., T. M. Stearns, P. D. Reynolds, and B. Miller. 1994. New venture strategies: The development with an empirical base. *Strategic Management Journal* 15 (1): 21-42.

Cavalluzzo, K. S., L. C. Cavalluzzo, and J. D. Wolken. 2002. Competition, small business financing and discrimination: Evidence from a new survey. *Journal of Business* 75 (4): 641-79.

Chaganti, R., and P. Greene. 2002. Who are ethnic entrepreneurs? A study of entrepreneurs' ethnic involvement and business characteristics. *Journal of Small Business Management* 40 (2): 126-43.

Coleman, James. 1990. *Foundations of social theory*. Cambridge, MA: Harvard University Press.

Cooper, A. C., F. J. Gimeno-Gascon, and C. Y. Woo. 1994. Initial human and financial capital as predictors of new firm performance. *Journal of Business Venturing* 9:371-95.

Covin, J., and D. Slevin. 1997. High growth transitions: Theoretical perspectives and suggested directions. In *Entrepreneurship 2000*, ed. D. L. Sexton and R. W. Smilor. Boston: Upstart Publishing.

Davidsson, P., and J. Wiklund. 2000. Conceptual and empirical challenges in the study of firm growth. In *The Blackwell handbook of entrepreneurship*, ed. D. L. Sexton and H. Landstrom, 26-44. Oxford, UK: Blackwell.

Dees, J. G. 1998. The meaning of social entrepreneurship. http://www.fuqua.duke.edu/centers/case/documents/dees_sedef.pdf.

Fairlie. R. 1999. The absence of African-American owned business: An analysis of the dynamics of self-employment. *Journal of Labor Economics* 17:80-108.

Gerlach, A. 2003. Sustainable entrepreneurship and innovation. Presented at the 2003 Corporate Social Responsibility and Environmental Management Conference, June 30–July 1, University of Leeds, UK.

Granovetter, M. 1985. Economic action and social structure: The problem of embeddedness. *American Journal of Sociology* 91:481-510.

Greene, P. G., and J. Butler. 1996. The minority community as a natural business incubator. *Journal of Business Research* 36:51-58.

Hebert, R., and A. Link. 1982. *The entrepreneur: Mainstream views and radical critiques*. New York: Praeger.

Jack, S., and A. R. Anderson. 2002. The effects of embeddedness on the entrepreneurial process. *Journal of Business Venturing* 17 (5): 467-87.

Jones, O., and S. Conway. 2000. The social embeddedness of entrepreneurs: A re-reading of "against the odds." Working paper, Aston Business School Research Institute, Aston University, Birmingham, UK.

Kirchhoff, B. 1994. *Entrepreneurship and dynamic capitalism*. Westport, CT: Praeger.

Kirzner, I. 1973. *Competition and entrepreneurship*. Chicago: University of Chicago Press.

Light, I., and E. Bonacich. 1988. *Immigrant entrepreneurs: Koreans in Los Angeles, 1965-1982*. Berkeley: University of California Press.

Light, I., and S. Gold. 2000. *Ethnic economies*. San Diego, CA: Academic Press.

Lowrey, J., & Associates. 2005. *The new agenda for minority business development*. Boston: Boston Consulting Group.

Lowrey, Y. 2005. *Dynamics of minority owned establishments, 1997-2001*. Washington, DC: U.S. Office of Advocacy.

Lumpkin, T., and G. Dess. 1996. Clarifying the entrepreneurial orientation and linking it to performance. *Academy of Management Review* 21 (1): 135-49.

Monti, D. 1999. *The American city*. Oxford, UK: Blackwell.

Penrose, E. 1959. *Theory of growth of the firm*. New York: John Wiley.

Porter, M. E. 1985. *Competitive advantage*. New York: Free Press.

———. 1995. The competitive advantage of the inner city. *Harvard Business Review* 55:71.

Portes, Alejandro. 1998. Social capital: Its origins and applications in modern sociology. *Annual Review of Sociology* 24:1-24.

Portes, A., and J. Sensenbrenner. 1993. Embeddedness and immigration: Notes on the social determinants of economic action. *American Journal of Sociology* 98 (6): 1320-50.

Putnam, R. 2000. *Bowling alone: The collapse and revival of American community*. New York: Simon & Schuster.

Reynolds, P., N. Carter, W. Gartner, and P. Greene. 2004. The prevalence of nascent entrepreneurs in the United States: Evidence from the Panel Study of Entrepreneurial Dynamics. *Small Business Economics* 23:263-84.

Robb, A., and R. Fairlie. 2007. Why are black-owned businesses less successful than white-owned businesses? The role of families, inheritances, and business human capital. *Journal of Labor Economics* 25:289-323.

Robinson, K. 2004. Understanding entrepreneurship development as a local problem-solving strategy. Working paper presented at the meeting of the Rural Sociological Society, Sacramento, CA.

Schumpeter, J. 1935. *The theory of economic development*. New York: Oxford University Press.

Sexton, D., and J. Kasarda, eds. 1997. *The state of the art of entrepreneurship*. Boston: PWS Kent.

Simmel, G. 1971. Group expansion and the development of individuality. In *Georg Simmel: On individuality and social forms*, ed. D. Levine. Chicago: University of Chicago Press.

Timmons, J., and S. Spinelli. 2007. *New venture creation*. 7th ed. New York: McGraw-Hill.

Uzzi, B. 1997. Social structure and competition in inter-firm networks: The paradox of embeddedness. *Administrative Science Quarterly* 42 (1): 35-68.

Woolcock, M., and D. Narayan. 1999. Social capital: Implications for theory development, research and policy. *World Bank Research Observer* 15:2.

Tax Refunds and Microbusinesses: Expanding Family and Community Wealth Building in the Borderlands

By
BÁRBARA J. ROBLES

The Earned Income Tax Credit (EITC) is the largest antipoverty fiscal policy program for working families administered by the Internal Revenue Service (EITCs totaled $42 billion in 2003). For the 2004 tax season, U.S.-Mexico border county EITC refunds reached $1.9 billion while total tax refund amounts for low-income borderlands families topped $2.6 billion. Questionnaires administered during the tax-filing season to working families in Texas, New Mexico, Arizona, and California border counties collected more than forty-five hundred surveys that canvassed respondents on a variety of financial behaviors and tax refund expenditures. Additionally, researchers recorded data on tax filers using their tax refunds to capitalize microbusinesses and respondents' desires to know more about operating a microbusiness. Empirical analysis employing logistic regression produces results that parallel previous findings in the literature and suggests actionable policy prescriptions that may support family and community entrepreneurial activities in the borderlands.

Keywords: Earned Income Tax Credit; microbusiness and self-employment; asset building programs

In Latino ethnic enclaves, family formation often entails multiple earners, multiple generations, and a larger number of dependent children. This implies that family income is distributed among more family members (and family not residing in the households) than the typical American nuclear family. The degree of unemployment along the U.S.-Mexico border plays a profound role in the ability of families in the borderlands to secure a financially stable future for their children and has a positive relationship with poverty rates. Fifty-five percent of all Hispanics in the United States (42.7 million) reside in the four border states: Texas, New Mexico, Arizona, and California (U.S. Census Bureau 2006). The high concentration of Latinos in the region corresponds to a greater incidence of seasonal jobs, low-wage service sector jobs, and a larger labor pool with lower educational attainment characteristics. As

DOI: 10.1177/0002716207303602

public assistance income declines with more stringent eligibility rules legislated by the 1996 Welfare Reform Act, more families are engaging in self-employment and microbusiness activities, and the number of earners in families continues to increase.

The amount of informal economic activity is also related to stagnant job creation, high unemployment rates, and chronically depressed wages (Servon and Bates 1998). As more entrepreneurial activity increases in the region, formalizing "income patching" (families engaging in entrepreneurial activities that help "patch" their wages) becomes a crucial policy issue both for individual families (using microbusiness and self-employment as asset-leveraging vehicles) as well as local governments (capturing new revenue streams). A large portion of the microbusiness and self-employment activities in both the informal and formal markets along the southwest border are highly correlated with economic survival strategies and are often the second or third job for the working adult (see Figure 1).

What constitutes an informal economic activity? Informal economic activities range from bartering goods, to extending reciprocal favors in the form of babysitting and housecleaning, to day labor and odd jobs as well as taking in laundry for cash or in-kind services without a recorded transaction occurring. Another frequent cash or service exchange is ethnic and cultural food preparation. Working poor families often engage in cash and in-kind activities as a means to supplement low-wage formal work. Even as informal economic activity serves to buffer erratic income flows for families on the borderlands and can be identified as an asset-enhancing activity, the lack of recorded exchange of services for a fee represents a challenge for community-based organizations engaged in financial and tax education and tax preparation services (see Figure 2).

On the one hand, informal economic activity helps keep struggling working poor families from experiencing stressful economic and financial losses during periods when seasonal work is unavailable. On the other hand, formalizing such activities can be used to leverage asset- and wealth-building opportunities for low-resourced Latino families. The challenge lies in educating workers and families on their tax rights and documenting income streams from services provided. This helps create a track record for the individual; opens up avenues of

Bárbara J. Robles joined the College of Public Programs at Arizona State University as an associate professor in August 2005. She currently sits on the Board of Economic Advisors for the U.S. Hispanic Chamber of Commerce. She is a coauthor of The Color of Wealth: The Story Behind the U.S. Racial Wealth Divide *(New Press, 2006) and author of* Asset Accumulation and Economic Development in Latino Communities: A National and Border Economy Profile of Latino Families *(Filene Research Institute, 2006). She is a research fellow at the Filene Research Institute.*

NOTE: The Annie E. Casey Foundation, the Filene Research Institute, and the Frontera Asset Building (FAB) Coalition are partners in the creation of a new regional data source. My excellent research assistants were instrumental in processing the data. I thank the Kauffman Foundation for research support. I particularly benefited from the discussions and presentations by colleagues at the summer Entrepreneurship Bootcamp conferences at the University of North Carolina at Chapel Hill.

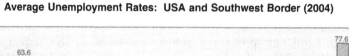

FIGURE 1
AVERAGE UNEMPLOYMENT RATES: UNITED STATES AND
SOUTHWEST BORDER, 2004

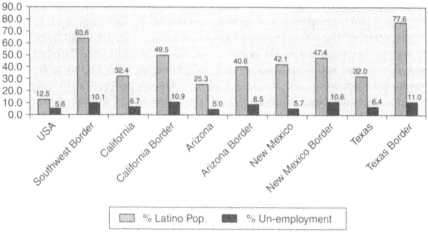

SOURCE: Monthly, state and local unemployment statistics, U.S. Bureau of Labor Statistics, author's calculations.

FIGURE 2
EMPLOYMENT CREATED BY MICROBUSINESS IN
BORDER COUNTIES BY STATE, 2003

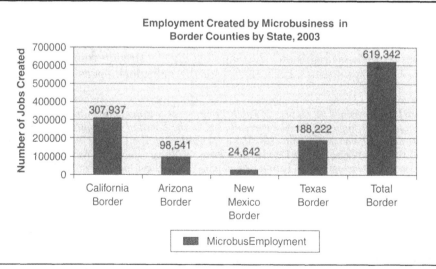

SOURCE: Nonemployer statistics, county business patterns, full-time and part-time county employment statistics, U.S. Department of Commerce, American Enterprise Opportunity (www.aeo.org).

leveraging informal work activity by transitioning into formal business activity; and creates new sources of fiscal revenues for local, state, and federal government.

Working poor families often engage in cash and in-kind activities as a means to supplement low-wage formal work.

Tax Refunds and Tax Filing

Many studies focusing on the African American population in the United States offer innovative public policies that have aided the black population in building community financial assets and resources.[1] Such research has helped shape newly emerging policies on housing, enterprise zoning, and taxation relief for families, individuals, and microenterprise minority businesses. In approaching the subject of asset and wealth building in low-income Latino communities, especially those communities located on the U.S.-Mexico border, awareness of educational attainment levels becomes central to understanding the degree of disenfranchisement that exists in many of the *colonias*[2] and border communities.

Financial and economic choices are fundamentally intertwined with consumer skills that are generally learned through intergenerational transfer of knowledge and frequent exposure to mainstream markets. For native-born, middle-class Americans, basic financial concepts are often learned by watching parents or adult caretakers engage in monthly budgeting, bill paying, and consumer purchases. For non-native-born working poor families arriving from countries with class-oriented financial institutions (limited to serving wealthy customers) and severely underdeveloped credit systems, these concepts and activities are skills to master. Moreover, for native-born families residing in isolated communities in the United States that rely on cash and informal barter systems, familiarity with mainstream financial services and products is difficult to acquire since mainstream financial institutions are often absent.

Understanding income tax responsibilities and rights are also asset- and wealth-building skills and are often overlooked as a component in financial education curricula and outreach. Studies and research indicate that the Earned Income Tax Credit (EITC) has been successful in providing substantial economic relief to a growing segment of the U.S. population: low-income workers (see Table 1).[3]

TABLE 1
DISTRIBUTION OF TAX PROVISIONS: U.S. EARNED INCOME TAX
CREDIT (EITC), 2003 (TAX YEAR 2002)

Income Class	Joint Returns		Head of Household and Single Returns		All Returns		Average EITC Refund
	Number	Amount	Number	Amount	Number	Amount	
$0-$10,000	510	$816	5,062	$6,129	5,572	$6,945	$1,246.41
$10,000-$20,000	1,033	$2,851	4,505	$10,901	5,538	$13,752	$2,483.21
$20,000-$30,000	1,327	$3,007	3,207	$6,758	4,534	$9,766	$2,153.95
$30,000-$40,000	1,229	$1,543	1,765	$1,976	2,994	$3,519	$1,175.35
$40,000-$50,000	397	$262	210	$130	608	$392	$644.74
$50,000-$75,000	36	$37	2	$2	38	$39	$1,026.32
$75,000 and over	0	$0	0	$0	0	$0	
All returns	4,533	$8,516	14,752	$25,896	19,284	$34,412	$1,784.48

SOURCE: U.S. House (2004).
NOTE: Number of returns in thousands, amounts in millions except in the average EITC Refund column.

National data on labor force participation rates indicate that Latinos have higher rates of labor force participation. For example in 2005, Latinos with less than a high school degree have a 61 percent participation rate compared to whites (46 percent) and blacks (40 percent). Latinos with a high school diploma have a 74 percent participation rate in the labor force, while whites with comparable education have a 63 percent rate and blacks have a 68 percent rate.[4] Thus, regardless of family type, more Latinos are eligible for the EITC, yet research shows that Hispanics are least likely to be aware of this refunded tax credit and less likely to claim it compared to whites and blacks (Maag 2005; Staveteig and Wigton 2000). As Table 2 indicates, $302 million in potential EITC refunds went unclaimed in tax year (TY) 2002.

Survey Design and Descriptive Indicators

In 2003, a series of roundtable conversations among borderlands family and community asset-building practitioners was convened. One outcome from the roundtable discussions was the formation of a four-state borderlands tax education, preparation, and asset-building community nonprofit coalition: the Frontera Asset Building (FAB) Coalition. The community-university FAB coalition partners designed a Financial Behaviors and Needs Survey (FBNS) that is administered at participating Southwest border tax preparation and filing locations during

TABLE 2
EARNED INCOME TAX CREDIT (EITC) BORDERLANDS AVERAGE REFUND
AMOUNTS, RETURNS FILED IN 2003 (TAX YEAR 2002)

	Total EITC Claimed (Returns)	Total EITC Claimed (Amount in Millions)	Estimated Eligible EITC Unclaimed (Amount in Millions)	Estimated Eligible EITC Nonfilers (Returns)	Average Claimed EITC Refund (Amount)	Average Eligible EITC Refund (Amount)
Southwest border	705,001	$1,419	$302	181,131	$2,013	$1,812
California border	209,916	$354	$95	62,101	$1,688	$1,529
Arizona border	102,083	$187	$27	24,820	$1,827	$1,672
New Mexico border	37,831	$76	$4	5,127	$1,931	$1,921
Texas border	355,171	$805	$175	89,083	$2,268	$2,035

SOURCE: Stakeholder Partnerships, Education and Communication (SPEC), Internal Revenue Service, Austin Territory, 2004, proprietary data.

tax season. During the 2004 tax-filing season (TY2003), more than fifty sites located in rural and urban border counties in Texas, New Mexico, and Arizona successfully administered 1,992 surveys (pilot data). In the 2005 tax season (TY2004), 4,689 surveys were collected at fifty sites in California, Arizona, New Mexico, and Texas (baseline data). For summary statistics and modeling results, I rely on the 2005 tax season survey baseline data.

Many of the community-based organizations administering the survey were community development corporations (CDCs) operating community development financial institutions (CDFIs) that provided microbusiness support services. We designed the survey to capture microbusiness owners' financial behaviors and needs (see Figure 3) and their use of tax refunds to capitalize their operations.

The results of the 2005 tax season survey provide an instructive and compelling empirical snapshot of families with an average adjusted gross income[5] (AGI) of $11,780 and an average total tax refund of $1,309 (which includes EITC). In contrast, the results for the microbusiness owners subsample provides a differing snapshot of the tax season 2005 survey respondents ($n = 202$). For example, the microbusiness owners had a lower average AGI at $9,845 but a higher average total tax refund of $1,460. Also, they had a greater degree of lending to and borrowing from family members, 55 percent compared to all border filers, 47 percent (see Table 3).

· Three relevant findings provide a deeper understanding of how tax refunds are leveraged into asset- and wealth-building activities (see Figure 4): (1) microbusiness owners expend tax refunds on schooling for themselves or their children to a higher degree than the total border tax-filing population, (2) microbusiness owners expend their tax refunds on property taxes to a higher degree, and (3) microbusiness owners allocated their tax refunds on acquiring a home to a greater degree.

FIGURE 3
FINANCIAL BEHAVIORS AND NEEDS SURVEY, TY2004

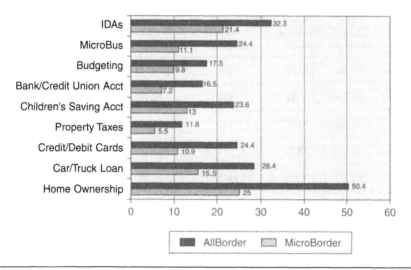

Would you like to learn more about:

SOURCE: Proprietary data from the Financial Behaviors and Needs Survey, Tax Year 2004, Tax Season 2005.
NOTE: AllBorder, n = 4,689; MicroBorder, n = 202.

Logit Model Results and Discussion

The variables used in the logistic estimation capture how low-wealth tax filers expend their tax refunds on microbusiness and self-employment activities. The variables[6] consist of demographic, socioeconomic, and behavioral characteristics that contribute to understanding the resiliency of low-resourced entrepreneurs engaging in income patching and income-generating opportunities. These variables are presented in Table 4.

The first logit model (model 1) investigates the usage of tax refunds on microbusiness or on self-employment. The qualitative binary dependent variable takes on the value of one if a tax filer used his or her tax refund on microbusiness or on self-employment and takes the value of zero otherwise. The explanatory variables are AGI (total dollars), refund amount (total dollars), years of education (total years), use of a mainstream financial institution (dummy variable), number of dependents (total number), English-language survey used (dummy variable), tax refund used for property taxes (dummy variable), use of tax refund on school expenses (dummy variable), and expressed interest in knowing more about microbusinesses or self-employment (dummy variable) (see Table 5).

The results of the logit estimation for model 1 indicate that English proficiency, using tax refunds to pay property taxes (proxy for homeownership), using

FIGURE 4
FINANCIAL BEHAVIORS AND NEEDS SURVEY, TY2004

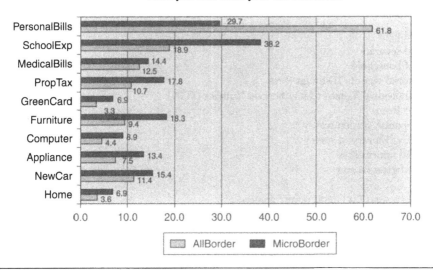

Have you ever used your tax refund for:

SOURCE: Proprietary data from the Financial Behaviors and Needs Survey, Tax Year 2004, Tax Season 2005.
NOTE: MicroBorder, $n = 202$; AllBorder, $n = 4,698$.

tax refunds on school expenses, and wanting to learn more about self-employment and microbusiness ownership (a proxy for wanting to gain access to business operations information) are all statistically significant and directly contribute to increasing the probability of using tax refunds to capitalize microbusiness or self-employment activities. The mainstream financial services and education coefficients are negative and statistically significant, albeit the usage of bank or credit union dummy coefficient is significant at the 10 percent level. Both tell interesting stories: as years of education increase, the probability of using tax refunds to capitalize microbusiness ownership and operations declines. This result is entirely unsurprising given that increased education provides a greater degree of self-employment and microbusiness capitalization options, while the increase of mainstream financial services usage also decreases the probability of using tax refunds to capitalize self-employment and entrepreneurial activities. These results make sense: more education and increased bank or credit union usage lead to a wider menu of options for capitalizing entrepreneurial activities.

The second logit model (model 2) examines the probability of the tax filer expressing interest in wanting to know more about self-employment or microbusiness ownership. The qualitative binary dependent variable takes on the value of one if the tax filer wants to know more about self-employment or

TABLE 3
SUMMARY STATISTICS FOR MICROBUSINESS OWNERS,
TAX YEAR 2004/TAX SEASON 2005

Filing status	
Single	46.9%
Married-joint	20.3%
Married-separate	0%
Head of household	32.8%
Using social security ID on tax form	94%
Using Individual Taxpayer Identification Number (ITIN) on tax form	6%
Using Spanish version survey	37%
Using English version survey	63%
Financial information	
Adjusted gross income	Mean = $9,845, median = $7,071
Earned Income Tax Credit refund amount	Mean = $819, median = $220
Total tax refund amount	Mean = $1,460, median = $1,049
Informal group savings participation	3.8%
Informal group maximum amount saved by individual	$5,000
Informal group total amount saved	$9,300
Percentage sending money to family not in household	27%
Percentage borrowing/lending from family	55%
Percentage using money order to pay bills	47%
Percentage using mainstream financial services	76%

SOURCE: Proprietary data from the Financial Behaviors and Needs Survey, Tax Year 2004, Tax Season 2005.
NOTE: Observations = 202.

microbusiness and zero otherwise. The explanatory variables in the model are AGI (dollar amount), tax refund received (dollar amount), years of education (number), number of dependents (number), English survey used (dummy variable), use of mainstream financial institution (dummy variable), tax refund used for education expenses (dummy variable), tax refund used on microbusiness or self-employment activity (dummy variable), and tax refund used to pay property taxes (dummy variable) (see Table 6).

The results for model 2 provide a snapshot of the microbusiness owner/self-employed aspirant. The two variables associated with education, actual years of education and using tax refunds on educational expenses, increase the probability of wanting to know more about microbusiness ownership and self-employment information. Similarly, using tax refunds to capitalize self-employment or microbusiness activities increases the probability of wanting to know more about

TABLE 4
SUMMARY STATISTICS FOR VARIABLES IN LOGIT MODEL (N = 2,138)

	Mean (or Proportion if Dummy Variable)	Standard Deviation	Minimum Value	Maximum Value
Dependent variables				
Used tax refund for microbusiness	.017	.129	0	1
Wants to know more about microbusiness	.081	.269	0	1
Explanatory variables				
Adjusted gross income (AGI)	$12,978	$12,397	$0	$82,465
Tax refund amount	$1,458	$1,669	–$1,837	$7,498
Years of education	11.2	3.9	0	28
Number of dependents	1.8	1.3	0	7
Explanatory dummy variables				
Uses English survey	.763	.425	0	1
Uses bank/credit union	.777	.416	0	1
Uses tax refund for property taxes	.098	.298	0	1
Uses tax refund for education	.166	.372	0	1

SOURCE: Proprietary data from the Financial Behaviors and Needs Survey, Tax Year 2004, Tax Season 2005.

entrepreneurship. Additionally, the refund dollar amount also increases the probability of wanting to acquire more business and/or self-employment information. In model 1, neither AGI nor tax refund amount contributed to the probability of using the tax refund on microbusinesses (neither was statistically significant). In model 2, the tax refund amount has a direct relationship with the probability of wanting to know more about self-employment and microbusiness operations.

Taken together, the findings from the two models provide insight into the role that education and tax refund expenditures play in the economic resiliency behaviors of low-resourced tax filers with limited leveraging options for entrepreneurial activities. What is clear from these suggestive results is that tax refund recipients who expend on education increase their capacity to engage in wealth-enhancing activities. These findings parallel the results previously reported in the literature by Servon and Bates (1998) and Bates (1990) for low-resourced individuals engaged in service sector small business operations. Continuing education and engaging in wealth leveraging activities (paying property taxes with tax refunds and capitalizing microbusiness and self-employment activities with tax refunds) create opportunities for asset building and economic stability for income-constrained entrepreneurial aspirants.

TABLE 5
LOGIT MODEL 1

Coefficient Variable	Model 1: Dependent Variable = Tax Refund Used for Microbusiness/Self-Employment (n = 1,318), Estimated Coefficient
Adjusted gross income (AGI)	−0.00004 (−1.56)
Refund	0.0002 (1.20)
Education	−0.107 (−2.15)**
Dependents	0.059 (0.318)
Bank/credit union usage	−0.902 (−1.86)*
Survey English	1.12 (1.83)*
Used tax refund for property taxes	2.06 (4.10)***
Used tax refund for education	1.07 (2.34)**
Wants to know more about self-employment/microbusiness	1.18 (2.11)**
Likelihood ratio (zero slope)	36.37***

NOTE: t-statistics are given in parentheses.
*Significant at .10. **Significant at .05. ***Significant at .01.

What is clear from these suggestive results is that tax refund recipients who expend on education increase their capacity to engage in wealth-enhancing activities.

Conclusions, Policy Recommendations, and Future Research Directions

The borderlands has a significant Latino population with specialized family formation characteristics. The slow growth of low- to medium-skilled wage employment plays a decisive role in economic resiliency and entrepreneurial behaviors in both the rural and metropolitan areas of southwest border counties. However, the economic conditions that create challenges for struggling communities are also opportunities for microbusiness and entrepreneurial initiatives. To continue to grow tax revenues at local and regional levels, policies that encourage formalizing informal entrepreneurial activities are crucial to realizing community productive capacity.

TABLE 6
LOGIT MODEL 2

Coefficient Variable	Model 2: Dependent Variable = Wanting to Know More about Self-Employment or Microbusiness Ownership (n = 1,318), Estimated Coefficient
Adjusted gross income (AGI)	−0.00001 (−1.07)
Refund	0.00014 (1.93)**
Education	0.074 (2.49)***
Dependents	0.088 (0.978)
Bank/credit union usage	0.028 (0.107)
Survey English	−0.248 (−0.964)
Used tax refund for property taxes	−0.486 (−1.26)
Used tax refund for education	0.569 (2.40)**
Used tax refund for microbusiness/ self-employment	1.21 (2.22)**
Likelihood ratio (zero slope)	28.54***

NOTE: t-statistics are given in parentheses.
*Significant at .10. **Significant at .05. ***Significant at .01.

From previous literature (Servon and Bates 1998; Bates 1990; Velez-Ibanez 2004; Robles 2006), policies promoting education and skills-building benefit two groups of entrepreneurs: (1) those with college education who can leverage their human capital into growing enterprises while requiring more mentoring from established entrepreneurs helping them to expand their market reach and commercial banking networks beyond ethnic enclaves; and (2) those with limited education who require policies focused on basic entrepreneurial skills and basic knowledge of formal market entry where community organizations offering microbusiness support services act as mediators and facilitators for mainstream financial institutions and formal markets. Each group requires a specific policy action aimed at its particular life cycle and human capital profile. A one-size-fits-all policy for entrepreneurs of color does not create permanent change; nor does it reflect the intragroup diversity of nascent and established entrepreneurs, those "income patching," or those engaged in stabilizing and expanding operations.

This study has focused on the second group of aspiring microbusiness owners and the self-employed. Through tax and asset-building outreach programs connected to skills-building, community-based support services, many of the hard-to-reach entrepreneur aspirants can be connected to formal business operations and mainstream financial institutions. We have seen that despite low-resourced status, borderlands tax filers strategically use their tax refunds in ways that increase wealth-enhancing opportunities. These findings support previous findings in the literature that education is a crucial factor in asset building for families and, consequently, for communities. New data sources and ongoing data collection efforts help create new research findings and policy directions. Data collection that creates an intersection between financial behaviors, economic resiliency choices, and wealth-building opportunities brings with it more understanding of low-resourced community needs.

Notes

1. For low-income families, research such as Caskey (1994), Sherridan (1991), and Shapiro and Wolff (2001) focus only on "low-income status." For the African American population, research that identifies the unique historical, cultural, and racial legacy of policies include Conley (1999), Oliver and Shapiro (1995), Shapiro (2004), and Darity and Myers (1998).

2. The term *colonia* is a Spanish word for neighborhood or community. However, the term colonia conveys a unique meaning along the U.S.-Mexico border. These *colonias* are areas of nonincorporated townships that may lack basic water and sewage systems, paved roads, safe and sanitary housing conditions, phone service, and school and public health facilities (Federal Reserve Bank of Dallas 1996).

3. The Earned Income Tax Credit (EITC) is the largest single source of federal support for low-income families (Stanfield 2002).

4. See U.S. Census Bureau (2007).

5. Adjusted gross income (AGI) is defined as taxable income from all sources including wages; salaries; tips; taxable interest; ordinary dividends; taxable refunds, credits, or offsets of state and local income taxes; alimony received; business income or loss; capital gains or losses; other gains or losses; taxable IRA distributions; taxable pensions and annuities; rental real estate; royalties; farm income or losses; unemployment compensation; taxable social security benefits; and other income minus specific deductions including educator expenses, the IRA deduction, student loan interest deduction, tuition and fees deduction, Archer MSA deduction, moving expenses, one-half of self-employment tax, self-employed health insurance deduction, self-employed SEP, SIMPLE, and qualified plans, penalty on early withdrawal of savings, and alimony paid.

6. The original survey collected 4,698 tax filer respondents answering financial questions that are reported in Figures 3 and 4. The tax data (AGI, refund, number of dependents) was reported by volunteer tax preparers. Combining the tax data with the respondents' information reduces the sample size to 2,138 observations.

References

Bates, T. 1990. Self-employment trends among Mexican-Americans. Working Paper CES 90-9, Center for Economic Studies, U.S. Census Bureau, Washington, DC.

Caskey, J. 1994. *Fringe banking: Check-cashing outlets, pawnshops and the poor.* New York: Russell Sage Foundation.

Conley, Dalton. 1999. *Being black, living in the red: Race, wealth, and social policy in America.* Berkeley: University of California Press.

Darity, W., Jr., and S. Myers Jr. 1998. *Persistent disparity: Race and economic inequality in the United States since 1945.* Northampton, MA: Edward Elgar.

Federal Reserve Bank of Dallas, Community Affairs Department. 1996. *Texas Colonias: A thumbnail sketch of the conditions, issues, challenges and opportunities.* http://dallasfed.org/ca/pubs/colonias.html.

Maag, E. 2005. Disparities in knowledge of the EITC. *Tax Notes*, March 14: 1323.

Oliver, M., and T. Shapiro. 1995. *Black wealth/white wealth: A new perspective on racial inequality.* London: Routledge.

Robles, B. 2006. *Asset accumulation and economic development in Latino Communities: A national and border economy profile of Latino families.* Filene Research Institute Monograph, July, Filine Research Institute, Madison, WI.

Servon, L., and T. Bates. 1998. Microenterprise as an exit route from poverty. *Journal of Urban Affairs* 28 (4): 419-41.

Shapiro, T. 2004. *The hidden cost of being African American: How wealth perpetuates inequality.* New York: Oxford University Press.

Shapiro, T., and E. Wolff, eds. 2001. *Assets for the poor: The benefits of spreading asset ownership*. Ford Foundation Series on Asset Building. New York: Russell Sage Foundation.

Sherridan, M. 1991. *Assets and the poor: A new American welfare policy*. Armonk, NY: M. E. Sharpe.

Stanfield, R. 2002. *Social policy and the tax system*. Washington, DC: Tax Policy Research Program, The Urban Institute. http://www.urban.org.

Staveteig, S., and A. Wigton. 2000. *Racial and ethnic disparities: Key findings from the survey of America's families*. Series B, No. B-5, February. Washington, DC: New Federalism Program, The Urban Institute.

U.S. Census Bureau. 2006. *U.S. Census Bureau News*, CB06-72, May 10. Washington, DC: U.S. Department of Commerce.

———. 2007. *Statistical abstract of the United States: 2007*. Table 578, Labor Force, Employment and Earnings. Washington, DC: U.S. Census Bureau, U.S. Department of Commerce. http://www.census .gov/prod/2006pubs/07statab/labor.pdf.

U.S. House of Representatives, Joint Committee on Taxation, Ways and Means Committee. 2004. *Green book, 2004*. Washington, DC: Government Printing Office.

Velez-Ibanez, C. 2004. Regions of refuge in the United States: Issues, problems and concerns for the future of Mexican-Americans in the United States. *Human Organization* 63 (1): 1-20.

QUICK READ SYNOPSIS

Q
R
S

Advancing Research on Minority Entrepreneurship

Special Editors: TIMOTHY BATES,
Wayne State University;
WILLIAM E. JACKSON III,
University of Alabama

and

JAMES H. JOHNSON Jr.,
University of North Carolina at Chapel Hill

Volume 613, September 2007

Prepared by Herb Fayer, Jerry Lee Foundation

DOI: 10.1177/0002716207305590

Latino Self-Employment and Entrepreneurship in the United States: An Overview of the Literature and Data Sources

Bárbara J. Robles, Arizona State University; and
Héctor Cordero-Guzmán, City University of New York

Background   While attention has been paid to Latino growth and its contribution to the U.S. labor market, less scholarly and popular media attention has focused on Latino self-employment, entrepreneurship, and business growth.

- A gap exists in our knowledge about the accelerated growth in Latino small business ownership across the United States.
- This article provides an overview of the current state of research on Latino entrepreneurial activities and recommends a broader research agenda that includes community based organizations as part of the entrepreneurship landscape in high-density Latino communities.
- The most recent results from the *Hispanic Owned Business Survey: 2002* indicate that 1.57 million Hispanic-owned businesses operate in the United States and are growing at a rate of 31 percent (three times the national average).
- Although both current data availability and previous policy initiatives have substantive limitations, the authors are encouraged by the debate among Latino small business scholars who have pioneered investigating Latino entrepreneurial activity in the United States.

Research Needs Although the data collected on Latino business owners and the self-employed have improved over time, continuing analyses of the available data creates questions arising from scholarly findings for this particular community.

- Does successful management of small businesses despite low levels of education and low family wealth relate to a family member (especially an extended family member) having owned a business?
- For researchers seeking to understand the entrepreneurial activities of particular Latino groups, the Decennial Census and Current Population Surveys are the only large data sources that specifically capture Latino country of origin data.
- The self-employed as described in the Public Use Microdata database is only one segment of a diverse Latino entrepreneurial landscape.

Findings From the overview of Latino self-employment and entrepreneurship research, a consistent set of findings emerge that help explain both the accelerated growth of Latino entrepreneurial activity while capturing the barriers to successful small-business life-cycle transitions.

- Low educational levels continue to be statistically significant and may be a driving force in the push into self-employment while contributing to the marginal existence of many Latino small businesses.
- Lack of financial resources (personal wealth or access to capital) for operation/expansion purposes contributes to block business growth.
- Latino entrepreneurial activity continues to be concentrated in the service sector.

NOTE: These three persistent indicators have not changed significantly for the Latino population over the past twenty-five years. Policies crafted in a one-size-fits-all mold, however well intentioned, have contributed to the unchanging nature of the Latino business community indicators.

Conclusion Research that continues to uncover the facets of the social and community links between the micro-entrepreneur and self-employed sector with the economic realities of community revitalization, gentrification, sustainable urbanism, transnational migration, ethnic biculturalism, and the permeable boundaries of the ethnic enclave would provide us with a deeper understanding of the role of the smallest entrepreneur in Latino communities.

- The college-educated pool of Latino entrepreneurs is becoming more visible and requires researchers to recognize the bimodal nature of policy application for different entrepreneurial stakeholders.
- Policy prescriptions aimed at the Latino college-educated entrepreneurial population anchored in university-business partnerships and collaborative programs that bring more entrepreneurship-skills programs and business leadership mentoring into the postgraduate, university, and community college environment could prove to have more permanent and positive outcomes.
- Policies that include a pipeline component that creates linkages to community-based Latino serving organizations engaged in micro-enterprise lending and financial education services would provide an upwardly mobile avenue for the less educated aspiring entrepreneur.

Q
R
S

Mexican-Hispanic Self-Employment Entry: The Role of Business Start-Up Constraints

Magnus Lofstrom, University of Texas at Dallas and Institute for the Study of Labor; and Chunbei Wang, University of Texas at Dallas

Q
R
S

Background

This article contributes to the minority entrepreneurship research by analyzing self-employment among Mexican-Hispanics, an important minority group that has been relatively overlooked in the entrepreneurship literature.

- A major focus of the literature is on the role of access to financial capital:
  - Do capital constraints shape self-employment entry and exit?
  - The data reveal that Mexican-Hispanic males are substantially less likely to be business owners, relative to whites.
- Greater assets, measured as inheritances, lead to higher probability of business survival, suggesting that liquidity constraints are binding.
- Owner educational background is a major determinant of business survival and the financial capital structure of small business start-ups.
- Other factors linked to the self-employment entry decision include managerial ability; risk aversion; nonpecuniary benefits of owning one's business; and intergenerational links, including parental wealth.
- Another factor is differential treatment in the credit market. Credit constraints impact the types of industries that minorities seek to enter.

NOTE: Like African Americans, Hispanics are a disadvantaged minority group. There are a number of differences between the two groups, however, particularly regarding family composition, educational attainment, immigration status, and historical experiences in the United States. This article focuses on the largest Hispanic group in the United States, Mexican-Hispanics.

Self-Employment

The authors address the role of differences in the industry composition of entrepreneurs in explaining the relatively low Mexican-Hispanic self-employment rate.

Potential Barriers

The self-employment entry difficulties Mexican-Hispanics may face are possibly due to low endowments of human capital, as well as limited access to financial resources.

- Close to one-half of self-employed Mexican-Hispanics have not completed high school, and only 9 percent are college graduates.
- There appear to be significant differences in human capital endowment, and possibly financial resources, between Mexican-Hispanics and whites. Mean business equity is found to be lower among Hispanic-owned businesses than white-owned businesses.
- Self-employment entry by industry groups shows that the lower self-employment entry rate among Mexican-Hispanics is due to lower business start-up rates in the medium- and high-barrier industries.
- The result of limited access to capital is higher failure rates.

NOTE: Mexican-Hispanics are more likely than whites to become business owners in the low-barrier industry group, the industry group where Mexican-Hispanic business start-ups are concentrated.

Conclusion   The findings in this article are consistent with the hypothesis that the lower self-employment rate among Mexican-Hispanics, relative to whites, is at least partially due to human and financial capital start-up constraints.
- The lower educational attainment levels among Mexican-Hispanics appear to restrict business start-ups to low-barrier industries.
- Policies aimed at increasing the currently low average Mexican-Hispanic schooling levels may also succeed in increasing the Hispanic self-employment rate.
- An important issue for future research is to assess whether there are differences in the success of self-employed Mexican-Hispanics and whites within industry groups.
- The entry barriers addressed in this article may also affect the success of Mexican-Hispanic entrepreneurs, which may be one of the mechanisms that lead to the observed low Mexican-Hispanic self-employment rate.

Q
R
S

Access to Financial Capital among U.S. Businesses: The Case of African American Firms

Alicia M. Robb, University of California, Santa Cruz;
and Robert W. Fairlie, University of California, Santa Cruz,
and National Poverty Center, University of Michigan

Background   African Americans are found to have levels of wealth that are one-eleventh those of whites.
- The median level of net worth for black households is only $6,166.
- Blacks are much less likely to start businesses than are whites, which results in a substantially lower rate of business ownership.
- Among black entrepreneurs successful in starting businesses, it is found that they invest much less capital at start-up on average than white entrepreneurs.
- Lower levels of start-up capital among black businesses appear to also limit their ability to grow and succeed.
- Racial disparities in start-up capital contribute to higher failure rates, lower sales and profits, and less employment among black-owned businesses.
- Evidence from the Survey of Small Business Finances suggests black-owned businesses face significant barriers to access to capital, which are possibly due to lending discrimination.
- Black businesses are less likely to have loans approved and are more likely to not apply for loans because of fear of denial.

NOTE: Given the importance of financial capital in a firm's formation and ability to survive, credit market imperfections can have profound implications for business performance and viability. Minority-owned businesses lag behind non-minority-owned businesses in terms of sales, profits, survivability, and employment; facing greater obstacles in obtaining financing for their businesses implies that an already difficult situation worsens.

The Study   This study addresses issues of low levels of black personal wealth, limiting the formation of new businesses and lower levels of start-up capital resulting in less successful black-owned businesses relative to white-owned businesses, including the following:

- *Black-white disparities in business ownership and outcomes*—White non-Latinos and Asians have the highest self-employment rates, whereas blacks have the lowest rates.
- *Wealth inequality*—Blacks are overwhelmingly more likely to have low asset levels and less likely to have high asset levels than are whites.
- *Personal wealth and business entry*—Current findings are consistent with the presence of liquidity constraints and low levels of assets, limiting opportunities for black entrepreneurs to start businesses.
- *Start-up capital*—Black entrepreneurs invest less start-up capital in their business because they have less access to capital.
- *Borrowing patterns and discrimination in lending*—Black and white entrepreneurs differ in the types of financing they use for their businesses. (Although these differences are likely to be caused by many factors, they may be partly due to differences in personal wealth and lending discrimination.)

Conclusions   Several important policy implications evolve from this research.
- Address potential discrimination in the lending market.
  - This may be accomplished through additional oversight by the lending community.
  - This could entail improved training for internal loan review practices in financial institutions.
- Technical assistance programs to assist minority-owned businesses with starting and operating a business, applying for a loan, and financial literacy and accounting training are some other types of programs that could benefit minority-owned businesses and help them access credit markets.
- Finally, programs like individual development accounts and first-time homeowner programs that help low-income people build assets and human capital could also help these individuals build the financial and human capital needed to start and succeed in entrepreneurship.

Small Firm Credit Market Discrimination, Small Business Administration Guaranteed Lending, and Local Market Economic Performance

Ben R. Craig, Federal Reserve Bank of Cleveland;
William E. Jackson III, University of Alabama; and James B. Thomson,
Federal Reserve Bank of Cleveland

Background   Minority entrepreneurs more often report that access to adequate capital is a major problem than do their majority counterparts.
- Black small business owners are three times as likely as white small business owners to face this problem.

- The likely sources of capital access constraints on minority-owned small businesses points to discrimination.
- The primary research question addressed in this article is, Does Small Business Administration (SBA) guaranteed lending lessen the negative impacts of discrimination on minority entrepreneurs and their communities?

NOTE: The authors' results suggest that high-minority markets are positively impacted by SBA guaranteed lending. Moreover, the impact for high-minority markets is three times as large as it is for low minority markets. This result has important implications for public policy in general and SBA guaranteed lending in particular.

Discrimination   There are at least two reasons why discrimination against minority-owned firms might be observed in small business credit markets.
- The first is simply prejudicial-type discrimination behavior.
- The second is related to differential levels of asymmetric information and credit rationing.

NOTE: One method likely to reduce the costs of asymmetric information-based discrimination is to reduce the amount of asymmetric information, especially for minority-owned firms. One practical method is to encourage lenders to make profitable loans that they would not otherwise make via resources such as the SBA guaranteed lending program.

Information   Many economists contend that private lending institutions may indeed fail to
Problems   allocate loans efficiently because of fundamental information problems in the market for small-business loans.
- The lack of perfect information in loan markets may cause two effects that allow the interest rate itself to affect the riskiness of the bank's loan portfolio.
  - Adverse selection impedes the ability of markets to allocate credit using price by increasing the proportion of high-risk borrowers in the set of likely borrowers.
  - Moral hazard reduces the ability of prices to clear lending markets because it influences the ex-post actions of borrowers.
- As a result of these two effects, a bank's expected return may increase less for an additional increase in the interest rate and beyond a certain point may actually decrease as the interest rate is increased.
- And because the value of collecting information on borrowers may be less in high-minority markets (because of expectations of less aggregate per capita lending), the levels of imperfect information may be higher, in equilibrium, in high-minority markets.

The SBA   By reducing expected loss associated with a default, the SBA guarantee increases the expected return to the lender—without increasing lending rates.
- To the extent that the loan guarantees do reduce the rate of interest, external loan guarantees will help mitigate the moral hazard problem.
- Lowering the rate increases the number of low-risk borrowers applying for credit, which increases the likelihood that the average risk of firms applying for loans is representative of the pool of borrowers.
- Hence, external loan guarantees help mitigate the adverse selection problem.

NOTE: If SBA loan guarantees indeed reduce credit rationing in high-minority markets for small business loans, then there should be a relationship between measures of SBA guaranteed lending activities and economic performance. This study finds evidence consistent with this proposition.

Conclusion

The study results should be interpreted with caution because of at least five issues noted by the authors.

- We are unable to control for small business lending at the local market level—we do not know whether SBA loan guarantees are contributing to economic performance by helping to complete the market or are simply substituting for small business lending in the market.
- We are not able to test whether SBA guarantees materially increase the volume of small business lending in a market—a question that is related to who captures the subsidy associated with SBA guarantees.
- We do not have direct measures of whether SBA guaranteed lending is really reducing discrimination at the microeconomic level.
- We do not have any measures of the actual demand for credit by potential and existing minority small businesses in the local market.
- We do not include measures of the costs of SBA guaranteed lending, which would include the performance of granted SBA loans.

NOTE: All of these issues relate to a larger question: what is the optimal level of SBA guaranteed lending in U.S. small firm credit markets? Future research may seek to shed additional light on this larger question.

Traits and Performance of the Minority Venture-Capital Industry

Timothy Bates, Wayne State University;
and William Bradford, University of Washington

Background

This study analyzes the performance of investments made by venture-capital (VC) funds that specialize in financing minority business enterprises (MBEs).

- The apparent existence of a discriminatory financing environment creates an underserved market and, hence, attractive opportunities are available to firms capable of identifying and serving MBE financing needs.
- The minority VC funds are earning yields on their realized investments that are at least equivalent to those of the broader VC industry.
- This study analyzes the nature and performance of the VC funds that specialize in financing large-scale, minority-owned businesses.

New Entrepreneurs

A new African American entrepreneur has emerged, who is young, well educated, and operating increasingly in nontraditional industries.

Minority VC Investment

An important trait differentiating the minority-oriented VC sector is its broad diversification regarding industries in which the funds invest.

- Mainstream VCs are heavily concentrated in several high-tech sectors while minority VCs are widely diversified across high- and low-tech fields.

- One fact is clear: equity capital invested in MBEs has grown enormously.
- The ability of the minority-oriented VC industry to expand its MBE investments depends critically upon its ability to attract capital from institutional investors.

Conclusions The authors conclude that the returns to the minority-focused funds are certainly no lower, and perhaps higher, than those of mainstream funds.

- Furthermore, their market risk of investments is not higher than the risk of the mainstream funds.
- Thus, one can accept the hypothesis that minority-focused funds are investing in an underserved market niche with attractive returns. This conclusion is tempered by the reality of underlying databases that are not perfectly comparable.
- The evidence, nonetheless, clearly suggests that, during the period observed, the investment performance of the minority-focused funds was at least equivalent to that of their vintage mainstream funds.

The Future As we look to the future, we see reasons why mainstream VC funds will not exploit MBE investment opportunities.

- First, fund general partners obtain the bulk of their investment opportunities through contacts and relationships built over time.
- Second, most minority funds are not high-tech oriented and do not fit the technical focus typifying mainstream VC funds.
- Third, the existence of discrimination can result in distaste for minority persons, spilling into distaste for investing in minority businesses.

NOTE: To the extent that general partners prefer not to work with ethnic minorities and are willing to forgo economic profits to avoid transacting with minority owners, fund entrance will be (self-) restricted. We conjecture that each of these factors plays a role in creating a profitable niche for minority-focused VC funds.

Secrets of Gazelles: The Differences between High-Growth and Low-Growth Businesses Owned by African American Entrepreneurs

Thomas D. Boston, Georgia Institute of Technology and EüQuant; and Linje R. Boston, EüQuant

Background Until this study, no one had explored why some African American–owned businesses have achieved high rates of growth while others have not.

- Specifically, high-growth firms in the data were less likely to compete on the basis of price, but the small number of variables found to be statistically significant shows need for further study.
- David Birch labeled fast growing companies "gazelles"—defined as firms that have achieved an annual rate of growth of at least 20 percent.

- In this study, gazelles were compared to
  - low and moderately growing small businesses called growth-oriented firms and
  - firms whose annual employment growth was less than 1 percent or negative, called no-growth firms.

High versus Low Growth

Kim and Mauborgne (1998) found that high-growth entrepreneurs may be distinguished from low-growth entrepreneurs along several dimensions.
- These include greater strategic intentions, entrepreneurial intensity and growth, greater willingness to incur the opportunity costs of growing, more decentralized firm structure, higher levels of financial resources, and a greater variety of funding sources.
- Their research indicated that high-growth-oriented entrepreneurs are more likely to pursue market expansion through product and service innovation and increased advertising expenditures.
- They are also more likely to pursue technological avenues, spend more time searching for financing, engage in operations planning, and devote more resources to organizational development and training.

NOTE: High-growth entrepreneurs, in contrast to small business owners, are highly motivated, have a greater propensity for risk-taking, engage in innovative activities, exhibit a psychological profile that is consistent with the goal of growth and profitability, and plan systematically.

Comparisons

In this study, the authors compared the responses of gazelle owners to the responses by owners of no-growth companies in several business categories.
- In traits and self-perceptions, the differences were not significant.
- Gazelle owners do hold slightly more positive views about the economy; however, the difference can be attributed to chance.
- While a greater proportion of gazelle owners are more satisfied with their current positions as entrepreneurs than are owners of no-growth firms, the difference is not statistically significant.
- While a slightly greater proportion of gazelle owners reported that their skills were inborn compared to the percentage of no-growth owners, the differences were not statistically significant.
- Fewer gazelle owners (80 percent vs. 87 percent for no-growth owners) rate control over their destiny as a significant motive for entering into business, and again, this difference is not statistically significant.
- The results confirmed that the pursuit of power and social status is much less important to gazelle owners.
- Gazelles were attracted to opportunities, not pushed by adverse circumstances like prior loss of a job.
- Other questions asked if owners entered business because they wanted to overcome racial barriers, to serve their communities, or if they were inspired by someone outside of their family—none of the differences were statistically significant.
- Seventy-four percent of gazelle owners considered the desire to use their experience and education as a significant factor to enter business.

Owner Attributes

As to owner attributes, none of the group differences in responses to questions in this category were statistically significant.
- The data revealed that there was only a two-hour difference in the reported average number of hours spent weekly in the enterprise.
- Eighty-three percent of gazelle owners compared to 75 percent of no-growth owners founded their business.

Growth

More gazelle owners than no-growth owners indicated a willingness to take their company public if the opportunity arises.
- An equal percentage of both groups of owners feel the same about the impact of discrimination on the ability of their firm to grow.

Competitive Strategy

Respondents were asked about their pricing strategy, and responses suggest that gazelles are less likely to engage in competitive pricing strategies.

Marketing

The results show that gazelles received a smaller percentage of their total revenue from African Americans.

Conclusion

The differences in rates of growth among African American–owned firms cannot be explained simply by evaluating differences in owner attributes, firm attributes, characteristics of markets, and environmental constraints.
- Firms experiencing rates of growth of 40 percent annually are very similar to firms experiencing declining rates of growth.
- The real explanation of high growth remains a "black box."

Exploring Stratification and Entrepreneurship: African American Women Entrepreneurs Redefine Success in Growth Ventures

Jeffrey Robinson, New York University; Laquita Blockson, College of Charleston; and Sammie Robinson, Illinois Wesleyan University

Background

This article focuses on African American women in entrepreneurship as a starting point for exploring the influences of social stratification on entrepreneurship and vice versa.
- The authors note that, according to a study in which the survival rates of firms owned by women and minorities were examined, African American women–owned firms fared better than those owned by African American men.
- Trends pointing to the increasing presence of women in African American entrepreneurship have implications for the U.S. economy. They provide a road map for economic development in the African American community through productive entrepreneurship.

Social Stratification

Social stratification and entrepreneurship interact in at least three ways.
- Entrepreneurship can be a means of social mobility–it can create ventures that create wealth and allow the entrepreneur and their families to move from lower status to higher status positions.

- Entrepreneurship can play a role in addressing the challenges of a fractious, stratified society.
- Social stratification influences the process of entrepreneurship for those actors who hold lower status positions in society.

NOTE: For those entrepreneurs who hold disadvantaged positions in the social structure, social stratification can have profound effects on how they identify, shape, and pursue entrepreneurship.

Lack of Research

To fully appreciate the dearth of research in this area, the authors considered Brush's (1992) review of the women in entrepreneurship literature.

- She noted that only two of the fifty-seven articles on women and entrepreneurship she analyzed from 1977 to 1991 focused on minority women.
- In addition, the authors found only seventeen research dissertations related to African American women entrepreneurs and self-employment.
- The macro-level of analysis of African American women entrepreneurs is by far the least studied area of all.

NOTE: Since 1991, there has been a marked increase in number but not necessarily in the breadth or depth of the research.

New Research Approach

From the literature review, it is clear that there is much to be gained from exploring social stratification and entrepreneurship together.

- The multidimensional nature of social identity can be accounted for.
- This approach allows one to move beyond the functionalist paradigm to understand how entrepreneurship unfolds differently for these subjects.

NOTE: The authors argue that we must also acknowledge the inequality that exists in the United States and other nations and consider how that inequality interacts with the identification and the shaping of entrepreneurial opportunities by constraining some activities and providing opportunities for others.

Definition of Success

While the history of American/Western business values has conditioned us to believe that economic indicators of success are predominant, entrepreneurial success is defined much more broadly in other cultures and environments.

- Werbner (1999) described it best when she noted that success may be defined as "the competitive achievement of prestige or honor, and of the symbolic goods signaling these, within a specific regime of value."
- Things that are valuable (or deemed significant) to entrepreneurs when defining success for their ventures (and/or themselves) often cannot be translated cleanly into economic terms.
- Noneconomic measures of success may be viewed as being as valuable as, if not more valuable than, economic measures of success.

NOTE: The authors' observations would validate Werbner's argument. Using solely economic indicators to determine entrepreneurial success may mask whether they are, indeed, successful. Based upon their preliminary observations, the authors argue that the context of African American women is important for this discussion and has implications for the field of entrepreneurship.

Implications What do we learn from studying these entrepreneurs and what are the implications of this research?

- The process of entrepreneurship may have many similarities across contexts, but the process is influenced by society's norms, values, rules, regulations, and public policies—*context matters*.
- Studying African American women in entrepreneurship with an eye on social stratification perspectives provides an opportunity to use different research approaches in entrepreneurship research.
- The recognition of the importance of context and relevance of research approach will lead to more informed policy making.

Conclusion The goal of this article was to present the usefulness of analysis that addresses the complexities of race, gender, class, wealth, and entrepreneurship.

- As a result, the implication is that further research in this area should be conducted from an interpretivist perspective. By adopting a lens that considers several important factors,
  - entrepreneurship may be defined as a process, noting the different measures of success; and
  - entrepreneurship research should take into account both the complexity within society and the multidimensional nature of social identity and its relationship to social stratification.

Q
R
S

Building Ventures through Civic Capitalism

Candida Brush, Babson College; and Daniel Monti, Andrea Ryan, and Amy M. Gannon, Boston University

Background An exploratory study of urban entrepreneurs participating in a technical assistance program finds that they focus both on the bottom line and an explicit wish to improve their community.

- This integrated combination of economic and social values, a kind of civic-minded capitalism, guides their positioning for growth and yields a business that can best be called a "civic enterprise."
- Entrepreneurship and business development are vehicles for accelerating the revitalization of urban areas.
- Many depressed urban neighborhoods have mostly minority populations whose rate of population growth vastly outstrips their ability to develop their own businesses.
- Even though minority business development is growing at a rate of 10 percent annually, it is lower than the national average for all businesses.
- The prevalence of entrepreneurial behavior among black men and women is 50 percent greater than for whites—for Hispanic men, 20 percent greater—though business survival rates are low.
- There is an unfortunate gap in our knowledge of how smaller urban and minority businesses position for growth that calls for a more organizational approach to studying minority businesses.

Three Ms

Key factors influencing business growth and success are money, market access, and management capability—the three Ms.

- The relative lack of access of minority businesses to the three Ms has been crucial to their lack of success and slow business growth.
- Markets are important to all businesses, but may be even more so for minority businesses who are located in predominantly minority communities and/or inner cities. It is also important to extend the market beyond the local community to enable growth beyond what might be expected.

NOTE: Given the relative lack of success of minority businesses, we must ask both what helps to foster their growth and what barriers sit in the way.

The ICE Study

The subjects of this study participated in a technical assistance program, Inner City Entrepreneurs (ICE), which was launched in Boston.

- The sample of entrepreneurs was 55 percent minority and 45 percent white, 65 percent male and 35 percent female, with nearly 80 percent of the sample having four years of college.
- Most of the entrepreneurs (62 percent) started their ventures from scratch, and 25 percent of them have owned two or more ventures.
- Personal values and goals were related to the decision to start a business.
- The overwhelming majority of the ventures are small, with 70 percent having fewer than ten employees.
- They were more likely to say their goals were to provide jobs than to make a profit or create personal wealth. The more popular ways of "giving back" to the community include providing jobs to local people; offering in-kind contributions, free services, and donations; making referrals for people looking for assistance; letting their business be used for meetings and as a site for public announcements; and participating in neighborhood initiatives and celebrations. What may be unique to this sample is that nearly 20 percent believe that having a broader social mission or "social consciousness" is what distinguishes them from the competition.

Conclusions

Based on the qualitative and quantitative results in this exploratory study, the authors conclude that to understand the processes of growing ventures in urban neighborhoods, we must understand the interactions of people and place and how these interactions affect the economic and social missions of these ventures.

- The dual mission of these *civic capitalists* influences many decisions the entrepreneurs make and can sometimes create special challenges.
- Ethnicity and culture also play a role in creating both advantages and disadvantages.
- If they wish to grow, particularly in communities with relatively weaker institutional infrastructures and more unstable economic situations, they encounter a variety of challenges:
  - For *civic capitalists*, a poor balance of social and economic missions can put the business at risk.
  - As a business grows, the entrepreneur becomes less involved in every decision, perhaps making it more difficult to manage both missions well.
- Given all the challenges, how does a venture ensure that the dual social and economic missions are held by the organization itself and not simply part of the owner's approach?

QRS

NOTE: Their ability to survive and their motivation to succeed puts these businesses in a better position to positively impact the economic and social environment of urban communities—to create jobs, serve the community, and become entrepreneurial leaders.

Tax Refunds and Micro-Businesses: Expanding Family and Community Wealth Building in the Borderlands

Bárbara J. Robles, Arizona State University

Background

The Earned Income Tax Credit (EITC) is the largest antipoverty fiscal policy program for working, low-income families administered by the IRS.

- Unemployment plays a profound role in the ability of families in the Borderlands to secure a financially stable future for their children.
- The high concentration of Latinos in the region corresponds to a greater incidence of seasonal jobs, low-wage service sector jobs, and a larger labor pool with lower educational attainment characteristics.
- As public assistance income declines, more families are engaging in self-employment and micro-business activities.
- Informal economic activity is also related to stagnant job creation, high unemployment rates, and chronically depressed wages.
- A large portion of the micro-business and self-employment activities along the Southwest border are highly correlated with economic survival strategies and are often a "second or third" job.
- Formalizing informal economic activities can be used to leverage asset and wealth-building opportunities for low-resourced Latino families. The challenge lies in educating workers and families on their tax rights and documenting income streams from services provided.

Economic Choices

Financial and economic choices are fundamentally intertwined with consumer skills that are usually learned through intergenerational transfer of knowledge and frequent exposure to mainstream markets.

- For non-native-born working poor families arriving from countries with class-oriented financial institutions (limited to serving wealthy customers) and severely underdeveloped credit systems, these concepts and activities are skills they need to master.
- Moreover, for native-born families residing in isolated communities in the United States that rely on cash and informal barter systems, familiarity with mainstream financial services and products is difficult to acquire since mainstream financial institutions are often absent.
- Understanding income tax responsibilities and rights are also asset- and wealth-building skills and are often overlooked as a component in financial education curricula and outreach.
- Although the EITC has been successful in providing substantial economic relief to a growing segment of the U.S. population and although Latinos are eligible for the EITC, Hispanics are least likely to be aware of this refunded tax credit and less likely to claim it compared to whites and blacks.

Tax Refunds   Three relevant findings provide a deeper understanding of how tax refunds are leveraged into asset- and wealth-building activities:

- Micro-business owners expend tax refunds on schooling for themselves or their children to a higher degree.
- They expend their tax refund on property taxes to a higher degree.
- Micro-business owners allocated their tax refunds to a greater degree upon acquiring a home of their own.

Studies   The findings from two study models provides insight into the role that education and tax refund expenditures play in the economic resiliency behaviors of low-resourced tax filers.

- Tax refund recipients who expend on education increase their capacity to engage in wealth-enhancing activities.
- Continuing education and engaging in wealth-leveraging activities create opportunities for asset building and economic stability for income-constrained entrepreneurial aspirants.

Conclusion   The slow growth of low- to medium-skilled wage employment plays a decisive role in economic resiliency and entrepreneurial behaviors in both the rural and metropolitan areas of Southwest border counties.

- The economic conditions that create challenges are also opportunities for micro-business and entrepreneurial initiatives.
- Continued growth of tax revenues at local and regional levels—which realizes community productive capacity—requires policies that encourage formalizing informal entrepreneurial activities.
- Promoting education and skills-building benefits two groups:
  - those with a college education, who can leverage their human capital into growing enterprises; and
  - those with limited education, requiring policies focused on entrepreneurial skills and the basics of formal market entry.

Future   Through tax- and asset-building outreach programs connected to skills-building community-based support services, many of the hard-to-reach entrepreneur aspirants can be connected to formal business operations and mainstream financial institutions.

- Education is a crucial factor in asset building for families and, consequently, for communities.
- New data sources and ongoing data collection efforts help create new research findings and policy directions.
- Data collection that creates an intersection between financial behaviors, economic resiliency choices, and wealth-building opportunities brings with it more understanding of the needs.

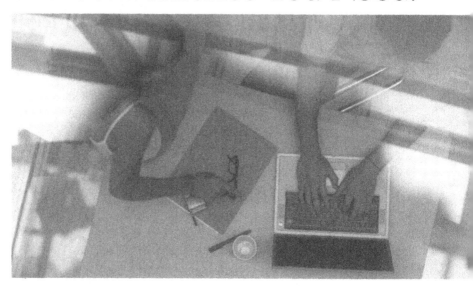